Behold, the way for man is narrow,
but it lieth in a straight course before him,
and the keeper of the gate is the Holy One of Israel,
and he employeth no servant there;
and there is none other way save it be by the gate;
for he cannot be deceived,
for the Lord God is his name.

2 Nephi 9:41

CHIEKO N. OKAZAKI
DISCIPLES

Deseret Book Company
Salt Lake City, Utah

Author's note: Some of the addresses included in this book were given while I was serving in the general Relief Society presidency of the Church, but I offer them here as "just Chieko."

© 1998 Chieko N. Okazaki

All rights reserved. No part of this book may be reproduced in any form or by any means without permission in writing from the publisher, Deseret Book Company, P.O. Box 30178, Salt Lake City, Utah 84130. This work is not an official publication of The Church of Jesus Christ of Latter-day Saints. The views expressed herein are the responsibility of the author and do not necessarily represent the position of the Church or of Deseret Book Company.

Deseret Book is a registered trademark of Deseret Book Company.

Library of Congress Cataloging-in-Publication Data

Okazaki, Chieko N., 1926–
  Disciples / Chieko N. Okazaki.
      p.   cm.
  Includes bibliographical references and index.
  ISBN 1-57345-413-3 (hc.)
  1. Christian life—Mormon authors.   I. Title.
BX8656.O44   1998
248.4'89332—dc21   98-27282
                                                        CIP

Printed in the United States of America

10 9   8   7   6   5   4   3   2   1   72082 - 6406

To the daughters of my heart
Christine Wynn Okazaki
and
Kelle Smart Okazaki

CONTENTS

IN THE SHELTER OF HIS WINGS

I'd like to talk about two images of wings from the scriptures that will bring us closer to Christ. The first is the image of wings as shelter. As we read in Psalm 63:10, "Because thou hast been my help, therefore in the shadow of thy wings will I rejoice." The second is the image of wings as empowerment. Doctrine and Covenants 124 contains an inspiring revelation of the Lord to William Law, an early Church leader, through Joseph Smith. The Lord promises:

> And these signs shall follow [William]—he shall heal the sick, he shall cast out devils, and shall be delivered from those who would administer unto him deadly poison;
>
> And . . . shall mount up in the imagination of his thoughts as upon eagles' wings.
>
> And what if I will that he should raise the dead [?] Let him not withhold his voice. (D&C 124:98–100)

Even raising the dead! So think with me about wings as shelter and wings as power.

Wings as Shelter

Let's begin with the image of wings as shelter. I always feel the sadness of Jesus when he looked over the city of Jerusalem and lamented, "O Jerusalem, Jerusalem, . . . how often would I have gathered thy children together, as a hen doth gather her brood under her wings, and ye would not!" (Luke 13:34). They rejected the shelter of his wings. I have never wanted to do anything that would make me refuse to be gathered. As a disciple, I have always wanted instead that feeling of physical and emotional closeness, of being cherished and protected under the Savior's wings.

I remember, when I was a child on the big island of Hawaii, swimming with the other children. Even when it was cold, we wouldn't come out until we were blue and our teeth were chattering. I remember all of us skinny little children huddling together with chattering teeth. I'd make my two younger brothers creep as close to me as they could come with the other children, and then wrap a big bath towel around us as far as it would go. We would make a shelter under my wings, and in a few minutes we would warm each other up.

When World War II broke out, my father, even though he was Japanese, went off with the other men to guard the lighthouse. My mother was alone with me and my two brothers, ages nine and four. We were only five hundred yards from the beach. We didn't know if there were Japanese submarines on the coast, preparing to land soldiers on our shore. We didn't know if American soldiers were coming down the lane looking for Japanese people. We had to keep the windows tightly covered for the blackout and be very careful with the lights. I was afraid of what might be in the darkness. I was afraid of the unknown. I was afraid of being alone. I was afraid for all of us.

Even though I was only fourteen, I knew that my mother sensed my fears and that she knew my little brothers were afraid too. She pulled the mattresses into the living room and arranged them like a sleeping nest, snuggling a little brother in each arm, with room for me to sit beside her so that I could feel the comfort of her touch as well. We did that for several nights. When I think of being sheltered under wings, it is the image of my mother, holding our fears away by nesting with us, that comes to me.

We all want safety, peace, and shelter. We all have situations that challenge and frighten us. The Old Testament is very candid about the fallen nature of the world we live in, how often we feel afflicted and oppressed, and what a great need we have for a refuge, a feeling that there is a safe place of love and shelter where we can seek respite from the storms that assail us. Look at these beautiful scriptures about the shelter of God's wings:

> I have called upon thee, for thou wilt hear me, O God . . . Shew thy marvellous lovingkindness, Keep me as the apple of the eye, hide me under the shadow of thy wings. (Psalm 17:6–8)
>
> Thy mercy, O Lord, is in the heavens; and thy faithfulness reacheth unto the clouds. Thy righteousness is like the great mountains; thy judgments are a great deep: . . . How excellent is thy lovingkindness, O God! therefore the children of men put their trust under the shadow of thy wings. (Psalm 36:5–8)
>
> Thou hast been a shelter for me, and a strong tower from the enemy. I will abide in thy tabernacle for ever: I will trust in the covert of thy wings. (Psalm 61:2–4)

I don't know how those scriptures make you feel, but they reassure me in a deep and abiding way that God is real and that he is present with his disciples in their troubles.

It is not news to anyone that nobody gets through this life without adversity. It comes to all of us, though it comes in different ways, in different intensities, and at different times. We also know that adversity is part of our Heavenly Father's plan—not some terrible aberration or failure of the plan. We don't like adversity and we don't want it, but we need it. Ralph Waldo Emerson said, "When it is dark enough, men see the stars." The same idea is expressed in an old Oriental proverb: "All sunshine makes a desert." We need darkness to see the stars. We need both rain and sunshine for healthy plants. We need opposition in all things, even when we don't want it or like it.

A wise Jewish rabbi wrote:

> Mature people are made not out of good times but out of bad times. Man's extremity is God's opportunity. It is in a crisis that the best in us comes to the fore. This very age in which we live, which is so turbulent, so confusing, so uncertain, is an anvil upon which God can remake us for the good, for the better. . . .
>
> What I am asking for is a mature outlook, reasonable expectations, a calm and steadfast mind and the patience with which to meet whatever comes with courage and faith in God, instead of with bitterness and resentment.[1]

Nobody wants trials. Nobody likes adversities. Nobody secretly prays, "Pile on the adversity, Lord, so I can really impress my friends with how mature I am." Nor should we seek to make life more difficult than it is. We'll get enough difficulties just in the normal course of living, without seeking out problems on purpose. But there are a few ways we can make those inevitable problems even harder for ourselves. For instance, as disciples we cannot seek the shelter of the Lord's wings if we turn our backs on him, if we grow angry and bitter, or if we deny that the wings exist. We have to do our part by exercising faith and by not making things worse than they are.

I'm not saying we should deny our pain or pretend that things are rosy when they're not. We don't make things better by wearing masks. I'm just saying that we usually have a choice about our attitudes, and the biggest difference we can make is in where we choose to focus when something is hurting us.

I came across this poem, now more than a hundred and fifty years old, in the *Times and Seasons*, published in Nauvoo. It describes this idea of being able to accept both good times and bad times by retaining a focus on the Lord. The first two stanzas read:

When streams of pleasure gently flow,
And skies are clear, and comforts glow;
In all prosperity, would I
To Jesus turn my grateful eye.

Or should the storms of sorrow lower,
Afflictions, pain, temptations pour;
In all adversity, would I
To Jesus turn my patient eye.[2]

Can you sense how the author of this poem has stability because he or she maintains a focus on the Savior, whether the circumstances are good or bad? If we allow the pain to make us focus all our attention on ourselves, then we can't find peace and comfort under Christ's wings.

When times seem very difficult for you, keep your focus on the Savior, and I promise you that his wings will be there to shelter you. There is a beautiful prayer in Psalm 57:1: "Be merciful unto me, O God, be merciful unto me: for my soul trusteth in thee: yea, in the shadow of thy wings will I make my refuge, until these calamities be overpast." And when our hope is in the Savior, then we are sheltered under wings that will never fail.

"Jesus, Lover of My Soul," hymn number 102, has always been a favorite of mine. Maybe it comes from growing up on the big island of Hawaii, where the ocean is a constant fact of life and where we are so keenly aware of what storms, rolling water, and tempests can do to unprotected souls on land and on the sea. The last verse is an expression of trust in the Savior:

Other refuge have I none;
Hangs my helpless soul on thee.
Leave, oh leave me not alone,
Still support and comfort me.
All my trust on thee is stayed,
All my help from thee I bring.

Cover my defenseless head
With the shadow of thy wing.

I hope, if you need a song to sing to yourself when the storms of life are beating down upon you, that you'll think of this one and of the safe refuge under strong wings that is waiting for us. The promise of refuge under his wings is a promise the Savior made and a promise that he will keep because he is a God of miracles. He is Jesus Christ, our Savior, our Redeemer. He was born on earth to show us how to live. He fulfilled the Atonement and submitted to crucifixion. And after three days, he rose "from the dead, with healing in his wings; and all those who shall believe on his name shall be saved in the kingdom of God." And I hope that we, with Nephi, can say, "Wherefore, my soul delighteth to prophesy concerning him, for I have seen his day, and my heart doth magnify his holy name" (2 Nephi 25:13).

Wings as Power

The second idea I'd like to discuss is the image of wings as power for disciples of Christ. Let's read some scriptures that use this image of wings as power, renewal, and strength. These scriptures tell us about support from the Savior as we testify of him. Isaiah 40:31 says: "But they that wait upon the Lord shall renew their strength; they shall mount up with wings as eagles; they shall run, and not be weary; and they shall walk, and not faint." We're familiar with the last part of that scripture because it sounds very much like the physical renewal of our health and strength promised in Doctrine and Covenants 89 to those who keep the Word of Wisdom. Well, I'd like to apply it to us in the sense of emotional and spiritual renewal as we fix our faith upon Christ and testify of him.

This next scripture contains a promise that I think we can apply to ourselves. In the Doctrine and Covenants, the Lord encouraged an early missionary named Lyman Wight with a revelation given through Joseph Smith:

> It is my will that my servant Lyman Wight should continue in preaching for Zion, . . . confessing me before the world; . . . and I will bear him up as on eagles' wings. . . .
>
> That when he shall finish his work I may receive him unto myself, even as I did my servant David Patten, who is with me at this time, [David Patten was an apostle who was killed at the battle of Crooked River in Missouri] and also my servant Edward Partridge, [he was the first presiding bishop of the Church. He was tarred and feathered in Missouri] and also my aged servant Joseph Smith, Sen., . . . and blessed and holy is he, for he is mine. (D&C 124:18–19)

What a beautiful promise! Imagine hearing the Lord say, "Deborah, you are mine. Matthew, you are mine." Isn't that a glorious promise? Don't you want to receive it for yourself? And the Lord has told us how we can—by "preaching in Zion," by "confessing" Jesus before the world. It means by bearing testimony of the Savior. What do those phrases mean? Are they only for missionaries? No, they're for any disciple to whom the Savior is a living presence.

Let me share with you some recollections from the first days of the mission that my husband and I served in the Japan Okinawa Mission. This was a new mission. The Northern Far East Mission was divided in two, with the current mission president continuing to supervise the work of the Japan Mission in the north while we took over the newly created Japan-Okinawa Mission in the south.

We got there in August 1967, with everything to invent from scratch. Ed and I were both converts. Although we had known and loved many missionaries, we'd never served a mission, worked in a mission presidency, or had much to do with missionary work except for feeding missionaries and giving them referrals. We were drowning in the details of setting up the mission office, opening new cities, getting to know the missionaries and members, coping with the language, finding a mission home, setting up office procedures, getting our boys settled in school, even finding places to shop.

We found a small house on Shinohara Honmachi in Kobe and set up the mission office there while we were still looking for an office. Every room in the house did double duty. The ditto machine was in the kitchen. Whenever I had to cook, I'd say, "Elder Johnson, come get this!" All of the mission records were on the table, and whenever it was time to eat, I'd say, "Elder Johnson, set the table!" So everything would go in piles on the floor until after the meal, when he could spread them out and work again. I remember doing something as simple as trying to buy pencils and paper clips. Elder Van Orden and Elder Powell, our most experienced elders, would drive us, but, of course, the mission was new to them as well. They would stop to ask directions of the neighborhood police in their excellent Japanese—which still sounded very American—and the police officer would look at these two Caucasians in the front seat and then see two Japanese people sitting in the backseat, and so they would explain the directions to Ed and me because they thought we'd understand. Of course, no matter how we looked, we didn't understand Japanese! It was very funny and very frustrating at the same time.

We had missionaries coming in every month, and Ed was trying to find a corner to interview them in, hold orientations, and give them assignments when he wasn't even sure where the map was. Although only the family—Ed, me, and our two teenage sons—were living in the house, I'd feed everyone who was there for lunch, and that was about ten people per meal. I'd have to go shopping every day, because the cupboards and refrigerator were so small. The washing machine was just apartment-sized. One pair of Ken's jeans was about all it would take.

So that was how our mission began, with an enormous amount of work and an enormous amount of frustration when even the simplest tasks seemed incredibly complicated. It was only about a month until we found an office, even though it seemed like forever. But none of those realities were important at all. What was important was the love. We felt the love of God for us. We felt Christ's love for the Japanese people. We felt such abundant love for the missionaries who were trying so hard. And truly, we felt lifted up on the wings of eagles.

Just a few weeks later, in September, we held our first zone conference. I remember that the opening song was one of Ed's favorites: "It May Not Be on the Mountain Height," with its inspiring chorus: "I'll go where you want me to go, dear Lord." Ed and I and our boys—they were there, too—sang those words with a great deal of meaning, and so, I imagine, did the missionaries. We had all left things that were important to us to come to this country, this mission, and this meeting. I remember Ed, standing up and starting to welcome the missionaries, but suddenly stopping and standing there speechless at the podium, with tears running down his cheeks. I remember looking out at the missionaries' faces and then suddenly not being able to see them because of the tears that filled my own eyes. We knew this was the work of the Lord. When Ed was able to speak, the first words he choked out were simple words of gratitude that we were where the Lord wanted us to be. Many of the missionaries were weeping too, as they felt the same spirit. We were being lifted up on eagles' wings, the wings of love.

Let me say it as simply as I can. Power comes from love. Achievement and ability come from love. We can try to do it on our own, or we can really achieve with the Savior—by accepting his love and by being willing to love others in return.

I've talked about examples from the mission field. We were in a formal mission situation. Our duty and responsibility and calling as missionaries was to testify of the Lord Jesus Christ in as many ways and on as many occasions as we could. And certainly, missionaries are blessed with many opportunities to do just that, because that's their full-time job. But your full-time job is something else. Perhaps you are a full-time student, with additional duties that may feel just as full-time. You might have obligations to your employer, to your parents, to your children, or to all of the above. And I hope that you also have callings in the Church that provide you with opportunities to serve others.

In each of these jobs and callings, can you testify of Christ? Can you be a disciple? Of course you can. Testifying of Christ is not one more burden to be added to your already heavy load. It's not another link in the chain that attaches you to an enormous weight on your ankle that you're trying to drag around. Testifying of Christ is your simple, honest acknowledgment of the role he plays in your life, the source of strength that he is to you, the joy in the Spirit that you feel, the confirmation that comes from prayer, and the trust you feel, even in adversity, that things will work out for the best because he is there blessing you. Christ lifts you on the wings of eagles by filling you with his own love—his love for you and for the people around you.

I remember those days in the mission field, not as troubled and exhausting days, although they were long and arduous. I remember them as being filled with sunshine and joy, with the zest of learning, with enthusiasm for each new task to be accomplished, and especially with love—such enormous love for my husband, who was growing in wisdom and spirituality before my very eyes; and for my sons, who were coping with their own adjustments to the new culture, the strange environment, the immersion in a difficult language that was not their native tongue, and their dual responsibilities to be both students and also active parts of the missionary work. And I felt about each missionary as though he or she were my son or daughter.

I'm sure you have days that are as complicated and as frustrating as those days were for me, days in which you must work hard at many demanding tasks and deal with many people. I give you this challenge: Can you make them disciple days? Can you see in each of those people a beloved son or daughter of our Father in Heaven? Can you feel the love for each one of those people that inspired the Savior to face the ordeal of the Atonement with unwavering will? Can you feel that love in your own heart? The Savior testified before Pilate: "To this end was I born, and for this cause came I into the world, that I should bear witness unto the truth. Every one [and this means you, Chieko, and David, and Heather, and Jason—everyone] that is of the truth heareth my voice" (John 18:37). Do you hear that voice? Do you feel that truth in your heart?

Can I put it into other words? We are testifying of Christ when we feel his love for us and let that love take the many spontaneous forms of expression that love finds—service, kindness, a withholding of judgment, a willingness to listen.

When I was assigned to visit Japan and Korea as part of my calling in Relief Society, I met with Han In Sang, a Korean General Authority, while I was preparing myself to go so that I could understand the people and know better how I might help. Brother Han said, "We need to train leaders to show love, to come to Christ through love. We've taught people how to implement the handbook in perfection, but we haven't taught them what they need to know about loving each other."

He told me about interviewing a young bishop who was very anxious about his responsibilities, who urgently wanted to do what he was supposed to do, but who was so concerned and intense that there was very little room for joy. At the end of the interview, moved by compassion for this worried young leader and filled with love for him, Elder Han put his arms around him and gave him a hug, telling him that he loved him and that the Lord loved him. To his astonishment, the young bishop burst into tears. Tears came to Elder Han's eyes as he told me this experience. The young bishop said that it was only the second time in his life that anyone had ever hugged him.

Is there someone in your classroom or your home or your office who knows everything in the handbook but doesn't know that Heavenly Father and Jesus love him or her? Is it possible that you have enough love to go around? Have you taken shelter under the Savior's wings? Have you experienced the healing in his wings as you have gained a testimony of the Atonement? Have you felt uplifted by the Savior's wings of love? Then you have a disciple's testimony and you can share it. You can bear witness of the Savior, and he will uplift others who hear you.

We've talked about the shelter of the Savior's wings for us in times of adversity, and we've also talked about being uplifted on the wings of eagles as we bear testimony of Christ in our lives. Let your heart follow the wings you see, dipping and soaring above this world. Let your thoughts be lifted in praise to God and in thanksgiving for the wings in your life. And seek the shelter of his wings.

I want to conclude with a story about the Savior that comes from a special witness of the Lord Jesus Christ. Elder Melvin J. Ballard was an apostle and the grandfather of Elder M. Russell Ballard, currently a member of the Quorum of the Twelve. He had administrative problems to solve as part of his calling that were very troubling to him personally. There were no precedents or guidelines. In other words, this was a situation that the handbook didn't cover! He sought the Lord repeatedly for inspiration and help. Then he wrote:

> That night I received a wonderful manifestation and impression which has never left me. I was carried . . . into a room where I was informed I was to meet someone. As I entered the room I saw, seated on a raised platform, the most glorious being I have ever conceived of, and was taken forward to be introduced to Him. As I approached He smiled, called my name, and stretched out His hands toward me. If I live to be a million years old I shall never forget that smile. He put his arms around me and kissed me, as He took me into His bosom, and He blessed me until my whole being was thrilled. As He finished I fell at His feet, and there saw the marks of the nails; and as I kissed them, with deep joy swelling through my whole being, I felt that I was in heaven indeed. The feeling that came to my heart then was: Oh! if I could live worthy, though it would require

four-score years, so that in the end when I have finished I could go into His presence and receive the feeling that I *then* had in His presence, I would give everything that I am and ever hope to be![3]

I am thrilled with this story. I recognize in it the echoes of my own experiences with the Savior, though never in a manifestation of such concreteness, that have also filled me with divine love and have inspired me to be true to my covenants as a disciple. I notice—and I think we all have to smile over it—that Elder Ballard did not receive answers to his questions about his administrative responsibilities or how to proceed. In other words, he wasn't given this manifestation to fill out missing places in the handbook. He was given this experience because the Savior loved him and wanted him to know it, and so that he could testify of the Savior's love. I think, once he had been filled with the love of the Savior, he understood his problems in a new way, and perhaps he also understood how love was the solution to those problems.

We can seek the same witness of divine love in our own lives. As Doctrine and Covenants 93:1 promises: "Verily, thus saith the Lord: It shall come to pass that every soul who forsaketh his sins and cometh unto me, and calleth on my name, and obeyeth my voice, and keepeth my commandments, shall see my face and know that I am" (D&C 93:1). The witness of divine love may not come to you in a vision, but I know it will come.

A stake patriarch tells of giving a talk one Sunday in a BYU student ward when President Marion G. Romney made an unexpected visit. This stake patriarch's talk, he says, was about

> the experience of Enos and the need that we all have to know that we have been forgiven. During the course of my remarks I stressed several times that we didn't have to hear a voice as Enos did, but that we would know by the power of the Spirit when we had been forgiven. At the conclusion of the meeting President Romney was asked to speak to the congregation. I

remember how emphatically he testified, "I want you to know that you *can* hear a voice!"[4]

I too testify that the voice of the Lord is speaking to us even now, even as we stand confused and perplexed in our troubles and distress—discouraged, inadequate, limited in our understanding and limited in our abilities. The Savior is with us, ready to shelter us under his own wings and to lift us, soaring with him, on the wings of eagles. May we seek his face, hear his voice, be grateful for the shelter of his wings, and praise the power that sends us soaring.

QUESTIONS FOR A DISCIPLE

I'm sure you've read or watched fantasies and adventures, and learned the myths of heroic journeys in search of knowledge. On these journeys, there are always tests for the hero. Imagine that I'm the wise old woman (I have the hair for it!) asking you the great questions that will prove if you are worthy to receive the knowledge that has been hidden from the world, knowledge that will be a shield and a sword to you, knowledge that will save you and your people—in short, questions for a disciple.

These questions aren't original with me. They are all questions that Jesus posed to the people who followed him. Here they are:

Number one: "What wilt thou that I shall do unto thee?"

Number two: "Who is my mother and who are my brothers?"

Number three: "Whom say ye that I am?"

The Desires of Our Hearts

This first question, "What wilt thou that I shall do unto thee?" is a question about the desires of our hearts. Are we truly the stuff of which disciples are made?

In Luke, chapter 18, the story is told of a blind beggar by the road to Jericho who heard the commotion of people coming down the road and asked, "What is happening?" The people who were near said, "Jesus of Nazareth is going by." The blind man immediately cried out, "Jesus, Son of David, have mercy on me!"

The scripture says, "They which went before rebuked him, that he should hold his peace." I visualize this as being the people leading the group—perhaps some disciples of Jesus, or perhaps townspeople or important officials of Jericho. In any case, they told the blind man to be quiet, but he shouted even more, "Son of David, have mercy on me!"

Jesus heard him and stopped. He asked that the blind man be brought to him. When people led the blind man to him through the throng, Jesus then asked this great question: "What wilt thou that I shall do unto thee?" meaning, "What do you want me to do for you?"

The blind man replied, "Lord, I want to see."

Jesus' answer to him—without touching him, without praying for him, without any formalities of any kind—came very promptly: "Receive thy sight: thy faith hath saved thee." In other words, he said, "Then see. You are healed because you believe."

And the blind man *was* healed. He immediately followed Jesus, praising and glorifying God. And everyone who saw this miracle also praised Jesus.

Now, what if Jesus were asking you this question? What if he were coming nearer and nearer and you had the chance to lift your voice and tell him the desire of your heart, your most dearly held wish, your most desperately yearned-for hunger? What would it be? Maybe you hesitate to acknowledge that hunger even to yourself. Maybe you think you have prayed before and your prayers have not been answered. Maybe you are reluctant to ask because you feel you cannot be worthy of your heart's desire. There are other scriptures that explain such circumstances, set up conditions, and warn of alternative responses. But not in this experience. Here, on the road to Jericho, Jesus heard a cry for mercy, asked his question, and granted the speaker's exact request as soon as he heard it.

Did you notice that the blind man knew exactly what he

wanted? Similarly, we have to know what we really want. This isn't always as easy as it seems. We hear lots of messages telling us what we should want, or what is appropriate for people our age to want, or what other people like us want, or what somebody would want if they were us. There were people around the blind man who didn't want him to ask, thought he was interrupting, and tried to get him to hush. Maybe there are people in your life who don't want you to ask for your heart's desire—for any number of reasons. Well, this isn't between you and them. It's between you and Jesus. You'll notice that Jesus didn't take a vote or an opinion poll. He asked the blind man, "What do *you* want me to do for you?" And he listened to the answer.

Did you also notice how quickly and willingly and even joyfully Jesus granted the blind man's desire? He didn't rebuke the blind man for asking. He didn't consider it an interruption. He didn't ask the blind man if he was worthy, or if he was *sure* this was what he wanted. He didn't check with the blind man's mother or his neighbor or his rabbi to be sure that the blind man was sufficiently mature enough to handle sight. He instantly said, "Receive thy sight."

And did you notice what the effect was of Jesus' blessing? The blind man prayed for the removal of a physical handicap that represents a spiritual, moral, and intellectual one as well. He wanted to *see*. But on a metaphoric level, isn't this really what we all want in one way or another? Don't we want to see, to gain insight, to understand, to comprehend the vision? And how can we think, even in our shakiest moments, that the Lord will not grant this desire willingly and joyfully?

Do you remember what Joseph Smith was praying for when he went to the Sacred Grove? He said, "I kneeled down and began to offer up the *desires of my heart* to God" (Joseph Smith–History 1:15). And it was the desires of his heart that Heavenly Father and Jesus Christ answered. The reason Joseph Smith had the courage to go to that grove in the first place was because of James's encouraging promise that when we lack, we can ask God, who giveth "liberally" to all "and upbraideth not" (James 1:5). Don't you love the generosity of that term? *Liberally.* With no scolding.

Psalm 37:4 tells us, "Delight thyself also in the Lord; and he shall give thee the desires of thine heart." And we all remember Jesus' kindly urging: "Ask, and it shall be given you; seek, and ye shall find; knock, and it shall be opened unto you" (Luke 11:9).

We can ask for the desires of our hearts. We can ask confidently, in faith, knowing that a loving parent listens to us and will willingly grant those desires when he can. The question Jesus asks the blind man offers a glorious promise that we can have hope. And remember, it hinges on the question of Christ, "What do you want me to do for you?" This is the question he asks us still. Give him your answer and then praise God when you see.

The Family of God

The second great question for you as a disciple is one Jesus asked when he was teaching the people thronged around him. Someone brought the message, "Your mother and brothers are standing outside. They want to talk to you." Jesus asked a great question: "Who is my mother and who are my brothers?" (Matthew 12:48). Then he answered it. He pointed to his followers and said, "Here are my mother and my brothers. My true brother and sister and mother are those who do what my Father in heaven wants."

In other words, we belong to two families: the family of our kinfolk and the family of disciples of Christ. Let me focus for a few minutes on this second family. I don't know your responsibilities, your daily schedule, or your tasks. I don't know what constitutes good work or bad work in your life. I suspect that you, like most of us, are involved in what Emma Lou Thayne calls "hand-to-hand combat with lists" of chores, jobs, schoolwork, family responsibilities, activities, service to neighbors, spending time with friends, and Church callings to fulfill. For most of us, the world of kinfolk and the circle of other believers comprise a good part of our world.

Could I ask you to think very seriously and carefully about belonging to the family of disciples when you are dealing with people both inside and outside of your family? To run efficiently, any relationship, any family, any school, any job, or any organization has to develop rules and procedures and protocols and structures and reports and standards and checkpoints and accountings. Learning how to accommodate and use these rules and procedures is part of what we need to be able to do and do well, but let's also remember that our job here on the earth is not to build perfect organizations but to build perfect people. What if we were to ask God himself what his work is? If we were to pose this question to our Heavenly Father: "What is *your* work?" I think he would answer us as he has already answered Moses: "Why, *you* are my work and my glory. What I work for is to bring to pass *your* immortality and eternal life" (see Moses 1:39). It's easy to see how we are working toward this goal when it comes to our church activities or family life, but sometimes it is less easy to see the same goal in our professions or at school.

At the Maritime Museum in Stockholm, I learned about a ship called the *Wasa*. It was a beautifully constructed three-masted ship, typical of the late Renaissance. If you've seen pictures of the battle between the English fleet and the Spanish Armada, you'll have the basic idea. One of the first things you see in the exhibit is a large painting of the ship itself, slowly toppling over to one side, with sailors spilling off the sides.

Was this ship lost in a great battle? No, it wasn't. The *Wasa* is the oldest existing ship of the Royal Swedish Navy. It was constructed in Stockholm harbor and set on its maiden voyage on August 10, 1628. Before it even left the harbor, it capsized in a light squall and sank. There was an immediate inquiry into the cause, but no one could give a convincing explanation. It stayed there on the bottom of Stockholm's fine, deep harbor for 333 years, then was raised in 1961 and became part of the museum's study.

Curt Borgenstam, who heads the project, has continued to ask a great question of his own: "Why did the *Wasa* sink?" He admits at this point that they probably will never, after three hundred years, have enough information to answer this question completely, but he has been able to determine a number of factors. Perhaps the most important was that the *Wasa* followed the Dutch style of building, which made it quite flat-bottomed, rather than the English style, with very deep hulls. As a result, the *Wasa* had limited space for ballast and was so high with its double deck and its double row of cannon above the water line that it was very unstable. Its ballast consisted of cobblestones loaded into the hull, but these were not enough to lower the center of gravity to the point of safety. Ironically, Curt Borgenstam's calculations show that if the center of gravity had been only five to ten centimeters lower, the ship could have made it out of the harbor safely. Of course, out on the open sea it would have encountered greater waves and certainly more severe winds. By capsizing in the harbor, it allowed most of the crew to be rescued, so the ship was lost but lives were preserved.

But how big is ten centimeters? Hold up your fingers and measure ten centimeters in the air. That's right. It's just about four inches.

What is our ballast? I think it is personal service, with an eye to the same work and the same glory as God. Kindness and service are the ballast to our souls. Sometimes we feel that the little ships of our family are so top-heavy with rules and procedures and guidelines that they can barely wobble. Sometimes we feel that programs and policies have put on all sails and are running over everything in the harbor. And then sometimes we wonder why our ship just sank.

Please remember that our ballast should be what Jesus called the "weightier matters of the law." Jesus didn't rebuke people very often, but he severely chastised the scribes and the Pharisees as hypocrites. "Ye pay tithe of mint and anise and cummin," he said, "and have omitted the weightier matters of the law, judgment, mercy, and faith. These ought ye to have done, and not to leave the other undone" (Matthew 23:23).

Ed Hayes, a Christian writer, made this statement, which I love: "Our lives are fed by kind words of gracious behavior. We are nourished by expressions like 'excuse me,' and other such simple courtesies. . . . Rudeness, the absence of the sacrament of consideration is but another mark that our time-is-money society is lacking in spirituality, if not also in its enjoyment of life."[1] Did you hear that phrase? "the sacrament of consideration."

You'll have many opportunities in the course of your daily activities to do extra-mile service, with family members, with friends, with co-workers, with ward members, or with the server who takes your order at McDonald's. Will you see what little miracles might happen when you consider your interactions as opportunities to help others solve their problems and meet their needs?

Susan Easton Black, who teaches at BYU, tells a story about having a family home evening lesson on service during which her sons decided to perform some service to Sister Washburn, their next-door neighbor, who was a widow in her eighties. One of her very creative little boys volunteered to shovel the snow from her walk. The only problem was that it was August. However, they made cookies for her that month, and Susan remembered Todd's promise.

After the first snowfall a couple of months later, she reminded him of his service project. Reluctantly, he hunted up his coat, tugged on his hat, boots, and gloves, and trudged out the back door. In only a few minutes, he was back, announcing, "I cannot possibly shovel her walks."

When Susan got ready to encourage him with a few brisk words, he quickly explained, "I can't shovel the walks; Sister Washburn has already done it."

Susan must have exclaimed, "I feel so embarrassed. What if someone saw this elderly woman shoveling her own walk when a family of boys lived right next door?"

But Todd wasn't through yet. "You think you are embarrassed now," he said, "wait till you look out the window." There was

Sister Washburn, shoveling *their* walks.[2] Sister Washburn was one of those who looked around her neighborhood—not to ask, "who will take care of me?" but to ask, "Whom can I take care of today?" And a few inches of snow were her opportunity.

Please remember the great question of Jesus: "Who is my mother and who are my brothers?" The next time your phone rings, it will almost certainly be a member of the family of disciples. Please respond to them with a sense of kindness and helpfulness.

A Testimony of Christ

The third great question for the disciple is the question that Jesus asked Peter: "Whom do ye say that I am?" (Matthew 16:15). This event occurred after the miracle of feeding the five thousand, and after the Pharisees tried to trick Jesus into doing a miracle to prove to them that he was the Christ. Jesus retired from them with his disciples and then posed the question that was running throughout the region that day as a rumor: "Who do people say I am?"

His disciples reported the rumors: "Some say you are John the Baptist. Others say you are Elijah, and still others say you are Jeremiah or one of the prophets."

Then Jesus asked the great question, the question that he asks us today, the greatest question we can answer in this life or the next: "And who do *you* say I am?"

This time, the answer was so enormous, so staggering in its implications, that only Simon Peter, the impetuous apostle, answered: "Thou art the Christ, the Son of the living God."

Think what a testimony means to you. Think of the power of knowing beyond doubt that Jesus Christ lives and loves you, and that he died for you. Think of the power of his companionship in your life, so that you are never without the strength of that eternal compassion, that abundant love, that bright vision of the importance of this life in the eternal scheme of things.

Think of your parents, your children, your brothers and sisters, your loved ones whether they are far or near. Think what it means in this life and in the next for you to share with these loved ones a firm conviction of a testimony of the Savior. Joseph Smith was talking about you in the vision he had of the celestial glory. Let me share one passage from that revelation, paraphrased slightly so that it speaks directly to us:

> We are those who have received the testimony of Jesus, and believed on his name and been baptized . . . by being buried in the water in his name, according to the commandment which he has given—
>
> That by keeping the commandments we might be washed and cleansed from all our sins, and receive the Holy Spirit by the laying on of the hands of him who is ordained and sealed unto this power;
>
> We are they who overcome by faith, and are sealed by the Holy Spirit of promise, which the Father sheds forth upon all those who are just and true. . . .
>
> We are they into whose hands the Father has given all things—
>
> We are priestesses and queens, who have received of his fulness, and of his glory;
>
> Wherefore, as it is written, we are gods, even the daughters of God—
>
> Wherefore, all things are ours, whether life or death, or things present, or things to come, all are ours and we are Christ's, and Christ is God's.
>
> And *we shall overcome all things.* (See D&C 76:51–53, 55–60)

This is how Jesus sees you. We talk about having a testimony of the Savior, but do we realize that he has a testimony of us, too? He has a testimony of you as immortal, glorified, perfected, a queen, a priestess, and a god. When Jesus asks, "Whom say ye that I am?" respond from a heart full of faith, "Thou art the Christ, the son of the living God." And if your faith is not yet strong enough to say this, then build it with love and hope until the words ring inside your own heart.

Let's remember the three great questions Christ posed. He asks: "What wilt thou that I should do for thee?" This is an invitation to tell him the desires of our heart in full confidence that he will respond with the same joyous willingness with which he said to the blind man, "Receive thy sight." Second, in answer to the question, "Who is my mother, who are my brothers?" let's remember that we belong to a family of disciples as well as to a family of kin, and that our entrance into that second family requires believing in the Savior and then doing the will of the Father. Remember the *Wasa*, so top-heavy with sails and cannons and a high deck and so flat-bottomed that it couldn't hold much ballast. Think of it being capsized by a light puff of wind. Let us ballast ourselves with daily acts of kindness, the "weightier matters" of the law: "judgment, mercy, and faith."

And third, let's remember the searching, ringing question of Christ, "Whom say ye that I am?" And let us answer that question as Peter did, with all our hearts—"Thou art the Christ, the son of the living God."

STEADFAST DISCIPLES

As I thought about what the scriptures say about steadfastness in Christ, I was interested to notice that the word appears over and over again in the account of the Savior's appearance to the Nephites in the Promised Land. For instance, before Christ's birth, the people who doubted the prophecies of Samuel the Lamanite began to taunt the believers, threatening them with death and torture, jeering that the time had passed for the sign and that their faith in Samuel was misplaced. The believers didn't know whether they were right or not. They had no way to get more information. There were no arguments they could use against these people who were not only trying to make them feel ashamed of their faith but threatening their lives.

> And the people who believed began to be very sorrowful, lest by any means those things which had been spoken might not come to pass.
> But behold, they did watch *steadfastly* for that day and that night and that day which should be as one day as if there were no night, that they might know that their faith had not been vain. (3 Nephi 1:7–8)

Their faith was rewarded, the sign was given of Christ's birth, and, thirty-three years later, the signs of his death appeared in the terrible destructions that racked the face of the earth. When the shaken survivors gathered at the temple later, they were both confused and comforted to hear a voice speaking to them. They could not tell what the voice was saying the first two times, but as it came a third time, they "did open their ears to hear it; and their eyes were towards the sound thereof; and they did look *steadfastly* towards heaven, from whence the sound came" (3 Nephi 11:5).

And of course, they understood the voice the third time and knew it was the voice of the Father, announcing the coming of his Beloved Son to them.

The third occurrence of this word came when Jesus had preached to the people, given them the Sermon on the Mount, and called twelve disciples to minister to them. Then he told the people to go to their homes and think about what he had said, and that he would return on the morrow. "And it came to pass that when Jesus had thus spoken, he cast his eyes round about again on the multitude, and beheld they were in tears, and did look *steadfastly* upon him as if they would ask him to tarry a little longer with them" (3 Nephi 17:5).

His heart was touched and he could not refuse the yearning of their hearts. He healed their sick, and angels ministered to their children. There was an outpouring of the Spirit so great that Jesus could not refrain from weeping because of the fullness of his joy. Then he prayed for them, praying that their faith would be strengthened, that they would be purified in him, and that he would be glorified in them. It is a prayer of the magnitude of eternity. And when he had finished, "he came again unto his disciples; and behold they did pray *steadfastly*, without ceasing, unto him; and he did smile upon them again; and behold they were [transfigured] even as Jesus" (3 Nephi 19:29–30).

So we have this word, *steadfastly*, that appears four times in the account of the Savior's ministry. First, the people fear that they might have been deceived, that their hopes might have been misplaced, but they do not waver or turn aside. Despite their fears, they continue steadfastly watching.

Second, the people cannot even understand the words Heavenly Father is speaking to them, but they look steadfastly in the direction of the voice. They don't give up, even though they are bewildered by the destruction and grief-stricken for the devastation and death that surround them. They look steadfastly toward the voice, and finally they can understand what it says.

Third, they look upon the Savior steadfastly, their hearts filled with a desire for the blessing of his presence. And by the fourth time this word is used, they are transfigured in the presence of Christ, their faces glowing with pure light, just as his is, while they pray without ceasing to him. In other words, the concept of steadfastness in this particular story begins with doubt and confusion and ends with transfiguration and glory.

I want to talk about how these four ways might apply to us as well, four circumstances in which we as disciples need steadfastness: steadfastness in the face of adversity, steadfastness in seeking understanding, steadfastness in persistence for a blessing, and steadfastness in thanksgiving and celebration for the goodness of God.

Steadfastness in Adversity

Let's begin with a situation that we're all familiar with: affliction and adversity. What can deliver us from affliction? What can preserve us so that we can endure affliction and emerge from it intact? Is it our own strength? Is it our own intelligence or good planning?

I believe in miracles. I believe in a God of miracles, someone who fights our battles for us, someone who is mighty to save and on whose arm we can rely. What other alternative do we have? Surely none of us believes that we can actually be lucky enough or smart enough or fast enough to avoid the adversities that come to every human being born on the earth. Sometimes we are slow to see miracles in the course of our daily lives, and so, sometimes, we're reluctant to pray for miracles.

I love the stories of the Old Testament—not because I understand them all and certainly not because I think they're all edifying, but because so many of them testify that God is a God of miracles. Let me give you just one example. Think about the way the Lord fought the Israelites' battles in the Old Testament. The first battle was that of the Israelites against the Amalekites as they were entering the Promised Land.

Moses instructed Joshua to select his army and go to battle against the Amalekites while Moses would watch the battle from a nearby hilltop "with the rod of God in [his] hand." Aaron and Hur went with Moses, and they watched, all the next day.

> And it came to pass, when Moses held up his hand, that Israel prevailed: and when he let down his hand, Amalek prevailed.
>
> But Moses' hands were heavy; and they took a stone, and put it under him, and he sat thereon; and Aaron and Hur stayed up his hands, the one on the one side, and the other on the other side; and his hands were steady until the going down of the sun. (Exodus 17:8–13)

And Israel won that battle.

The second battle involved Gideon (Judges 6–8), selected by an angel to deliver his people from the Midianites. He was dubious—a younger son in a minor house in one of the weaker tribes of Israel. He tested the angel's words by asking for signs on two separate nights, which were given to him. He raised an army of thirty-two thousand, but the Lord said, "The people that are with thee are too many for me to give the Midianites into their hands, lest Israel vaunt themselves against me, saying, Mine own hand hath saved me" (Judges 7:2). So Gideon sent back all who were afraid—twenty-two thousand, leaving ten thousand. That was still too many for the Lord, so he had Gideon take them to the stream to drink. Everyone who knelt down by the water and put his face to the surface of the stream to drink, the Lord sent away, keeping only the three hundred who scooped up water in their hands to drink. Gideon armed these three hundred with trumpets and lamps inside empty pitchers. Silently they surrounded the Midianites at night. At a given signal, they blew their trumpets, threw down the pitchers, and held the lamps up as they cried, "The sword of the Lord, and of Gideon!" (Judges 7:19–22). With that, the Midianites panicked and began fighting each other, then fled.

The third extraordinary battle occurred later in Israel's history, under the leadership of Jehoshaphat, king of Judah and a descendant of David. When a coalition of the Moabites and the Ammonites came to battle against them, Jehoshaphat assembled all the people—men, women, and children—before the Lord and prayed in the temple asking for help. Then the spirit of the Lord fell upon a man in the congregation, who stepped forward and promised, "Ye shall not need to fight in this battle; set yourselves, stand ye still, and see the salvation of the Lord" (2 Chronicles 20:17). And that's exactly what happened. The Israelites went forward to the place of battle the next morning, and Jehoshaphat gave them their instructions: "Believe in the Lord your God, so shall ye be established; believe his prophets, so shall ye prosper" (v. 20). Singers went before the army to "praise the beauty of holiness" and to sing anthems of praise to the Lord. "And when they began to sing and to praise," the Lord stepped in (vv. 21–22). He turned the Moabites and the Ammonites against each other so that they slew and destroyed each other. After the battle was over, the Israelites passed over the field of battle, collecting the spoils of this battle they had not fought. The two hostile armies were so richly dressed and wore so many precious jewels that it took the Israelites three days to take away the plunder (see vv. 22–25).

Visualize it this way: Imagine a class in tactics at West Point. The uniformed cadets march to class, where they are introduced to a guest lecturer who promises three surefire ways to win a battle.

"The first method," he tells them, "is the Moses strategy. During the fighting, you get the president of the United States to hold a Bible in his uplifted hands as he watches the battle from some vantage point. If he gets tired, call on the secretaries of state and defense to hold his arms up. As long as his arms remain aloft, the United States will win.

"The second method is the Gideon way. Pick the most unlikely general you can—one from a small family on the wrong side of the tracks who has a fearful, negative attitude. Put him in charge. Reduce your standing army by more than 90 percent. Do away with all weapons and give the men musical instruments and flashlights. Surround the army at night. Play your instruments, turn on your flashlights, and holler about God and your chicken-hearted general. The enemy will become confused and kill each other and flee. You are sure to win.

"Finally, there's the Jehoshaphat plan. Gather everybody in church and let the president lead in a prayer confessing the utter weakness of the country. Then gather a choir, and let them take the front lines as they sing praises to God. The enemy will be defeated."[1]

When you phrase it in practical terms, these tactics are pretty absurd, aren't they? The Israelites weren't stupid or primitive. They knew this wasn't how you won wars. But that *was* how the Israelites did it, because their God was a God of miracles. All of these battles were times when the Israelites perceived clearly the grace of God—simply because there was no other way to explain what happened. Disciples believe in miracles.

I believe in miracles. I have seen miracles in my own life, and I have been the beneficiary of miracles. When I was in labor at the birth of our second son, I felt my spirit drifting upwards out of my body. I struggled against the feeling, fighting to get back to deliver the baby, but I felt helpless against the powerful force drawing me away. Meanwhile, my husband, Ed, was in the waiting room. (This was before fathers were allowed to be present and help at the births.) Suddenly, he felt a great anxiety for me. He knew that I needed the strength of his faith. He looked for a private place in which he could pray, and the only room he could find was a tiny toilet off the hallway. He went in, knelt down, and prayed humbly for me. The terrible force acting on my spirit ceased, I returned to my body, and our son was born safely.

This was a time when I was in grave danger, even though I did not understand why. A miracle, actuated by my husband's steadfast faith, saved my life. Adversity will come to all of us, and in the midst of adversity, we will be tempted to look for a hiding place, to start scrambling to put a defense together. I pray that we will remember the lesson of the steadfast Nephites and watch steadfastly for deliverance.

Steadfastness during Confusing Times

The second aspect of steadfastness that the Nephites exercised came when they had survived the adversity. The sun was shining, the sky was clear. In fact, they probably wished that they could not see so clearly, because their cities were laid waste by earthquakes, thunderings, lightnings, and darkness, and the "fair ones" of their people lay dead. I'm sure they were mentally and emotionally exhausted, struggling to understand. Under these circumstances, they received a message, a message they could not understand, a message that was confusing to them.

Now, often, when we are confused, we try to find someone who can explain things to us. We look for an expert. Or we pool our ignorance with people who are just as confused as we are and hope that clarity will emerge. The Nephites instead looked steadfastly in the direction of the voice and worked hard to understand. At that point, at the third repetition, things became clear. I want to point out two facts. First, our Heavenly Father was patient with them. He repeated the message three times. But second, they had to work to understand it. Communication with the divine wasn't something that came without effort.

Think about how faith operates in our own lives. It's not a vacuum cleaner that we can plug in and suck up doubts or confusion. It's not a wind that blows away things we don't understand. Faith is a process. It's part of a living dynamic that takes our questions and works on them in the context of God's patience.

Let me give you some examples from the kinds of questions children have. These come from a book I really enjoy about children's prayers, where they got to say what was really on their mind. For instance, one little girl named Marnie wrote, "Dear God, On Halloween I am going to wear a Devil's Costume. Is that all right with you?" And another little girl named Martha wrote, "Dear God, can you marry food?" And Norma asked what I think is a really insightful question, "Dear God, did you mean for the giraffe to look like that or was it an accident?" And Barbara has a very practical question, "Dear God, Why don't you leave the sun out at night when we need it the most?"[2]

We find questions like these charming because we know the answers, even though it might be a little hard to explain to a second-grader how the solar system works or how a giraffe might have come to be. Our questions are just as real, just as searching, just as important. And God is just as patient with our questions as we are with the questions of these children.

What should we do when we are confused or when we have questions? I think we should first remember that God is delighted with our questions, because they show we're thinking. Many times questions are not welcomed at church or in classes because they seem to stop or disrupt the teacher's idea of how the lesson should go. Many times doctrinal questions are perplexing, because the Lord reveals concepts to us in language and images that we can understand. Also, our understandings evolve over time. Sometimes, we may have a question that just doesn't seem to be a question for anyone else, and so we feel shy about asking it.

I'm not saying that all questions should be discussed in

classes. Some of them may be the kinds of questions to be pondered privately in our hearts as we seek for answers. Sometimes we need to grow in understanding of other concepts before we can comprehend a particular answer. But as a teacher, I really believe in the value of questions.

When I was a little girl, I remember one of the few movies that we saw was a Japanese tear-jerker about a poverty-stricken mother who had had to give her daughter away for adoption to a family who could care for her. The mother would go quietly to where she could watch her daughter, happy and beloved in the new home. The pain of the mother's heart, yearning for her daughter, broke my nine-year-old heart. I cried and cried at the thought that a child should be separated from her mother.

After we had seen the movie, I asked my mother about two terms that confused me that the characters in the movie had said often: *umi no haha* and *sodate no haha*. I knew that *haha* meant "mother," but I didn't know what the first words meant. My mother tenderly explained that *umi no haha* meant the mother who brought the child to earth, while *sodate no haha* meant the adoptive mother. She explained that both kinds of love were good, and that both mothers were good mothers. I felt so much closer to my mother, having seen this fictional presentation of a child who could not be with her mother. And at the same time, my mother strengthened in me a trust that others could love me and would take care of me if it were necessary.

Only six years later, when I was fifteen, my mother let me go into the care of strangers so that I could continue my education. Despite how much I missed my mother and longed for her, she had armed me with trust. If I had not asked the questions, if I had not struggled with the painful feelings aroused in me by the movie, I would not have had the feelings of increased closeness to my mother and increased trust in the love and care of others.

So when times are confusing to us and we are in turmoil, let us remain steadfast in looking toward the voice of our Father in

Heaven and steadfast in struggling to understand his message to us. Questions are blessings.

Steadfastness in Perseverance

The third way in which the Nephites were steadfast was in desiring the blessing of the Savior's continued presence after he had given them instructions to return to their home. We don't usually think of God as someone who changes his mind, but the force of the people's desire was so great that he could not resist their yearning and stayed with them again.

Are there blessings for which you yearn? Sometimes blessings flow to us like water from a spring, but more often, I think, they come to us from a well, when we are willing to do the hard work of letting down a bucket and then pulling it up, heavy and dripping. Faithfulness brings forth these blessings.

When my husband was presiding over the Japan Okinawa Mission and I was president of the three women's auxiliaries, I desperately needed someone to help with managing the mission home, and the Lord sent me Sister Fumiko Tasaki. She was a very traditional Japanese woman, the sweetest lady in the world, and married to a well-to-do husband who was not a member. She was under no financial necessity of working, and I was curious about why she would take on household chores that were somewhat below her social station—and even learn to cook American food!

She had joined the Church very suddenly when Elder Kazutoshi Fujimoto, one of our missionaries from Hawaii, tracted her out. He bore a very strong, sweet testimony to her, saying, "I was sent by God with a message for you." Sister Tasaki said, "I was stunned by the idea that God had a message for me. I couldn't turn him down." And so she was baptized. She had a very strong testimony and had great joy in the gospel.

When she began working, the mission financial secretary asked her, "Would you like to be paid by the week, every other week, once a month?" She whispered to him shyly, "How often is it permitted to pay tithing?" He laughed and said, "You can pay anytime." She said, "Oh, then it does not matter." Then we realized that this dear, sweet sister, who became a right hand to me, had taken this work simply so she could keep the law of tithing.

Sister Tasaki was patient and persevering as she struggled to find a way to pay her tithing, and she obviously considered the housework to be an answer to her prayers. Can we likewise be steadfast in our seeking for desired blessings?

Steadfastness in Joy

The fourth way in which the Nephites were steadfast was in their praise of Jesus Christ, praying to him as their Savior while he was in their midst. And their faith had transformed them. One of the Psalms communicates this same idea:

> My heart is fixed, O God, my heart is fixed: I will sing and give praise. . . .
> I will praise thee, O Lord, among the people: I will sing unto thee among the nations.
> For thy mercy is great unto the heavens, and thy truth unto the clouds. (Psalm 57:7–10)

Being steadfast in prayer is the key to being steadfast despite adversity and confusion, being steadfast in desiring a blessing. It is because of steadfastness in our faith and our joy in the Savior that we can accept these other situations in our lives. I was very touched by the account in the March 1994 *Ensign* of Lynette Moss, a mother who found her two-year-old daughter floating unconscious in the swimming pool. She wrote: "I just knew she could be healed. As I began performing CPR, I had no doubt that the Lord would help me bring her back to life. The emergency team was surprised to find Jamie's heart already beating when they arrived, but I wasn't." This mother's faith remained strong and unfaltering during the hospitalization of her daughter. She had many blessings, and many people united their faith in her behalf. When she heard what she thought was a discouraged comment, her first reaction was to say that they must continue to have faith. But little Jamie did not get better. Still, the mother's faith did not waver. When she was praying, just before her daughter's death, she felt someone next to her with an arm around her shoulder, communicating strongly the feeling that "whatever happened would be right." Because of this experience, she could accept her daughter's death in faith.[3]

The reason I think this experience is important is because we all know about miracles that have happened as a result of faith. We have talked about some of them today, in the Lord's preservation of the people of Israel. But we also know good people, righteous people, upon whose behalf great faith has been exercised, but who have died—just like this child, and just like my husband. At times like this, we need to look steadfastly toward Christ so that nothing can separate us or drive a wedge between us and our faith in him. In this case, the mother desired the blessing of her daughter's recovery, but she desired something more: she desired to know and do the will of the Lord. That's why, I believe, she could accept her daughter's death and know that it was all right.

When we truly have a knowledge of the Savior and of his love for us, we can accept things from his hand that seem terribly painful and yet feel his love more strongly. This seems like a contradiction, but it's not. Remember Nephi, tied to the mast of the ship by his rebellious brothers, his hands and feet numb and swollen, without food, without water, the entire company in peril of death because of the recklessness and faithlessness of his disobedient elder brothers. What was Nephi's response? He said, "I did look unto my God, and I did praise him all the day long; and I did not murmur against the Lord because of mine afflictions" (1 Nephi 18:16). I believe Nephi's record. I think this is a wonderful example for all of us. But I think we have to remember that Nephi wrote this account many years after it happened, and he understood something that he goes on to explain. When he describes how Laman and Lemuel bound him with cords and treated him "with much harshness," he explains, "Nevertheless the Lord did suffer it that he might show forth his power, unto the fulfilling of his word which he had spoken concerning the wicked" (1 Nephi 18:11). I don't know if this is an understanding Nephi had at the time he was being treated so harshly. It may have come to him slowly, over time, as he put together the prophecies of what would happen to the wicked with the course that his unrepentant brothers finally charted for themselves after their father's death.

Can you see how steadfastness in communion with God involves all of the other forms of steadfastness that we've talked about?—steadfastness during times of adversity, steadfastness during confusion, when we're not sure we understand what's going on, steadfastness and persistence in seeking a much-desired blessing, steadfastness and patience as the Lord manifests his power and might according to his will.

Psalm 145 expresses the kind of joy and confidence in the Lord that we as disciples all desire to have in its fullness:

> The Lord is gracious, and full of compassion; slow to anger, and of great mercy.
> The Lord is good to all: and his tender mercies are over all his works.
> All thy works shall praise thee, O Lord; and thy saints shall bless thee.
> They shall speak of the glory of thy kingdom, and talk of thy power. (Psalm 145:8–11)

Nephi, writing to his people—and to us!—with great urgency, tells us to have "unshaken faith" in Christ and urges us to rely on the merits of the Lord "who is mighty to save."

> Wherefore, ye must press forward with a steadfastness in Christ, having a perfect brightness of hope, and a love of God and of all [people]. Wherefore, if we shall press forward, feasting upon the word of Christ, and endure to the end, behold,

thus saith the Father: Ye shall have eternal life. (2 Nephi 31:19–20)

Our testimony of Christ can give us this brightness of hope. It gives us a hunger for the scriptures so that we can feel our kinship with the children of Israel, who prayed for miracles but didn't quite believe them when they happened; with the steadfast Nephi, lashed to the mast of his ship; with my husband, struggling in the spirit for my life; with Lynette Moss, who had the faith to see her daughter healed and the even greater faith to give her back to Heavenly Father. Remember that our God is a God of miracles, who fought the absurd battles of Moses, Gideon, and Jehoshaphat that should never have been won.

When we can be steadfast disciples despite confusion, despite adversity, and despite the apparent withholding of blessings that we truly desire, then we can be transformed by our steadfastness and live with an eye single to the glory of God so that we will truly see his hand in all things.

4

WEAVING PATTERNS: MEN, WOMEN, AND PRIESTHOOD PRINCIPLES

I can't think of anyone more important for men to get along with today than women, and vice versa, especially in our marriages, in our homes, in our church jobs, and in the larger society. I've titled this chapter "Weaving Patterns" because that's the image I want to begin with.

Picture a simple checkered tablecloth, blue and white woven together in a pattern called plain check. It is the very simplest pattern you can make when you're weaving, because it introduces only one variation. Author Laurel Thatcher Ulrich talks about this pattern in her biography of Martha Ballard, an eighteenth-century midwife and diarist in New England. This is how Laurel describes the weaving process and draws some lessons from it:

> If Dolly [Dolly was Martha Ballard's oldest unmarried daughter] alternated bands of dyed and undyed yarn on the warp in a regular pattern, white stripe following blue stripe, then filled in the weft in the same way, alternately spooling both bleached yarn and blue, the resulting pattern would be a checkerboard of three distinct hues. Where white thread crossed

white thread, the squares would be uncolored, where blue crossed blue the squares would be a deep indigo, where white crossed blue or blue crossed white the result would be a lighter, mixed tone, the whole forming the familiar pattern of plain woven "check" even today.

Then this is the point that Laurel was making by describing the weaving: "Think of the white threads as women's activities, the blue as men's, then imagine the resulting social web. Clearly, some activities in an eighteenth-century town brought men and women together. Others defined their separateness."[1]

You may recognize Laurel's name. She is a founding editor of *Exponent II*, and in 1991 she became the third Mormon and the first Mormon woman ever to win the Pulitzer Prize for history. Her book also won the Bancroft Prize, the Joan Kelly and John H. Dunning Prizes of the American Historical Association, and the MacArthur Foundation Award (which came with a no-strings-attached $320,000 award). So she seems like a good candidate to talk about the social patterns of women and men!

I want to use her image of weaving and social life in Martha Ballard's village as the theme for this chapter, in the hope that we can all see how we, in our own lives and in our lives together, are weaving. In the eighteenth century, there were very strict, almost impermeable boundaries between the male world and the female world. Martha, for instance, did not go to town meetings. Her husband did. When she went to help a woman give birth, she always referred to the home as "Thomas's house" or "Mr. Lowe's house," never as the woman's house. It was the man who paid her fee as a midwife. Her husband was considered the only taxable citizen in the family, until her sons became a certain age, and the census records gave Martha's husband's name but simply listed the ages and genders of everyone else in the household, including Martha.

Now, what about the boundaries of the male and female worlds we live in? Think of the tablecloth again. Some squares are all-male activities, like priesthood meeting; some are all-women squares, like Relief Society; and some are squares of mingled composition. I'd like to think with you about areas in which our personal lives, our family lives, our educational, church, and professional lives might be better and might work more smoothly if we could find a way to enlarge the areas where we have mingled colors. We get more beautiful, complex, and interesting patterns if we can find creative ways to draw on the strengths of both men and women in partnerships.

Partnership: Making More Complex Patterns

Sometimes people feel uncomfortable when we talk about men's and women's roles in today's world. You may be thinking, "I don't know how much mingling we can do. Won't that change the pattern?" It might, but I think it will make the pattern better. Remember that the two-color checked pattern we've been discussing is the very simplest form of weaving. The diversity and color and beauty of the fabric you can weave are all dependent on your imagination, your creativity, and the number of bobbins you have on your loom. Let me tell you another weaving story to demonstrate.

Have you ever been to the Lion House? Do you remember the carpet there? It has a beige background and a floral pattern in the foreground, a lovely nineteenth-century pattern that has been the height of fashion, become old-fashioned, come back into fashion, and now is classic. That carpet is in the Lion House because of Florence Jacobsen, the former general president of the Young Women's Mutual Improvement Association.

At one point, there were plans to tear down the Lion House and use the space for parking. Florence, who is a granddaughter of both Joseph F. Smith and Heber J. Grant, realized along with many people that an inestimable historic treasure would be lost if that happened. The house had originally been part of Brigham Young's household, you know, but over the years it had been put to a variety of uses, including as a boarding house for country girls who were in Salt Lake looking for work—a kind of LDS YWCA—and as a schoolhouse for teaching domestic art classes and institute classes. Under Florence's leadership, the YWMIA took over the Lion House and remodeled it as a working house where lunches and dinners would be served in elegant, historic surroundings.

As the restoration began, Florence found, hidden way in the back of a closet, the end of a roll of carpet. She recognized it as the original carpet that had been in the house during Brigham Young's day. The New England manufacturer that had woven the carpet was still in business, and when she called them up, described the pattern, and asked if they could match it, they said, "Yes, of course." It would be a special order, so to make it worth their while and also to plan for the future, she signed the contract that the YWMIA would buy enough yardage to carpet the house, replace that carpeting completely one time, and have a good number of yards to make repairs as needed for many years to come.

Then the carpet manufacturer called in great dismay. The carpet contained seventeen colors. It had been their absolute deluxe line in the nineteenth century, but even their most elaborate looms could weave only twelve colors now. It was simply impossible. And Florence in her sweet, gentle, but very firm way said, "We have a contract. Let's talk about how you can fulfill that contract." And they found a way. They called a retired carpet weaver out of retirement to lay in the missing five colors by hand. They fulfilled their contract with pride and kept some of the carpet to show future clients what they could do if they really put their minds to it. And that beautiful seventeen-color carpet was installed in the Lion House. The point of this story is that there are very few limits to how we can use the strengths of men and women fully and simultaneously if we have the imagination, the creativity, and the contract!

Let me discuss the patterns woven in my own marriage. My husband, Ed, and I were partners all our married life. Our lives definitely were the interwoven squares in the checkered cloth. We didn't have too many areas that were separate blue or white. We supported each other in our career aspirations, in raising our boys, in maintaining the links with our extended families, and definitely in our church assignments. When I think of a period of intense partnership, where our lives were tightly interwoven like the mixed square in the weaving, I think of our mission.

Our call came at the beginning of summer; it was June 6, 1968, the last day of school. Ed called me at the office and said, "Hello, are you sitting down?"

I said, "No, I'm standing up."

He said, "Well, sit down." The secretary heard this and got me a chair.

He went on, "President Hugh B. Brown called and wants us to go on a mission."

I was in no mood for jokes. I said, "Ed, it's the last day of school and I'm busy. I don't want any kidding around. Now tell me what you called about."

He said, "I'm not kidding. I just got the call. President Brown wants us in Salt Lake on Monday. They want to call us on a mission."

I said, "You've got to be kidding."

"No, this is true."

"Are you really telling us we're going on a mission?"

"They want to interview us to go on a mission."

So there we were on the airplane with very mixed feelings. We brought Ken and Bob, who were fourteen and thirteen years old, with us. Now *they* didn't have mixed feelings at all. They said they were going to Salt Lake to tell the General Authorities their whole list of reasons why they were against this call. But as we visited with Elder Gordon B. Hinckley, they just quietly folded up the list and put it in their pocket. They couldn't say a word because of the tears in their eyes.

We were called and set apart right then. President Spencer W. Kimball set Ed apart, and Elder Richard L. Evans set me apart. In President Kimball's blessing to Ed, he said, "You will receive the gift of tongues." When I was set apart, I listened closely to Elder Evans to see if I would receive that same blessing, but I didn't. In a way, it was fair. Ed was so busy he didn't have time to study. He had to learn Japanese by standing up and speaking it—and he was able to do that. I couldn't. I had to learn Japanese through the help of the members and the missionaries. We both knew some Japanese because it had been spoken in our childhood homes, but it wasn't gospel Japanese, and after World War II, you can imagine that Japanese wasn't a popular language in the United States, so we had both concentrated on speaking English. But there we were, back in Japan, needing to know Japanese. So we both learned: Ed was blessed with the gift and I was blessed by study.

We had to be there on August 1. That was a busy summer. As we closed the door of our house, I looked at Ed and said, "Do you know anything about being a mission president or running a mission?" He looked back at me and shook his head. He said, "This is the first time I'm going to a job where I know nothing. We just have to depend on the Lord." So there we went.

When President Spencer W. Kimball interviewed us, he asked Ed, "What do you think your number-one job is?"

Ed replied, "To work with the members, to keep them strong, and to baptize others as members."

"No," said President Kimball. "Your number-one job is with the missionaries. You have the responsibility for two hundred children. See that their testimonies increase and that they complete honorable missions."

Now, this wasn't an easy goal. Ed and I were opening a new mission; and besides that, Expo '70 in Osaka was going to occur in our mission. We had to get ready to host six million people in our little pavilion in a way that would give them a glimpse of the gospel and interest them in knowing more. The Church sent us missionaries in batches of thirty-five or forty every few months. During our first year in Japan, the Language Training Mission began teaching in Japanese, so we received missionaries with very different levels of language preparation.

They also had very different levels of personal preparation. But caring for the missionaries was a partnership goal that Ed and I accepted together. Ed took administrative responsibility, and I took personal responsibility. In our monthly mission newsletters, Ed would give the elders and sisters practical and inspirational advice on how to implement the mission program, and I would give them advice on how to eat properly, using those unfamiliar ingredients.

We always wrote a welcoming letter to the missionaries, greeting them and telling them not to bring housekeeping items like sheets—just clothing, personal items, and the standard works. As each missionary came in, I cooked him or her a sukiyaki dinner, and Ed and I sent back a letter to the parents with a photograph telling what we appreciated about that missionary. Ed knew that they always wanted to buy a camera first thing, and he said, "We're going to get these things of the world out of the way." So, on the first day, he had the assistants take the new missionaries to a camera shop where they could buy good-quality cameras at a low price, then to other places to buy their sheets and other necessary housekeeping items. The first day, we got shopping out of the way.

The second day, we began the missionary program in language and lessons. We kept the new missionaries in the mission home for about a week and talked about culture, companion relationships, food, and communication with companions, with district and zone leaders, and with the president. Motivational and spiritual moments through talks, scripture reading, and testimonies were a major part of the program. Then we sent them off to the field with a prayer in our hearts.

Every time Ed visited the missionaries, I would send cakes or cookies. He had a stack of nesting trays made so he could carry the cakes without much trouble. In one branch, after the interviews, one missionary said, "Didn't Sister Okazaki send anything this time?" Ed said, "Oh, that's right. She sent you something." He gave them the cake, and the district leader took out his knife, cut this great big sheet cake into four pieces, and put one on each plate—and the four missionaries sat and ate the whole thing.

We were very close to the missionaries. My husband was determined that he would not send any missionary home, not one. And we didn't. Every time a missionary wanted to go home, we went out to talk to him or brought him in to the office, worked with him, talked with him, tried to identify where some of the pressures were, and tried to find ways to help him meet those pressures. (Ed had a secret weapon, too: For safekeeping, all of the missionaries' passports were locked in the office safe!) Of course, if any missionary had been absolutely determined to go home, no matter what, we couldn't have kept him or her, but we found that even the most discouraged didn't really want to leave the mission field. They just didn't know how to cope with the demands of missionary life. Those demands were real. It was hard to get used to the culture, the language, the food. Naturally it was difficult.

In the beginning, Ed used to say, "I wonder why the bishops send these missionaries. Why would they send these missionaries out in this condition?" Then after a little while he knew why they were sent. He said, "It's for me to take over to get them on this next step of their perfection, and this is one of the ways they'll need to get perfected." So then he said, "Send them all. Send anyone to me, and it'll be wonderful." We were thrilled with each new arrival.

I always traveled with Ed to visit the districts and branches every two months. While he was interviewing each missionary privately, I'd wait with the other missionaries, and I learned a lot about how things were going! Ed never told me anything that he learned in confidential interviews, but sometimes the missionaries discussed with me things that shed some light on an elder's individual problems. Ed and I felt like a team. We worked like a team. Each of us had strengths to bring to this new task that demanded every ounce of skill and energy and commitment and love we had. And because we gave it, our ability increased; and because we were focused on that task itself, our marriage also grew stronger and our ability to work together also increased. The nicest compliment Elder McConkie, our area supervisor, ever gave us was, "You two are a *team!*"

Now, the point about teams is that not everybody has the same strengths. The quarterback doesn't do the same job as the running back, and the pitcher doesn't do the same job as the catcher. Women and men don't have to have the same strengths to be on the same team. But I think it's absolutely essential that they feel like a team and work like a team.

What I'm suggesting, in short, is that we start thinking like partnerships and start acting like partnerships. I'm sure if we take this attitude we'll discover many, many wonderful new concepts that had never occurred to us before. I'd also suggest that we not think in terms of marital categories, either. Single people have a great deal to offer, both men and women, so I hope you will think about people in all stages of marital relationships in what I say next.

Let me paraphrase President Kimball's statement about marriage to apply to broader church circumstances: "When we speak of [Relief Society] as a partnership, let us speak of [it] as a *full* partnership. We do not want our LDS women to be *silent* partners or *limited* partners in that eternal assignment! Please be a *contributing* and *full* partner."[2] Many of you have seen the beautiful history of the Relief Society, *Women of Covenant,* published for the Relief Society's sesquicentennial in 1992. In the preface is this powerful description: "The Relief Society has been counterpart, companion, and complement to the priesthood quorums."[3]

Models from the Scriptures

I hope I've convinced you that we should be looking, not at all the all-white squares or at the all-blue squares, but at the squares where the colors mingle as the area of greatest potential growth for men and women as they explore priesthood principles in today's world. The scriptures are models for us in learning how to distinguish between gospel principles and social practices.

We sense the absolute centrality and importance of priesthood principles when we read Doctrine and Covenants 132:

47

> All covenants, contracts, bonds, obligations, oaths, vows, performances, connections, associations, or expectations, that are not made and entered into and sealed by the Holy Spirit of promise, of him who is anointed, both as well for time and for all eternity, and that too most holy, by revelation and commandment through the medium of mine anointed, whom I have appointed on the earth to hold this power (and I have appointed unto my servant Joseph to hold this power in the last days, and there is never but one on the earth at a time on whom this power and the keys of this priesthood are conferred), are of no efficacy, virtue, or force in and after the resurrection from the dead; for all contracts that are not made unto this end have an end when men are dead. (D&C 132:7)

This is a power that binds the living and the dead. Its principles are something to revere and honor, not to ignore or shun. But we need models to see how to explore new ways of partnership within priesthood principles. Where can we look? I'd like to suggest that we look, not to our history and not to models in the world around us, but to the principles and doctrines of the gospel as they are powerfully set forth in the scriptures.

I talk to many, many women who love the scriptures and read them regularly but are troubled because they do not seem to address the concerns of women as directly as they do the concerns of men. This seems to be particularly true in the Book of Mormon, where only six women are mentioned by name. Three of them are women from the Bible: Eve, Sarah, and Mary, the mother of Christ. The other three are women of the Book of Mormon: Sariah the wife of Lehi, Isabel the harlot, and Abish the Lamanite woman. Why, I've asked myself, do we hear so few stories of women in this all-important scripture? I've especially asked myself that question when I have read wonderful, powerful, empowering doctrinal statements in the Book of Mormon like this:

> [Christ] inviteth all to come unto him and partake of his goodness; and he denieth none that come unto him, black and

white, bond and free, male and female; . . . and all are alike unto
God. . . . (2 Nephi 26:33)

And the one being is as precious in his sight as the other.
(Jacob 2:21)

He imparteth his word by angels unto men, yea, not only
men but women also. (Alma 32:23)

And now, because of the covenant which ye have made ye
shall be called the children of Christ, his sons and his daughters;
. . . ye say that your hearts are changed through faith on his
name; therefore ye are born of him and have become his sons
and his daughters. (Mosiah 5:7)

Now, those are the principles of the gospel. Those are the doctrines of the Church. We believe them today just as the righteous
Nephites believed them. But those doctrines were enunciated by
prophets in a society that saw a very different role for women.
Francine Bennion, a devout and intelligent sister scriptorian,
looked at these very same scriptures in light of the social roles
assigned to women in the Book of Mormon. I'd like to share some
observations she made in an exciting address at a BYU/Relief
Society women's conference. It was as obvious to her as it is to us
that God valued women. By principle and by prophecy, women
were important in the Book of Mormon. But she also saw that
scriptures, in addition to the timeless principles they contain, also
contain a social message that is shaped for the people who
received it, in their own language, according to their own time and
understanding. This social message may or may not be harmo-
nious with the gospel principles embodied in the same scripture.
Sister Bennion comments that the Book of Mormon record keep-
ers saw women as "primarily accessories to men, dependent upon
them not only for survival but also for identity, which is presented
as a matter of relationship to a man, usefulness to a man, or use by
men. Whatever their strengths or virtues, women were subsidiary
to men, shown making decisions only when their men were absent
or helpless." So "why," Sister Bennion, asked, "was gender so

prime a determinant to Book of Mormon men and women if it apparently is not to God?"[4]

Now, that's facing a very tough question squarely, isn't it? And when we ask interesting questions—even if they make us a little bit uncomfortable because they're strange and unfamiliar—we can start to get some interesting answers. One of the answers Sister Bennion suggests is tradition.

> What matters is not only *what* the traditions were but also *that* they were the traditions. What matters is not only that the people inherited Old Testament, Middle Eastern, patriarchal traditions but that adherence to traditions of the fathers was equated with righteousness and honor for Nephites and Lamanites alike. They fought wars for hundreds of years because of "the traditions of their fathers." . . .
>
> To people who called themselves Nephites, Father Lehi was good, and therefore his ways were good and were the measure of goodness. To examine the roles of women would be to question core traditions of Lehi, and if such questioning were to occur (which, apparently, it did not), that questioning would by definition be neither right nor righteous. The place women had apparently was assumed to be the place God wanted them to have, as unchanged and unquestioned as ordinary air. (p. 174)

Ask yourself some questions about traditions. Are there some traditions in your Relief Society or your elders' quorum that perhaps were very functional a few years ago but that just aren't meeting people's needs now? Are there some things we do in our wards because that's the way we've always done them? Do we have stereotypes and attitudes about things that are left over from other days? Could the work move forward more effectively if we rethought some of those traditions?

Someone may think: "But if women aren't in the Book of Mormon, it's because God didn't want them in there." But the importance and fundamental equality of women is stressed in those very principles the prophets enunciated, which I have already quoted. I think a more reasonable answer is to see how revelation operates in the Book of Mormon. Sister Bennion points out:

> The visions of Nephi, Enos, and Moroni suggest a model: revelation is given to a seeker who takes his own questions and puzzlements to God. He expects God to answer, even if the answer is long in coming. He is an active participant in the revelation. . . .
>
> God does not erase the prophet's understanding with His own. God gives respect for agency, experience with His love, and awareness of Christ's mission as integral parts of the revelation, whatever the seeker's question, because these are relevant to all questions. But God speaks to us according to our own language and understanding, which at the same time both aids and limits us. (p. 175)

As just one example, have you ever applied that wonderful promise in Moroni 10:4, "And when ye shall receive these things, I would exhort you that ye would ask God, the Eternal Father, in the name of Christ, if these things are not true"? Yes, me too. Every missionary of the Church today, elder or sister, tells every investigator, male or female, to apply this promise in the sure faith of receiving an answer. Yet Mormon addresses these instructions to his "brethren."

Sister Bennion explains: "Nephi and Moroni suggest that God does not imprint revelation upon a blank mind. God answers, shows, tells. The receiver asks, sees, hears, takes part in creating understanding, and then acts upon that understanding. . . . As Nephites, Lamanites or Latter-day Saints, we bring our own sight and assumptions to scripture. God does not destroy this ability but has preserved it" (p. 176).

Sister Bennion's address prompted me to ask several questions:

Is this how I receive revelation—by taking my questions to

God and struggling to understand what he shows and tells me? Yes, it is.

Are there traditions of the fathers—*and* of the mothers—that represented goodness in times past but that may no longer be appropriate? Yes, certainly there are.

Are there some traditions that are still good ones and to which we should cling even more tightly? Absolutely!

How, then, do we tell them apart? Or will the prophet and our priesthood leaders tell us? I think it is inherent in the wonderful law of agency that God doesn't do our work for us and he doesn't expect us to do each other's work. The prophet's job is to receive revelation for the Church, not for individuals. Our job is to receive revelation for ourselves, not for the Church. We have a responsibility to take our questions to God and struggle with those questions in the process of receiving revelation.

Will my personal direction from God be the same as yours? I don't think so. We're individuals. God deals with us as individuals. This is the same God who made not just apples but pears and apricots and persimmons and grapes. He likes diversity. He invented it.

In short, the timeless principles of the gospel are embedded in social circumstances. It is easy for us to see how Nephite society was different from ours, or how Israelite culture differs from ours, but it's sometimes difficult to recognize the characteristics of our own culture—both its strengths and its weaknesses. We can do it if we will look at gospel principles instead of social practices.

I hope I have suggested to you some of the strengths that can come when men and women work together in partnership, following priesthood principles. Remember the blue-checked cloth and think about places where the work of both men and women can intermingle. Remember Florence Jacobsen, and the seventeen-color carpet she had created for the Lion House. Women are very different from each other and have very different gifts, depending on their personalities and circumstances. So do men. Think about ways to weave everyone into these lovely and complex patterns. Please remember that the Book of Mormon prophet who recorded the amazing words: "he denieth none that come unto him, black and white, bond and free, male and female; . . . and all are alike unto God" (2 Nephi 26:33)—this same prophet did not tell us about his mother or his wife or his daughters. And remember that it is gospel principles that are eternal, not any particular society's practices.

The gospel is a powerful countercultural force. It teaches women to teach, to speak, to organize, and to work together. It teaches men to put their families first, to love, and to serve. Surely women can accomplish very little if they do not understand, love, and respect the power of the priesthood and learn to work effectively with the men who hold it. Surely men will accomplish very little if they do not understand, love, and respect the power of the priesthood and learn to work effectively with the women and children whose lives can be blessed by priesthood principles. Surely all of us should shape our lives by the great principles enunciated in Doctrine and Covenants 121 about how priesthood power can and should be used: "Only by persuasion, by long-suffering, by gentleness and meekness, and by love unfeigned; by kindness, and pure knowledge, which shall greatly enlarge the soul without hypocrisy, and without guile" (D&C 121:41–42).

Our Father in Heaven does not want obedient slaves, anxious dependents, unthinking servants, loyal but incompetent children. He wants to give us all that he has. He wants to make us co-heirs with Christ. He wants us to become creators and peoplers of our own worlds, just as he is. In a word, he does not want inferiors. He wants partners. It behooves us, then, as disciples of Christ, to remove the obstacles in our own thinking and in our own traditions that may make it possible for us to look at any other brother or sister in the gospel and to think unkindly or demeaningly or uncharitably of them. Rather, let us say with Nephi and Jacob, "The one being is as precious in his sight as the other" (Jacob 2:21).

5

HONORING THE PRIESTHOOD

When I think of priesthood, three questions come to mind. First, what is the priesthood? Second, how can we, men and women alike, honor the priesthood? And third, how can men minister in the offices of their priesthood?

What Is the Priesthood?

Let's begin with a definition. What is the priesthood? I think the definition we hear most frequently is that it is the power to act in the name of God. We also hear that priesthood exists to bless lives. It has responsibilities like administering the ordinances, governing the Church in righteousness, and teaching the gospel to others. Sometimes we hear people speak as though *priesthood* were the same as "priesthood holders." Have you ever heard someone thank "the priesthood" for administering the sacrament or taking down the tables for the ward banquet? Sometimes this can be confusing.

I think we use the word *priesthood* in three ways. First, priesthood is Church government—it's that orderly list of offices from deacon to high priest, and it's also all of the separate callings that can come with each of those priesthood offices, such as missionary, bishop, or stake president. Second, it's the individual priesthood power that a righteous man, young or old, has by virtue of his ordination and of his living worthy to represent God. And third, it is an eternal principle that exists separately from the individual and even from the priesthood office itself. We're not sure if there will be teachers and deacons in the next world, but we're sure there will be priesthood.

I have a very simple definition that helps me think things through in my mind about the difference between power in the priesthood and the priesthood holder. I think of an umbrella. An umbrella is a sort of portable roof to keep off the rain. It makes a little house that we can carry around with us when we need to.

Let's say that this umbrella represents priesthood power. First, let's think of priesthood as an eternal principle. We know that there are times when the priesthood has been withdrawn from the earth during periods of apostasy, so those have been times, let's say, when the priesthood has been rolled up and left lying on a shelf, just as an umbrella is rolled up and put away on a sunny day. Whether the umbrella is actually working or not, it still exists. This isn't a perfect analogy, of course, but it gives us the idea of priesthood as a principle of eternal power.

Whether we know about priesthood or not, whether we're members of the Church or not, whether priesthood is on earth or not, whether it's operating in our lives in a way we understand or not, priesthood exists and is part of the divine plan of our Heavenly Father. So the priesthood can exist, separate from an office and separate from a priesthood holder, just as an umbrella can exist even if all it does is sit in the closet for twenty years.

Now, let's think about the other two meanings of priesthood. First is the idea of priesthood government. Imagine two men in a ward, Brother Smith and Brother Jones. Brother Smith holds the priesthood; Brother Jones does not. Where did Brother Smith get the priesthood? It was conferred upon him by another priesthood holder who had received authority from his bishop to perform that ordinance. The bishop or branch president received the power to authorize that ordination from the stake president or mission president. The stake or mission president received that authority, along with all the other authority he needed to govern the stake or mission, at the time he was set apart by a General Authority.

So Brother Smith has the priesthood, or, in the case of our analogy, he has an umbrella. Brother Jones doesn't. His hands are empty. If it rains, he's going to get wet. No umbrella. Now, let's say that he desires the priesthood, that he has been interviewed and found worthy, and he is ordained to the priesthood. An authorized representative takes an umbrella from its "eternal shelf" where it's just been waiting for Brother Jones to get ready, and gives it to him. This transfer of the umbrella is ordination. Brother Jones now has the priesthood. He has become a *priesthood holder.*

However, to illustrate the principle of church government, we know that usually with that ordination comes a specific function or calling. For example, if Brother Jones is ordained an elder, he might also be called to be a missionary. Or, he may be ordained to be a high priest and called to be a bishop. Of course, you understand that you don't stop being an elder when you're released from your mission call. The ordination remains in force, even if the callings change. Brother Jones can take his umbrella to Provo or to Paris or to Pakistan—lots of different positions, but the priesthood goes with him to every one. That's an analogy for priesthood as church government.

And now let's consider the third aspect of priesthood, personal priesthood. Imagine that Brother Jones has closed his umbrella and is just holding it in his hand. Here is this good priesthood *holder*—no office, no calling. But does holding the priesthood mean that he's using the priesthood? Is he blessing the lives of other people with it? Is it doing him or anybody else much good right now? No, because he's not exercising power in the priesthood. If it were raining, he would be getting wet.

If Brother Jones were to open the umbrella, it could shelter him. He wouldn't just be holding the priesthood, it would be blessing his life. Even if he never did anything else with the umbrella, it would still perform the function of keeping him dry.

As long as he honors his priesthood—or in other words, takes care of this umbrella—he will be protected by its power. But he can't punch holes in it or turn it upside down and store footballs in it or lean it against the wall and walk away from it. If he does any of those things, it will cease to function in his life and he'll start getting wet again.

But he can also use his personal priesthood to bless the lives of others, with or without a calling. Let's say without a calling, just to keep things simpler. Let's say that Brother Smith is in the hospital waiting for an operation the next day. At Brother Smith's invitation, Brother Jones can go to the hospital with another priesthood holder and give him a blessing. That's an exercise of priesthood power through an ordinance that's not attached to a calling.

Brother Jones can also exercise priesthood power just as a follower of Christ, doing the kinds of things that Christ did on the earth without a specific assignment. Let's say that it's raining, and Sister Brown is carrying her groceries home, and one of the bags starts to split. Brother Jones holds his umbrella over Sister Brown, takes the bag, holds the edges together, and carries it to her house. This isn't an ordinance; it's not a calling; it's just being a good neighbor and a kind Christian. But that's also one of the powers of Brother Jones's personal priesthood—which is the third definition of priesthood power.

And let's not forget the most important exercise of personal priesthood power. If Sister Jones were walking in the rain with her husband, what do you suppose Brother Jones would do with his umbrella? Wouldn't he hold it over both of them as they walked arm in arm? Both of them would be protected from the rain. Both of them would be functioning under the shelter of the umbrella. Sister Jones, by linking her arm with his, is sustaining him in upholding the umbrella, helping him hold it steady. And there's room under that umbrella for quite a few children. Because of the sealing in the temple, in an eternal marriage between a worthy, endowed man who holds the eternal principle of the priesthood and a worthy, endowed woman who sustains that same principle, the priesthood can be a protection to them as individuals, as a couple, and as a family.

I hope this little analogy of the umbrella helps you understand how priesthood can operate in three ways: first, as an eternal principle, separate from any earthly function or individual priesthood holder; second, as the organizational structure and ordering principle of Church government; and third, as a personal power to bless the lives of others, not only through your callings but as a follower of the Savior—a power that is yours as long as you exercise it righteously.

Honoring the Priesthood

So that's the first point: priesthood is an eternal principle, the order of church government, and a personal power. The second question I wanted to share some thoughts on is the topic of honoring the priesthood. How can we honor the priesthood?

I was once discussing the topic of honoring the priesthood with one of our former missionaries. He has since served in bishoprics and Sunday School presidencies and high councils, so he's certainly heard and probably given many lessons and lectures on the topic. He observed, "You know, we hear a lot about honoring the priesthood; but when it comes right down to it, what the speakers mostly talk about is not *dis*honoring the priesthood." I think he had a point. It's kind of like the way we usually teach about chastity. We don't teach about chastity as much as we teach about what's wrong with unchastity.

I'm not going to do that. Instead, I'm going to tell you two stories about my husband, Ed, that I hope will show you part of what honoring the priesthood means.

When we were living in Denver, some teenage neighbor boys were playing at the site of a house under construction, rocking back and forth on one of the big triangular-shaped roof trusses. One of the boys slipped off, and the section fell, hitting a younger brother, about age twelve, in the head. He stopped breathing, and the parents rushed him to the hospital, then called for Ed to come. Ed responded at once and administered to the boy while he was in an oxygen tank, struggling to breathe. All the way there, Ed had prayed, "Dear Heavenly Father, may I be worthy to give this child a blessing. If I've done anything that would prevent this boy from receiving a blessing from thee, forgive me, and make me pure so that the blessing can pass without hindrance to him." The next day, the boy had recovered, breathing, talking, and moving normally.

On the second occasion, one weekend, Ed was working in our garden when a woman came running to him from the neighborhood swimming pool, gasping, "Please come, Brother Okazaki. A little girl has been drowned." Ed ran with her to the swimming pool where the parents were working anxiously over this little girl. The ambulance was on the way, and it was a matter of life and death, but Ed still turned aside for a moment of private prayer, again asking the Lord with all the faith and humility in his heart to forgive him for any unworthiness in himself that might impede the Lord's blessing from coming with power to this child. He laid his hands on her head, pronounced the blessing, and saw the ambulance whisk her away. She lived, and the child's mother always, for as long as we lived in that ward, said that she was alive because of Ed's blessing.

I love to remember this event. Ed was wearing gardening clothes, covered with dirt and grass stains. He didn't even stop to wash his hands but placed them, stained with earth as they were, on the head of this child. His hands weren't important. His clothes weren't important. What was important was his heart, and for that he took time—to pray that his heart would be pure.

Ed did not confuse himself with the priesthood. He considered himself a vessel by which the priesthood power could be transmitted from its source—God—to its destination—those two children in danger. He was not casual about his priesthood. He was humble and sincere. He was not proud of his priesthood power. He considered it to be a weighty responsibility and a mighty stewardship. For him, it was part and parcel of his greater task of being a follower of Christ.

All of us honor priesthood when we honor our calling as Christians, when we honor the authority that conferred the name of Christ upon us. Long before a person is ready to serve a mission or go through the temple, he or she is a baptized, covenant member of Christ's church. Sometimes people talk to teenagers about missions so much that they unintentionally give the message that a person's identity during those teenage years is that of a future missionary, that who one is *right now* isn't as important or as valuable as the person one will be once he or she is old enough to become a missionary.

So when a topic like honoring the priesthood comes up, the young person thinks, "Well, that will be easy once I'm a missionary," or a young woman might think, " . . . once I'm married to a priesthood holder." Missionaries have a long list of things that missionaries do. They study the scriptures. They go tracting. They bear their testimonies and teach discussions. Maybe a young man even thinks, "When I'm a missionary, I'll know who I am because I'll be doing all of these things that will tell me I'm a missionary."

I want to tell young people this: you're valuable members of the Church right here and right now—not only at some point in the future, not just when you go on a mission or get married or have a baby. You twelve- and thirteen-year-olds are important—not just the grown-ups. The Savior has a job for you to do right here and right now, and it's being a Christian.

Think of it this way. Suppose that when you went to your closet this morning to get your shoes, all you found was a pair of missionary shoes. You put them on, but your feet aren't that size yet, so those shoes are slipping around. They're rubbing a blister on your left heel. You've almost walked out of them a couple of times. You kind of stumbled coming into the chapel because they were so big that they caught on the step and threw you off balance. You have to walk around really carefully so that you don't end up on the floor. You feel uncomfortable and off balance and

example, that we're all sitting in a meeting and we hear the sound of a car engine outside. It isn't a loud engine, but it's a powerful one. It swings around the corner effortlessly, just barely purring. We look through the windows. Yes, it's a big car and a powerful car—black, maybe, and inconspicuous. It doesn't have murals of surfers riding the waves at Waikiki painted on the side or flags flying from the hood or loud music blasting through the windows. But it's very well cared for. It's polished and gleaming, even though there might be a little dust on the fenders.

And then, through the windows we see that in the backseat is President Hinckley! He's heard about this meeting and has driven all the way down here to join us. We all rush outside and encircle the car. He's smiling and waving as the driver gets out to open his door, and the companion with him takes him by the arm to help him out. But the driver can't get the door open because we're all crowded around admiring the paint job on the car. "Ooh, look how shiny," one person says. "Look at those terrific hubcaps," says somebody else. "Have you ever seen a grill like that?" marvels a third. "If I start saving my money now, when will I have enough to make a down payment?" wonders a fourth.

What's going on here? Why are we paying attention to the car and no attention to President Hinckley? Let me compare the car to administering, and President Hinckley to ministering. Wouldn't we be foolish to give all of our attention to the vehicle that brings the messenger, and to pay no attention at all to the messenger? Well, that's what happens when we spend all our time polishing a shiny program until we can see our faces in it. We can't see the faces of the people that it's meant to serve, and we can't see the Savior's face either. And that's how we end up with empty programs, empty chairs, and empty hearts.

But at the same time, wouldn't it be foolish to say, "Oh, so administration isn't important. The vehicle to bring President Hinckley here isn't as important as he is. So here's a bicycle. Good luck, President Hinckley." There's no question about what's the most important, but there's also no question that good

administration is *essential*. I like to think of it as housework. If it's done well, it's just about invisible. You're simply aware of a feeling of comfortableness, of orderliness or peacefulness or security, of things going as they should. But if every chair is so cluttered that you can't sit down, and each one faces a different direction, it's hard to notice anything else.

Administration doesn't deserve the limelight. It shouldn't attract the attention. What it needs to do is deliver the messenger comfortably and graciously to the right location at the right time. All of us have a job to do, schedules to meet, groups to organize, tasks to do, programs to run. Let's administer in such a way that these arrangements and organizations, these tasks and timetables are done beautifully, on time, and unobtrusively. Let's not be the loud, rock-music-blaring surfer van. Let's be the quiet black car. Let's allow people to focus all their attention on the inspired messenger without being distracted.

Programs and handbooks are easy because they spell out the rules. But there isn't a rule book or a handbook for ministering sensitively. Efficient administration is a job for a manager. Ministering sensitively is a job for a loving Christian.

As a minister of the gospel, your real job is not to run programs but to love the people you serve. Usually the two jobs will not conflict. But what should you do if they do? What should take precedence? The people, every single time. Programs exist to bring you in contact with the people. Why do we have meetings? Not because there's something sacred about meetings—although something sacred happens if the meeting is sacrament meeting, where we renew our covenants with the Savior. But all those Sunday School meetings and quorum meetings and Relief Society homemaking meetings and Primary Inservice meetings and choir practices and seminary and Young Men and Young Women activities and Scout merit badge sessions—in all of those meetings, whatever their other purposes may be, their underlying and fundamental purpose is to bring people into contact with each other in a setting where they can share their faith and express their love

and learn more about each other so they can serve each other. We have Sunday School class at the same time every week and we conduct it in an orderly way to provide a comfortable place for the people. But it's the people, not the meeting, who are the important element.

Ministering leaders recognize that wards and stakes are happiest and work best when everyone—men, women, youth, and children—can share their knowledge, skills, and strengths to meet the needs of others. Administrators maintain rigid roles, rigid expectations, and rigid channels of communication. They expect to give orders and take orders. Ministering leaders and followers are flexible. They share, negotiate, and decide together based on the demands of the task. They work like a family, not like the army. There's a partnership, a sharing, a mutuality.

Priesthood isn't a matter of who's in charge and who gets to give orders. It's a matter of serving others. Every officer *and every member*, whether man or woman or child, needs that feeling of being sustained, both by members who hold the priesthood and by those who do not, so that *all* the members, men and women, can be strengthened.

I have a profound testimony of the power of the priesthood, as an eternal principle, as a principle of personal power in the lives of righteous men, and as the structure and order of our marvelous church. Ed has stepped on ahead of me, but somehow I don't feel that the priesthood influence is gone from my home. Even though that particular umbrella isn't close enough for me to reach out and touch whenever I want to, I still feel sheltered under the overlapping umbrellas of our bishop, of the righteous neighbors who are priesthood bearers, of my sons, and of the Church itself. I feel strongly that I share in the blessings of the priesthood, on the basis of my personal worthiness, because Ed and I made temple covenants together and are sealed together. It has also been a great privilege to work with General Authorities who honor their priesthood and see themselves as stewards of a great power that can be used to bless the lives of men, women, and children.

In conclusion, let me share with you a beautiful and powerful scripture that Moroni took the trouble to inscribe on the golden plates at the end of the existence of the Nephite nation. He says they were the words of his father, Mormon, but he doesn't tell us the context in which Mormon uttered them. Was he writing them in a letter? Was he speaking at a meeting? The fact that they are addressed to his "beloved brethren" suggests that perhaps they could even have been spoken at a priesthood meeting. He says:

> Charity is the pure love of Christ, and it endureth forever; and whoso is found possessed of it at the last day, it shall be well with him.
>
> Wherefore, my beloved brethren, pray unto the Father with all the energy of heart, that ye may be filled with this love, which he hath bestowed upon all who are true followers of his Son, Jesus Christ; that ye may become the sons of God; that when he shall appear we shall be like him, for we shall see him as he is; that we may have this hope; that we may be purified even as he is pure. (Moroni 7:47–48)

This my prayer, too: that we may be true followers of our Savior Jesus Christ, that we may be true sons and true daughters of God, and that we may be like him at his coming because we will have followed his path in this life.

6

KNIT TOGETHER IN LOVE

A favorite scripture of mine comes from that beautiful and tender letter of Paul to the Colossian Saints, where he prays "that [your] hearts might be comforted, being knit together in love, and unto all riches of the full assurance of understanding, to the acknowledgement of the mystery of God, and of the Father, and of Christ; in whom are hid all the treasures of wisdom and knowledge" (Colossians 2:2–3).

This scripture says we should be knit together in love. I enjoy knitting and I respect those who are consistent at it. It's a great satisfaction to wear something or display something that you yourself have made. I have, for instance, a sweater that Ken, my oldest son, started about five years ago that he asked me to finish. He actually asked me to finish it about three years ago, and I haven't made a whole lot of progress on it since then. Do you have projects around the house that you haven't quite finished yet?

We don't have to be skilled knitters of sweaters, though, to have something in our hearts that recognizes the knitting together of people. Why is it that we love to make connections, love to discover that we have something in common with the stranger sitting next to us on the plane, or are just delighted when we discover that the new sister who moved into our ward has a brother who served in the same mission as our son? It doesn't take much, does it, to make a connection, but the delight is real.

Let me tell you a little story that illustrates what I mean. About thirty years ago, my husband had some meetings in Washington, D.C., so the boys and I went along for the holiday. We took our motor home and rented a spot in a motor-home park for the week we were there. After a few days, I took our laundry over to the neat little laundromat in the park. Two other women were there, each with a book or magazine. I said, "Hello, hello," when I came in, then I put my laundry in, measured out the soap, put in the coins, and sat down with my own magazine. The wash cycle finished for all of us in sequence, and we each got up in turn and put the damp laundry into the dryers, put in our coins, and sat down again with our magazines. Then the drying cycle finished for our white things, so we each got up and took our clothes out of the dryer and plopped them down on the folding table. As the woman next to me and I began folding our clothes, almost simultaneously our eyes happened to fall on some very familiar items in each other's piles. We both looked up with the light of discovered sisterhood in our eyes and exclaimed, "Oh, are you LDS too?"

And suddenly, we were laughing and talking together excitedly, like two long-lost friends who had encountered each other by chance. The third lady was completely bewildered, trying to figure out what was going on. Finally she asked, "Er, have you two known each other long?"

No, we had not known each other long, but it was long enough. We arranged for our husbands to meet, and we had dinner together that night. The other couple, like us, were vacationing in the trailer park, and we discovered that we had a great deal more in common than just some items in our white laundry.

That was a short encounter, but some strands of our lives had touched and connected, and our hearts were, for that moment, "knit together in love."

I'd like to explore with you two aspects of being knit together in love that are particularly meaningful to me. The first aspect is how our partnerships with priesthood holders form effective teams—as marriage partners and as associates in the great work of building the kingdom. The second aspect is particularly dear to me, and that is how we, as women, can be knit together in the love of sisterhood in our shared faith in the Savior and particularly in the sisterhood of our Relief Societies.

Partnership

President Spencer W. Kimball held up the standard for partnership in the home and Church between men and women when he said in 1978, "When we speak of marriage as a partnership, let us speak of marriage as a *full* partnership. We do not want our LDS women to be *silent* partners or *limited* partners in that eternal assignment! Please be a *contributing* and *full* partner."[1] This is the goal for priesthood and Relief Society leaders in a ward as well.

In a partnership, the partners must both be strong, but they do not need to be strong in the same ways. Sometimes women think that their part of the partnership consists of being silent, sweet, and supportive under all circumstances. Well, I have trouble seeing the relationship between a doormat and a pair of muddy boots as a real partnership. Instead, I like to think of partnership as two hands, working together. There's not much that one finger can do by itself. It can point or prod or poke. But to comfort or hold or lift, it takes all five. (That's why Relief Society needs all the sisters, by the way!) And there's virtually no end to the good that two hands, gripping the same burden, can do. We need the support of this partner hand, the men of the priesthood. And they need our support, too.

Let me follow this image of the mutually helping hands a little bit further. I had been asked to speak on the sacrament meeting series that the Church tapes for the cable television network VISN, and I had used the same image of the fingers alone and then interlaced with the fingers of another hand.

At the end of January, I received a lovely framed and

decorated calligraphy from June Barrus, who was then just being released after six years of service as Relief Society president of the Springville Stake in Utah Valley. The calligraphy read:

> A finger alone can do very little
> But prod and point and poke.
> All fingers working together
> Are like a team within a yoke.
> Together they lift, grip, and carry along.
> Working together they are gentle and strong.

In the accompanying letter, she explained:

> While attending a General Board Open House, I was touched by a quote attributed to you. It concerned the uselessness of one finger compared to all fingers that work as a team. I pondered that concept, and how pointing fingers lack strength and are often used in a derogatory and intimidating manner, while fingers working together are strong and can be used to support, uplift, and encourage.[2]

Now, I do not know who had quoted my statement at the general board open house. Probably it was a member of the general board. But that unknown colleague forms a strong, though invisible, link between me and June Barrus, transmitting something from me to June that became a source of strength and a creative impetus to her. June returned this strength to me.

One October, Sister Michaelene Grassli, the general Primary president, and I had a lengthy assignment in Japan and Korea, giving regional women's conferences and training meetings and meeting with the priesthood leaders in each stake and region. In Japan I had the great joy of meeting again Setsuko Kubota Fujita, a dear sister who was the first woman baptized in Kochi. As we visited and reminisced, she reminded me of an incident I had forgotten. At a district conference I was attending with Ed, he was walking toward the stand, and she gestured for me to come sit by her. I smiled and thanked her and said, "I want to be with Ed."

"That taught me a lesson," she said. "I knew that I should also try to be with my husband. You'll never realize how closely my husband and I watched you and Ed. We learned many things about a relationship from you. We saw how frequently he conferred with you. We saw how intently you paid attention in meetings and how quick you were to speak when you saw a need. We saw how you and Ed would see a situation and exchange just a word or two, then both attack the problem together. There weren't many problems left after you were finished." The truth was: we worked as partners.

There are many differences in the partnership of a husband and wife as contrasted with the partnership of a priesthood holder and a woman involved in church work, but three things are the same: First, each partner has strengths to contribute. You do the partnership no good by denying or suppressing your strengths. Second, it is important to keep focused on the task, especially when it seems that personality differences might draw energies away from that task. A problem in the ward doesn't really care who solves it, as long as it is solved. And third, partnerships run on communication. Both partners must talk—really talk— candidly, honestly, and supportively. And both partners must listen—really listen—understandingly, with humility sometimes, and with a prayer for comprehension always in the heart.

Sisterhood

The sisterhood that springs up among women who share a similar faith in the Savior is a very real and very powerful source for good. In the spring of 1992, I addressed a conference of almost a hundred Mormon women from all over the West. Some had known each other for ten years. Others were there for the first time. We talked about our lives as women, our faith as Latter-day Saint women, the experiences we had in the Church, our experiences with Relief Society. Some of those experiences had been negative for these women. Other aspects were positive. It was a wonderful weekend for me, and I was so happy to be there with them.

A few months later, I received a book that had been compiled from the responses these women had written after they had gone home. One said:

> This was my first [meeting]. I enjoyed being in the midst of sisters who are intelligent, interesting, accomplished, powerful, thoughtful, capable, and friendly. I enjoyed the diversity of the sisters. I felt accepted and respected for just being there and came away feeling more empowered, capable, and comfortable with who I am and what I am doing.

A woman with a difficult political job wrote:

> I found . . . a forum [where I could get a reality check] and the safe haven I needed . . . It is like a breath of fresh air for me to be here! . . . I feel a sweet spirit of sisterhood when I'm with you and have been blessed by the many insights into the gospel you have shared with me over the years. My testimony has been strengthened through my association with you.

Another woman, who was there for the first time and had felt very panicky about coming, wrote:

> I spent . . . the weekend alternately wondering why I had been so afraid and reveling in the joys of sisterhood. When we sang, "Till We Meet," in the closing [session], I fervently wished that we didn't have to separate and go home. I thought, "If I could just stay here with these women or feel their strength in the gospel more often, it would make the journey back to Jesus' feet so much easier." . . . I felt that I had been heard by women who wanted to enlarge their perspectives, encouraged by the

experiences shared by others, and strengthened in my commitment to go back to my ward and use my voice and keep trying.

A woman who had been involved in the group for a long time wrote:

> Every year . . . I am noticeably strengthened by my experiences [here]. . . . I am much more accepting of imperfections in other people, myself, and the Church. I have more enthusiasm for what is really important in my life. I am also less concerned with details like apricots rotting on the backyard tree and an attic whose contents desperately want to be hauled to Deseret Industries.

One of the most thought-provoking statements to me was this:

> My most cherished remembrance about those days with all of you . . . is that rare and heady feeling of being surrounded by perfect love. I don't have to be smart or accomplished, orthodox or not orthodox, pretty or thin. It doesn't matter whether I'm married, single, or divorced—spiritual or pragmatic—rich or poor—I feel loved. That feeling so pervades all [of our gatherings] that I have terrible withdrawal symptoms and long for such acceptance in all places and with all people.

And I loved reading the response of women who felt committed to make their own Relief Societies places of love and acceptance. One woman wrote:

> Our gathering represents an ideal: what Relief Society could be and, perhaps, was in the beginning. . . . I come home charged with the power of women in community, inspired by the honesty which offers the agony and the epiphany, unedited by fear of rejection, and both shared in an act of love to further the experience of the whole. The trust and openness create a

palpable sense of caring and love. I feel determined to forge links with women in my ward community, to deepen the generally shallow relationships that are more draining than nourishing, to move personal interactions to a more positive base than fear of nonacceptance.

Another wrote:

> Many of my friends have decided to leave the Church. . . . At [our gathering] I made a commitment to stay; to improve and solidify the things I can have an effect on and not worry so much about the things I can't change. I discovered strong, courageous women who share my concerns and who champion each other. . . . What I discovered with joy was that I matter. I am healthy. I have great gifts to share. My Heavenly Father loves me for the differences I can make—though small.

I think that what all these women are talking about, in a way, is a form of grace—of love that was freely given just because they were there as sisters, rather than as a reward for something they had accomplished. In Relief Society, women should feel accepted and cherished just for being there. They don't have to prove themselves. They don't have to pay their dues. They don't have to serve on three committees or produce the most stunning centerpiece of the homemaking meeting. They are accepted and acceptable just because of who they are and where they are.

This is the grace that the Savior has for us. Certainly it's important that we keep the commandments and perform our duties. But our most anxious service and our most dutiful obedience are not sufficient to buy the love of Christ or make his atoning sacrifice worthwhile. In other words, he did not offer in the premortal existence to become our Savior because we were good— or because we were going to be good. He offered to become our Savior because *he* was good and because, as he says, "my grace is sufficient for thee," even with all our shortcomings (2 Corinthians 12:9).

What does this mean when it comes to our attitudes toward each other in Relief Society? It means that we are all daughters of Christ through our baptism. Our differences are less important than our shared testimonies of our Savior. Paul explained, "There is neither Jew nor Greek, there is neither bond nor free, there is neither male nor female: for ye are all one in Christ Jesus" (Galatians 3:28). Let me paraphrase with my own thoughts: In Relief Society there is neither old nor young, rich nor poor, valuable nor invaluable, feminist nor traditionalist, vigorously healthy nor chronically ill, serving nor served, for we are all one in sisterhood. Of course these different circumstances exist, but they are less important than our sisterhood as daughters of Christ who have accepted his name through baptism.

Let me be even more personal and share with you my own experiences in Relief Society. They can be most easily understood as three phases: first, the experiences of my childhood and youth; second, a long period of nonparticipation; and third, a period of intense and steadily intensifying involvement in the last twenty years.

First, my experience with Relief Society started when I was eleven and was investigating the Church in Mahukona. Our little branch's total membership was about forty or fifty people. I loved the hymns and seized hungrily on everything I learned about the Savior, but didn't understand much about the meetings. However, I noticed that at one point the men went one direction and the women and children went another, and those wonderful Hawaiian sisters just swept me along with them. There was no Primary, no YWMIA—just women and men—and I got to be a woman there. I learned that the name of that meeting was Relief Society, even though I wasn't sure what "relief" it offered or what a society was. I was baptized at age fifteen and remained involved through high school, faithfully attending meetings.

When I went to college, the Mormon students at the

University of Hawaii met with the resident members of Honolulu in Mission Branch. We held all of our meetings on Sunday, and I taught spiritual living lessons in the Relief Society. I don't recall hearing anything about visiting teaching. But these experiences, between ages eleven and twenty-two, gave me a foundation of love, acceptance, and knowledge, a foundation that endured for the next forty years while construction on the superstructure of my activity in Relief Society was, in some respects, suspended.

After the war, when Ed and I moved to the mainland, the weekday Relief Society meeting structure excluded me because I was working. In fact, I did not attend Relief Society again until I was president of all the mission Relief Societies in Japan and Okinawa. During the middle 1970s, I could begin attending second-session Relief Society meetings; and the block schedule during the 1980s gave me the opportunity to serve as president of our Relief Society in Littleton, Colorado, even while I was also principal of a newly opened, year-round, four-track school.

That was the beginning of the third period. You may know that I was called briefly as ward Relief Society president before I was called to the Primary General Board, and ultimately I served in the general Relief Society presidency.

What did those years mean? You need to remember the historical context. It was not until the early 1980s that all Mormon women automatically became members of the Relief Society. Up until that point, Relief Society was something you could *choose* to belong to, like a club or the PTA. If you chose not to, it did not mean anything about your activity in the Church or your commitment to the gospel. I did not feel rejected or excluded because I could not attend Relief Society. I was not made to feel "inactive." I was just left alone. I cheerfully paid my dues, carried the little card in my purse that identified me as a member of the Relief Society, and felt attached to the sisters in my heart.

Many individual women were kind to me. In 1973, when I was diagnosed as having breast cancer and had a mastectomy, Louise Erickson, a counselor in the Relief Society presidency, took me to radiation therapy, called me, and saw that my household functioned without me. It was the first time I'd received direct ministration from the Relief Society as an organization. She said, "Since you don't come to the meetings, we don't know you very well. I thought this was an opportunity to get acquainted with you." Now, of course, I knew women in the ward. Our family faithfully attended Sunday School and sacrament meeting. I taught YWMIA, since that was an evening calling. But I could tell that Louise meant "knowing" in some kind of special way. I understood that there was a way the Relief Society sisterhood knew each other that others did not.

These were wonderful experiences, but, looking back on that middle forty years of my life, I can see that Relief Society was not really a part of it, nor was I a part of Relief Society. In many ways, I was invisible in my ward. I was different because I worked outside the home. My schedule was different. My availability was different. Perhaps my Japanese ancestry and my convert status added to those differences. And my ward Relief Society had no way to accommodate those differences.

Now, here's the observation I want to make, and I want to make it very gently and lovingly, with only a little wistful regret. I am not blaming or accusing anyone. Nobody did anything wrong or hurtful. But my ward Relief Society did not *find* a way to accommodate my differences. It did not *seek* a way to reach across the separation caused by my different circumstances. I never heard announcements about Relief Society activities. I never received a handout from the Relief Society. I never participated in a Relief Society party. I never had a visiting teacher until 1984, and I wasn't called to be a visiting teacher myself until then. I was invisible to the Relief Society, outside its circle—until I had a dramatic need that they knew how to meet. I hope we can build a Relief Society today that is more flexible, better able to see and encircle women in many circumstances.

Now, I ask this question of all of us and lay this burden upon us: What circumstances are at work right now in our wards, silently separating one sister here and another sister there from the sisterhood of the Relief Society, marginalizing them, making them invisible? And what can we do about it?

When we traveled as a Relief Society general presidency and board members, we met with hundreds of women in all kinds of circumstances. We saw women struggling to make the best of those circumstances and living the gospel despite real challenges. I have no reason to believe that things are going to get easier for women. I think that social circumstances will continue to create difficulties. For example, LDS women are participating in the labor force in ever-increasing numbers. These women need Relief Society. They need the strength of sisterhood. They need to be understood. They need support with their families. They don't need to be told that they're selfish or unrighteous because they're working. They need to be told they are *loved*.

Here are some other demographic shifts: The number of never-married women in the Church is rising. So is the number of women who are the heads of household with dependent children. More women of color are joining our church, a church that is still predominantly white in its values if not in its actual population. The middle-class ethics of hard work and upward mobility are not universally shared around the world or even in America. It seems inevitable to me that we will have an increasing number of women, both converts and lifelong members, who are dealing with drug-related problems, with depression, with both the reality and the aftermath of abuse, with poverty, and with crime.

Millions of children are growing up in fluid family structures where parents divorce, remarry, combine existing families, and create new ones. Sometimes these are very successful, but even at best they are not without stress. Some of these children are the young women who are just now coming of age. Will Relief Society be a source of acceptance and stability in their life? Or will it be a place where they are marginalized because of their differences, where their life experiences are not recognized, or even where they find themselves blamed because of the realities of their lives?

These are real needs, real differences. Are we prepared to learn from and respect these differences, to welcome converts who are very different from us into the full circle of our sisterhood? Or will our answer be to marginalize them, to make them invisible, to erase them? Think of Jesus walking through the villages of Galilee. He didn't just talk with the prosperous and the well-adjusted. He reached out in love to the handicapped, the mentally ill, the poor, and the sinners. We need to follow him in our own daily walk.

Another shift that is going on in America is a gradual change toward a more equal partnership between men and women in business, government, education, family life, and many other aspects of life. Many of our daughters and granddaughters will have very different opportunities to develop and use their talents than we have had, and they will encounter different expectations from women of our generation about the place they will occupy in the world. We need to make room in the Church for all of their energy, intelligence, and ability, or we may lose many of them. All the sisters in the Church need to understand that they share equally in the blessings of the gospel, including the spiritual strength that comes from a personal testimony of the Savior.

Let us remember that being knit together in love is a promise that applies to all of us. It applies to our relationships with the priesthood holders in our lives—our husbands, fathers, brothers, sons, and our bishops and other priesthood leaders. It applies to our work in Relief Society, in being sisters to those who have a need for nurture in our wards and stakes—and sooner or later, that means everyone. The promise that our hearts can be knit together in love is a promise that is fulfilled wherever even two or three sisters gather together with love in their hearts for each other. For the Savior has promised: "There am I in the midst of them" (Matthew 18:20). May we fill our hearts with love so that he will always be with us.

7

STRENGTHENING EVERY HOME

President Gordon B. Hinckley issued a compelling invitation in his 1995 Easter message:

> What shall we do? . . . [This is] a day for resolution, my brothers and sisters, a day for making a decision within ourselves to be a little better than we've been, a little kinder, a little more merciful, a little more outreaching, with a little greater desire to bless those in distress and need. To be willing to go the second mile, to impart of our cloak, if need be, to do good where evil has been done against us, to be just a little more Christlike. I would hope that everyone here this day, before he or she retires for the night, would . . . think of some small way in which we might improve ourselves and draw nearer to our Lord.[1]

As we consider how we might "improve ourselves and draw nearer to our Lord," I want to discuss the power of strengthening every home. I want to stress *every* because often we think: "Oh, a home. That means a temple marriage, a husband who works full time, a wife who is home full time, and four or five or more children in the home." You know, that's an ideal that describes a certain life stage. Demographically, that statistic describes a very small percentage of the homes in the United States. What about the rest of the homes?

I don't know the stories of all women, but if we looked at a cross section of women in the Church, we would find a significant number of them to be single—either through divorce, through the death of a husband, or because they have not yet married. Some of them are single moms. Some are grandmothers, and the years of having little children in the home every hour of every day are in the past. But all of them have homes. All of them have families. All of them can be strong individuals and can build strong homes with strong families.

Motherhood

I would like to speak first of the importance of mothering. There is a wonderful Japanese proverb that says, "In a child's lunch box, a mother's thought."[2] As an educator, I know how important home can be in bringing children to formal education ready to learn, confident, curious, and compassionate to others. It's wonderful if you have the opportunity to be a full-time mom in the home—notice that I *don't* say "if you don't have to work"! All at-home mothers work, and they work very hard.

Being able to care for your children is worth making a sacrifice for, because those years of childhood will not come again. I want to share with you the experience of Jill Watson, the mother of five children spaced about a year apart, who are now teenagers. She wrote to Elaine Jack, the Relief Society general president:

> When President Kimball cautioned us to be "stay at home moms" it really concerned me, but I felt that I had to keep helping to support my family. My husband has always owned his own small business and money was always tight, so I would go out to substitute teach. This past year, however, my husband and I in fasting and prayer made the decision that I would no longer go out of the home to work. We really sensed that our family's spiritual growth was in need of help.
>
> My husband had been virtually unemployed at the time we

made this decision, but we put our faith in the Lord. We knelt in prayer and explained in detail our thinking to Heavenly Father. A warm, calm feeling came over both of us and we knew all would be well. We wanted Mom back in the home completely—raising the children even though they are older, and bringing a righteous spirit back into our home.

We have not once missed a bill payment or gone hungry. We have cut way back as a family on many things, and all of our children have learned to work hard and to support themselves financially. [And that's not a bad thing at all for children to do.] (One of our daughters in grade 9 really wanted to be in the band this year and she knew that there was no money, so she worked [at] babysitting and a summer job and paid for it herself. It was really hard as a Mom to have to sit back and not help, but she has really grown from this experience.) By the way, all of our children were included in praying and fasting, too, when it came time to make this decision. They all agreed that it was worth more to have me at home than to have all the extras. It hasn't been easy at times temporally, but spiritually it is fantastic! Heavenly Father has blessed us richly with his spirit in our home. Many people come to our home and they too mention that they feel a warm, good feeling. . . . The days are calm and peaceful in our home, too, for I truly find that the mother sets the mood in the home and Heavenly Father is right there to help us if we'll only talk to Him.[3]

Now, my reason in telling you this story is *not* to tell you that this woman's answer should be your answer. No, the important thing is the principle. Something was not working right in her family. When she prayed, she received inspiration—inspiration that was confirmed by the joint inspiration she and her husband received together. It was a decision that also made sense to the children so that they could make a unified decision. These are principles anyone can follow.

When you perceive a need in your family, pray for inspiration. Draw on the spiritual strength of your husband and other members of your family. Do not impose the decision on others, but talk it over with them, listen to them, share perspectives, and be persuasive. When you follow the inspiration you receive, there will be difficult moments that you should be prepared for, and ways in which that decision will require sacrifice, but have faith in your inspiration. Have the discipline to be obedient to the whisperings of the Spirit. Look carefully at the results. Let everyone who is involved in the decision also participate in the evaluation of that decision.

Single Motherhood

Not all women have the opportunity to be full-time mothers. Nor does the Church expect them to. Remember what President Hinckley said at his first press conference, when he was asked what counsel he had for women who needed to work to support their children or to supplement their husband's wages? He said, "Do your best." That's a recognition that we live in a world where not all situations are ideal.

Even though the message of the prophets has consistently been how important it is for mothers to be with their children, and how important it is for children to have both a mother *and* a father who love them and are involved in their care, no one says that children in single-parent families are doomed to disease, disadvantage, and disaster. If that were so, bishops would be subsidizing single mothers so they could stay home with their children. That doesn't happen. There is a sensitive recognition that it is harder for single mothers, since they bear responsibilities that should be shared by two. There is no condemnation. No one is willing to waste the children or throw away the next generation because a marriage ends.

I sometimes think, however, that we could all do a much better job of strengthening single-parent families instead of just saying, enthusiastically but vaguely, "That's too bad, but you can do it!" I think it begins with understanding and a willingness to listen. We have a great deal to learn from the strength and courage of single mothers.

Let me tell you a second story, the story of Deborah Hedstrom, who suddenly found herself a widow. She shares her insights about single parenting. "I remember very little about my youngest child's thirteenth birthday," she writes. "But somewhere between the torn wrapping paper and melted ice cream, I was struck by yet another implication of my husband's death: I was now the single parent of four teenagers. How could I possibly carry them through their metamorphosis from children to adults?" She describes two important principles that brought her peace of mind as she raised those teenagers:

> 1. Accept your limits. Three years after his wife died, a father found on his bed a note from his daughter. She had written, "I miss Mom, but you can't be like her. Just be a dad—please!" . . .
>
> Nothing is more stressful or frustrating than fervently trying to do what cannot be done. I know, because for a long time I tried to fill the dad gap in my teens' lives. I tried keeping our home just what it was when Dad was alive—but I wasn't him. I enlisted the help of male relatives and men from our church. They provided good role models and touched my children's lives, but they couldn't replace the missing father.
>
> The day I accepted the limits of my single parenting was the day I dropped a load God never intended me to carry and found a measure of peace.
>
> 2. Find positives. When I became a single parent, I dreaded that first vacation my kids and I would spend together without my husband. I knew they'd be off finding their own entertainment and that I'd have to "enjoy" things alone.
>
> When the vacation ended and we packed for home, I realized I had lacked for companionship—but I also realized that vacation had brought its share of good things as well. For the first time, I'd been able to browse through bookstores and tour museums for as long as I wanted. And I hadn't had to

build my day around mealtimes because while Dad had wanted three meals a day, the kids ate all the time.

In time, I found other positives about single parenting. For instance, my appreciation for friends and family has increased. Before, when they reached out to my kids, I'd pass it off lightly as a nice gesture on their part. Now, as a single parent, I *really* appreciate it.

Single parenting has also shown me my inner strengths. I've survived vehicle breakdowns, emergency hospital visits, and even teaching the kids to drive.

None of these positives came highlighted by a neon sign. In truth, the difficulties of a single-parent/teenage home are easier to see. But finding the positive is a great coping skill, as David recognized: "I would have lost heart, unless I had believed that I would see the goodness of the Lord in the land of the living" (Psalm 27:13, NKJV).[4]

Jesus doesn't care only about the children in intact families. He doesn't love and appreciate the efforts only of married mothers. He doesn't promise to help only people who are already perfect and have risen above their challenges. No, he is concerned about every individual and every family.

Blended Families

I don't know the stories of you women reading this book. Some of you are in the situation of Jill Watson. Others of you are coping with single parenthood like Deborah Hedstrom. Still others of you are engaged in blending families. I sat down with a piece of paper and figured out the configurations possible just in blended families depending on whether both or one partner was previously married and, if so, had children, and whether the second union had produced children. Do you know how many combinations there are? Thirty! Then add on the possibilities if the first marriage ended in death, instead of divorce, and you double it to sixty possibilities! So talking about blended family is a very complex situation.

No information is currently available on the rates of remarriage in the Church or the number of men and women who are involved as stepparents, but reliable researchers say that a fifth of the households in the United States headed by a married couple contain at least one stepchild under age eighteen. This figure, 20.8 percent, is up from 16.1 percent in 1980. Two and a half million families had various combinations of stepchildren, adoptive children, and biological children. Over ten times as many blended families consist of a biological mother and a stepfather as a biological father and a stepmother.

It's not your *fault*—but it could be your *opportunity*. Most students of blended families agree that, despite the challenges, it is the *process*, not the *structure*, that determines whether a family will function well.

We want to believe that when a man loves a woman, he will automatically love her children; or that when a woman loves a man, she will automatically love his children. The reality is that the love between husband and wife creates a *willingness* to love, but that love has to be built a step at a time, just like the love in any relationship. Furthermore, gender is directly related to conflict. Girls have a harder time getting along with stepfathers than boys do. Boys seem to have more trouble with stepmothers.

"All families must deal with problems to survive and be happy. But stepfamilies have some unique challenges," says Kristen Goodman from the Church's Research and Evaluation Department. Kristen has summarized eleven challenges that are particularly associated with blended families. (I am casting these challenges in terms of women, but they also apply to men.)

1. The ending of the first marriage requires emotional work during the second marriage as well. The history of the first marriage does not end with the second wedding.

2. Many of you women are helping to raise the children of

other women, and for some of you, at least some of the time, other women are involved in the raising of *your* children.

3. In most cases, your husband experiences at least some of the demands of the situation differently than you do. Some of those differences may involve how much time each of you spends in parenting, your parenting styles, what you want from the marriage, and the financial impact on your family.

4. At least occasionally you've heard messages at church about marriage and family that have made you heavy-hearted because they make you feel less valuable than people in traditional family configurations.

5. Remarriages are more likely to end in divorce than first marriages. Perhaps a spouse, knowing she has survived one divorce, may be more willing to end a second unhappy relationship. Or perhaps problems that created instability in the first relationship have not yet been resolved and continue to create problems in the second marriage. Children of remarriage may be committed to the first marriage, not to the second, and increase strains.

6. Relationships are often complex. Building new ones takes time and effort. Couples in a new marriage feel frustrated because they are swamped with so many needs that they feel they don't have time to build their relationship as husband and wife. Then each spouse must establish a new relationship with the partner's children and adjust the relationship with his or her own children. Stepbrothers and stepsisters may learn easily to get along, or they may be fiercely competitive, or anywhere in between.

7. Conflict is built into a new blended family because of the different histories and expectations of the participants. Good communication and conflict-resolution skills don't develop automatically. Decision making takes conscious effort. Who has which job? What behavior is appropriate in which circumstances? Which expectations are most important? How will a decision affect other family members? What's fair? How much time and affection should each child get?

8. How do you and your husband work out the pattern of

discipline in your home? How involved should a stepparent be in discipline of the stepchild? What do you do when the rules in the custodial parent's home are different from those in your home? Children need to know where boundaries are, but they also need to feel that the discipline is fair. They want to know who has the right to discipline them, and the form that discipline should take.

9. Moving more people into your house means that you have to reallocate *space*. *Money* has to be reallocated. Are the finances separate for each subfamily, or is there one pool for the blended family? And what happens when there's not enough money to go around—when, for example, a stepfather is making child-support payments to his former wife? Or when the divorced father is supposed to make child-support payments but doesn't?

10. Boundaries are important for stability and cohesion. Who is in the family and who isn't? Do you have to live in the same house to be a family? Obviously not. In most states, a stepfather has neither legal duties nor rights over his stepchildren unless he adopts them, but he is frequently more involved on a day-to-day basis with them than their biological father.

11. A remarriage doubles the number of grandparents, cousins, aunts, and uncles. And sometimes, the former extended family "writes off" the children after a remarriage so those children end up losing a favorite aunt or grandmother. Sometimes it's very hard for grandparents to accept stepgrandchildren as "real" grandchildren. Sometimes the extended family interferes with the newly blended family.[5]

I have been an at-home mom and a working mother, but I have never had the challenges of being a partner in a blended family. It seems to me that the Lord has a tender and powerful interest in these second-try marriages. Blended families should make him a partner in their enterprise.

Singles

I also fit in the next category of women—single women. As a widow, though, my experience is different from those of you for whom marriage is still in the future. If you are over the age of twenty-five and not married, you know that the statistical chances of finding an active, worthy, unmarried priesthood holder are very small. This is a reality. Being unmarried for many years—even for the rest of your mortal life—may be your reality.

I was twenty-two when I married Ed, but I had been facing the hard realities of being a single Mormon woman ever since I was sixteen or seventeen. I was a Japanese American immediately after World War II, I was a Mormon, and I was going to be a professional woman. The pool to choose from was very small. During my first year at school, I sometimes sat in our chapel and looked around at the people who were there. There were few unmarried men. They were all pleasant. I enjoyed being in meetings and activities with them. But none of them was appealing to me in a deeper way.

I did not dislike the idea of marriage, but I thought through the scenarios of my future if I were to remain single, and I found those scenarios acceptable to me—more than acceptable. I found them rich in happiness and service. I knew that as a teacher I would be surrounded by children. I had a lot of love to give them, and it would be a satisfying career. My brothers would probably marry, and I could be close to their children. If I did not marry, I would be able to take care of my parents as they grew older; I certainly owed them a great deal. I could be active in the Church and derive a great deal of satisfaction from serving there. Who knows? Maybe I could even be a missionary after I retired from teaching. So I decided to give up ideas of marriage, to stay close to the Church, and to concentrate on my education so that I would have a fulfilling and satisfying career. I felt that this was a set of choices that was honorable and acceptable to the Lord. I feel that anyone, before marrying, needs to envision the possibilities of singleness and think about what such a life would hold.

As matters turned out, that was not my future. There was Ed, and love, and marriage, and children. And I think one reason all of those blessings came to me is that I was prepared to be a strong, faithful, contributing individual without any of them. You can do the same thing. There are always opportunities to grow and opportunities to serve. I promise you that, as a widow, I will not define my life by what I do not have. And will you make me the same promise?

I don't want to be sentimental about this. I want to be clear. Singleness is not a sickness, a sin, or a problem. Single people are not broken, and they do not need to be fixed. Still, singleness is probably not a situation that any of us wants, sees as ideal, or seeks. Still, now that we have it, what do we do with it?

Here are my suggestions:

1. Let us consecrate our singleness, naming it specifically, to God. In the temple, when we make our vows of consecration, nothing is omitted or held back. Anything that can be used for building the kingdom is offered on the altar. What could the Lord do with our singleness if we offered it to him instead of complaining about it, suffering over it, or apologizing for it? A Catholic writer, François de Fenelon, has said, "All virtue consists in having a willing heart; God will lead you as if by the hand, if only you do not doubt, and are filled with love for him rather than fear for yourself."[6]

2. Discipline yourself for action. There are no limits on the amount of good you can do in the world if you build in yourself the spiritual muscles of self-discipline. The gifted teacher Maria Montessori, whose name has become synonymous with natural learning, pointed out: "The first idea that the child must acquire, in order to be actively disciplined, is that of the difference between good and evil; and the task of the educator lies in seeing that the child does not confound good with immobility, and evil with activity. . . . Our aim is to discipline for activity, for work, for good; not for immobility, not for passivity, not for [mere] obedience."[7]

I think that single people often see themselves as recipients: recipients of special programs (not all of them helpful), recipients of special attention (not all of it welcome), and recipients of promises for the future (if they can just manage to get through the present). With such an attitude, the glorious moments of mortality become a time of passive waiting. We become afraid that making plans, framing decisions, mobilizing resources, taking action, and changing directions are terribly risky behaviors that will move us into danger. Instead we think we need to coast, letting others make decisions for us and fitting into plans others make for us. If you've been thinking that your life needs some changes, then discipline yourself for action, for work, for good. Remember that a rut is just a grave with both ends kicked out!

3. Let us cling to our testimonies of the Savior. Let us nurture them. Let us cherish them. Let our testimonies grow strong, and let us grow strong with them. Not only does Jesus call us to come unto him, he is the pathway by which we come and our companion on the way, helping us over the rough spots, leading us on when it is dark, and encouraging us when our hearts sink.

Importance of Christ

It is very rare for me to separate women into groups and talk in this way about married mothers and single mothers, about remarried women and never-married women. Usually I am so consumed by the wonderful gospel that unites us that it is hard for me to talk about things that may separate us. And I know that sometimes women feel as if they're being categorized, as if only women in certain circumstances are valuable: that the mothers are more valuable than the nonmothers, that the mothers of many children are more valuable than the mothers of few children, that the young mothers are more valuable than the old mothers, that the young nonemployed mothers are more valuable than the young employed mothers.

The problem with that is that differences don't just remain delightful sources of diversity. They become occasions for us to judge each other. Christ did not come for a chosen few in favored circumstances. He is no respecter of persons. He has no quotas, no charmed circles, no special favorites. Each one of us is a precious

91

and beloved daughter of God. Each one of us must meet and know and worship Christ as an individual, and each of us will eventually be called to account for our lives in situations where husbands and children and houses and jobs are just accessories to who we are as individuals. Martin Luther said:

> The gist of the Gospel is this: No man [and we can add, no woman] is so high or may rise so high that he need not fear becoming the lowliest. Conversely, no one has fallen, or may fall, so deeply as to preclude all hope of becoming the highest. By saying: "The first shall be last" Christ takes all presumption away from you and forbids you to exalt yourself above any prostitute, even though you were Abraham, David, Peter or Paul. But by saying: "The last shall be first" He guards you against all despair and forbids you to cast yourself under the feet of any saint, even though you were Pilate, Herod, Sodom and Gomorrah.[8]

So I want to concentrate on what unites us as women, and that's our shared faith in Christ and his abundant love for all of us, no matter what our circumstances are.

The Savior is much more interested in us as individuals than he is in our marital circumstances. Yes, he cares about the quality of our relationship with our husband, if we have one, and he's vitally concerned with how we treat our children, if we have children. But he's also concerned with how we treat someone else's children—whether that's the five-year-old next door, the teenager down the block, the colleague at the next desk at work, or the clerk in the supermarket. That's because we are all brothers and sisters. We have a relationship with each and every individual on this earth. We can't divide them up into people we care about and people we don't have to bother about, because the Savior cares about each and every one of them. His arms are outstretched to each and every one. His heart yearns over each and every one. Our capacity to care may be limited because we are mortal, we are limited, we are finite human beings, but there is no end to his capacity to care.

Jesus Christ is our loving Savior. He is not some distant person in robes and sandals. He understands about the carburetor in our car, about ACT and SAT tests for our high-school senior, about a missionary cautiously trying tofu for the first time. We can share our whole lives with him. He doesn't want to see only the pretty, peaceful parts or the sections when we have a good day. Are there parts of our lives that we try to shove into the closet or sweep under the carpet when we pray or when we think we're trying to be righteous? I want to tell you that Jesus wants our whole hearts. He knows our whole lives. He's been through worse experiences than anything we have in our past. Do you remember when he told Joseph Smith in Liberty Jail: "The Son of Man hath descended below them all. Art thou greater than he?" (D&C 122:5–8).

I take what he says very literally. I truly believe that he understands our lives in detail, without flinching or turning away from even the most terrible things that have happened to us and even the most terrible things that we have done. I believe he knows about the messy, complicated physical realities of a woman's life. I believe that he understands the fear that swept my heart when I realized I had breast cancer. I think he was with me in the struggle after surgery, strengthening me as I thought through what it meant to me as a woman to be without a breast. I think he knows about childbirth and nursing.

Jesus did not tell people to ignore their bodies in an effort to become spiritual, or to blind themselves either to the beauties or to the horrors of the natural world. He lived in that world without shielding himself from it. He transformed that world by the miraculous power of his love. Remember the story of the leper who came to him, beseeching him, "If thou wilt, thou canst make me clean." Think of leprosy—the rotting flesh, the stench, the ingrained horror of physical and ritual contamination that Jesus would have learned from babyhood. Those are powerful physical and emotional barriers to overcome. Jesus not only overcame those barriers enough to be "moved with compassion," the scripture says, but he "put forth his hand, and *touched* him" (Mark 1:40–42; italics added). This was not long-distance healing. This was close, intimate, a refusal by the Savior to accept that there was anything in human life, no matter how repulsive it may have been to other people, that he could not transform into cleanliness and wholeness by putting his hand on it.

So when I say to share our whole lives with Jesus, I mean that very literally. I mean the parts that aren't pretty, too, the parts that we're not proud of. If we are struggling with an illness, we can talk to him in prayer about that struggle. Something miraculous happens in articulating exactly what something feels like and how it makes us feel. I think once we have said it, then we can give it to the Lord and let him carry it for us, take it away, or be with us in sharing the burden as we struggle to continue to carry it.

We are besieged and afflicted, not only by the ills of mortality and the dangers of society but also by our own human tendency to want to deny them. Isaiah says that the Savior is "a man of sorrows, and acquainted with grief" (Isaiah 53:3). He's acquainted with our grief. He knows our sorrow.

I tell you again: Jesus knows. He knows the size and the shape and the weight of your burden. He, who could not bear the weight of his own cross as the soldiers flogged him onward toward Golgotha, has already experienced the killing weight that makes your heart heavy. He is with you in bearing it, even if, in the wisdom of God, it cannot be lifted from you. But only if you share it with him.

He is our Savior because he paid the price to save us from our sins, from our imperfections, from our impurities, from our wounds and our ugliness. Isaiah tells us: "But he was wounded for our transgressions, he was bruised for our iniquities: the chastisement of our peace was upon him; and with his stripes we are healed" (Isaiah 53:5). Do you really think there are things that shock him? We can say words or think thoughts or do deeds that will increase his sorrow, but we can never think or say or do anything that he has not already experienced in taking that burden upon himself and carrying it out of love for us.

We don't need to partition off parts of our lives and say, "Oh, these don't count." We don't need to think that God wants only the spiritual part of our lives. The miracle of faith in the Savior is that it runs through our whole lives, like a drop of food coloring in the icing for a cake, transforming every bit. Our goal isn't to whittle away our material lives so that all we have left is the spiritual. Our aim isn't to expunge and erase our physical lives so that there is this pure cube of spirit left. No, it's to infuse our whole physical lives *with* the Spirit. We want there to be no activity, no thought, no word, no gesture of service, no impulse that is not steeped in the Spirit.

We are all women together in the Church, women who share a common belief in and love for the Savior. We all need him so much. And we need each other. All of us need each other. We have ideals of marriage, but no marriage is ideal. We have ideals of the family, but no family is ideal. All of them take work. All of them involve imperfect, struggling human beings. All of us *are* struggling, imperfect beings. There are times when we can all be mothers and times when we all need to be mothered. There are times when we all need a sister and times when we can all be sisters.

I bear my testimony to you that the Savior came to be with us in mortality—in the messy, confusing, heart-breaking, and heart-expanding mortal experience. I bear you my testimony that nothing human is foreign to him, that no human condition is one he cannot redeem if we will give him our hearts, that none of us is beyond his love. I pray that we will feel that love—feel it as a quiet spring bubbling in secret joy within us, and also feel it as a mighty flood, sweeping away our doubts and our fears, an inexhaustible treasure of living water that we may drink from forever and give to others who also thirst.

HEALING FROM SEXUAL ABUSE: EIGHT MESSAGES FOR SURVIVORS, FAMILIES, AND LEADERS

Some years ago, I was asked to speak at a regional conference in Portland, Oregon. This was certainly not a new type of assignment for me, but I felt a special sense of responsibility because the stake Relief Society president had, at my request, given me a list of problems she felt were particularly difficult for women in that area. One item on that list leaped out at me: sexual abuse.

I have never experienced sexual abuse, nor has anyone in my family, but many friends, acquaintances, and troubled Relief Society sisters have honored me with their confidences. President Gordon B. Hinckley and President Thomas S. Monson have condemned this shocking sin in strong terms that brought it sharply to my awareness.[1] I felt a burden laid upon me from the Spirit that this was the message I was to share in Portland.

This was a difficult thing for me to do. When I speak of love or faith or service or sisterhood, I often sense an easing of burdens and a brightening in the feelings of those I address. Would this topic add to the burdens and intensify the pain of those who were already suffering? Did I know enough to be helpful, or would I injure through clumsiness and ignorance?

I fasted and prayed. I thought deeply and continually during the period of preparation. I consulted the stake president in the area. Most of all, I sought the Spirit of the Lord, that I would fulfill the responsibility laid upon me in the way that he would have me do, that I would speak with clarity and with comfort from my own place of love and trust, that I could put an arm around a struggling sister and, for a few steps, help her walk the long, painful path of spiritual healing.

My prayers were answered. In Portland, I discovered that I had come to a place and a people prepared to hear this message. Several groups were already dealing explicitly with the support and healing of survivors. Priesthood leaders were supportive, informed, and understanding. I felt heard. People told me that they understood my message and felt the witness of the Spirit. It was both a sobering and an uplifting experience for me. I am very grateful for the opportunity to now address a wider audience and I pray, deeply and sincerely, that the same spirit will attend this writing.

The case of physical or sexual abuse poses particular challenges. In such cases, we have to simultaneously develop protection against the abuse, shape a moral and nonabusing pattern of life for ourselves, and develop the ability to forgive those who have violated our agency and damaged our trust. I have chosen to focus on trust because, out of all of the consequences of abuse— out of the pain and grief and shame and hurt and anger and sorrow and cynicism and rage and withdrawal and rejection of self and rejection of others—out of all these consequences, I think that the loss of trust may be the very worst of all. I want to talk about the betrayal of trust in the context of sexual abuse and then talk about how to restore it.

One of the most powerful parts of the gospel for me is its promise of peace. I love the Lord's reassuring words, "Peace I leave with you, my peace I give unto you: not as the world giveth, give I unto you. Let not your heart be troubled, neither let it be afraid" (John 14:27). That message, which he spoke to his apostles in Palestine in the context of teaching them about the second comforter, he repeated to Joseph Smith—but embedded in a very troublesome passage. The Lord told Joseph Smith:

> Therefore, renounce war and proclaim peace, and seek diligently to turn the hearts of the children to their fathers, and the hearts of the fathers to the children.
>
> . . . Lest I come and smite the whole earth with a curse, and all flesh be consumed before me.
>
> Let not your hearts be troubled; for in my Father's house are many mansions, and I have prepared a place for you; and where my Father and I am, there ye shall be also. (D&C 98:16–18)

Here he talks of war, of the hearts of fathers turned away from their children, of the cursing of the earth and the consuming of all flesh. This is a message that is very relevant, I believe, to sexual abuse. What the Savior told the Saints, in a message enunciated in his day and repeated in ours, is a very hard message: that war and unloving behavior and trouble and heartbreak and even betrayal are part of human life. We can count on our Heavenly Father, and we can count on the love of Christ as we struggle to love each other; but even at its best, no human love will be perfect.

Perhaps *betrayal* is too harsh a word for most of the difficult experiences that we have. A gentler way of saying it is that everybody is going to let you down. Your husband is not perfect. Your children will disappoint you in some ways. People in your ward won't always be thoughtful and neighborly. But *betrayal* is not too harsh a word for the situation in which the trust of innocent and powerless children does not protect them against physical and sexual abuse from a parent or another adult whose responsibility before God is to protect and nurture.

I have several messages that I want to share about the terrible betrayal of sexual abuse.

The first point is this: Sexual abuse is a problem for all of us, both men and women, whether we have experienced it personally or not. The most conservative statistic I have heard is that one woman in ten is sexually abused before she is eighteen. The worst I have heard is that the figure is closer to one in three.[2] One in three. The comparable statistic for the sexual abuse of boys is one in ten, and researchers feel that the sexual abuse of boys is even more severely underreported than the sexual abuse of girls.[3] There are no systematic studies of which I am aware done on Mormon women and men, but those who work with LDS women and men as counselors and therapists say they have no reason to believe that the statistics are any different for them than for the national population.

Think about that worst statistic, one in three. If you are a woman, it means that you have a 33 percent chance of being that woman. If you are a man, it means that your wife, your mother, or your daughter may be that woman. If you have three daughters, if you have three sisters, if you have three daughters-in-law, if you have three granddaughters, this terrible evil could have entered your family's life, with or without your knowledge. Consider the men in your life. Think about your sons, and grandsons, your missionary companions. Did one of them struggle silently with this spiritual burden? If you have worked in three elders' quorum presidencies or bishoprics or stake presidents, the statistical odds are that one of them bore this grievous, invisible wound. Think of your friends. Think of the women sitting in your Relief Society and the men sitting in priesthood meeting. Think of the children in your Primary. Sexual abuse is a problem for all righteous women and all righteous men everywhere.

The second message is that sexual abuse is not the child's fault. Sometimes we hear statements from people suggesting that sometimes a victim of sexual abuse has some kind of responsibility for the abuse. I asked a woman, a former Relief Society president who had been sexually abused by her father when she was a child, to help me understand why some people feel that women who are raped, or wives who are battered, or little girls or boys who are sexually abused, may have done something to cause this evil to come upon them. With her permission, I share part of her answer. She said:

> I think for some it must have something to do with an understandable desire to believe that parents cannot and, therefore, would not do this without some provocation from their children. [I don't know what will] . . . help those who want to believe that as Saints we are immune to such impulses.
>
> I often find myself wondering why even we, who know our parents as abusers, continued to protect them by idealizing them. At the heart of it, I think, is any child's self-interested hope of escaping pain. "He's not bad. I'm bad. If he's bad, I am inevitably at risk. If I'm bad, I can be safe because I can stop being bad. If I can believe that I am making my father do this to me, I can believe that I can make him stop." Accepting such responsibility becomes a way of not feeling the absolute despair of conscious powerlessness and the inevitability of recurring attack without possibility of rescue. Of course, the hope is in vain, but the time bought at the price of guilt and shame can save one's sanity. Eventually the little child must go back and feel the despair, but only when she has matured enough to bear it.

The third message I have is that women and men who have been sexually abused probably need professional help and certainly need personal support. In the vast majority of cases, they need professional help because sexual abuse, and particularly incest, attacks the very foundations of their identity. They need our personal support because they have learned not to trust other people and not even to trust themselves. Sometimes they have terrible memories, which they deny. Sometimes there are even more terrible gaps in their memories, which they are terrified to explore. Such profound isolation from other people can come close to a kind of insanity.

One man who shared his experiences of being sexually abused by his father told me, "I feel all alone at church a lot of the time. In fact, I have not attended my meetings sometimes for up to a year, because I cannot face the members." He told about his agony at sitting through a lesson in which our responsibility to forgive was presented as an absolute requirement. When he tried to suggest that sometimes it is not possible to forgive until some healing has taken place, his comment was received judgmentally and without understanding. The teacher rebuked him, and when he tried to explain his feelings, a "heated debate" developed. He said wistfully, "I wish that I felt safe and accepted during elders' quorum, [but] every time I enter that room that I am commanded to go into, I feel as though I am going in front of a firing squad."

Normal happy voices, respectful listening, and simple trust can sometimes be lifelines. If you have a friend who needs someone to listen, and if you can be a voice of steadfast love for her or him, please accept that burden if you can. If there are things you don't understand, please ask questions, but also say, "You may not want to talk about this." We must never seek to know more than a man or woman is willing to share. We must never violate the privacy of survivors, as their bodies and their sense of self have been violated in the past. And we must never betray their trust, for that would add one more betrayal to the burden they already carry.

Please be wise in your support. Don't take on more than you can handle and don't try to become a therapist. Instead, encourage your friend to get professional help, and maintain a close, loving contact.

Fourth, women and men who are coming to terms with sexual abuse need all the spiritual help they can get. Pray with them, if they wish. Pray for them. Encourage them to seek priesthood blessings. Read the scriptures with them, if they wish. Encourage them to read their patriarchal blessings. Attend church functions with them if they need companionship. Go with them to the temple if they want to go. My friend told me that a very important part of her own willingness to start working on her abuse was receiving a blessing from a priesthood holder when she was just beginning to suspect sexual abuse in her own past. Her own memories were chaotic and unclear, and she was reluctant to seek the blessing because, in her words: "I needed some guidance from the Lord that I wasn't able to trust myself to hear. You see, I very much did not want to open a door that could not be closed. I wanted to get on with my life. I feared destroying, by my becoming conscious of these things, the hard-won and fragile peace in my family. . . . And I was hanging on to the hope that I was making all of this up."

My friend was not making it up, of course, and the priesthood blessing told her things that she did not consciously know about until later. For instance, she was told in the blessing that her mother had played a role in her abuse. Later my friend discovered that her mother did, in fact, know about the abuse and had refused to help her.

Fifth, those of you who are teachers and leaders have a special role to play in supporting a man or a woman who is going through the aftermath of abuse. I would hope that every teacher in the Church will remember that in his or her classroom is almost certainly at least one person who has survived sexual abuse. With that person in mind, think of the stories you tell, the questions you ask, and, perhaps most importantly, the assumptions you make. Think of a seven-year-old girl whose father sexually abuses her. What does she feel when the Primary sings, "I'm So Glad when Daddy Comes Home"? Think of a twelve-year-old boy who is physically and sexually abused by an uncle who holds an ecclesiastical office. How does he deal with his confusion during a lesson that teaches us to obey our priesthood leaders because they want what is best for us? Think of a woman whose husband beats and rapes her. What feelings go through her mind as a Relief Society teacher explains that it is the wife's responsibility to maintain the spiritual atmosphere in the home and to support the priesthood? To these confused, despairing children and adults in pain, the teachers speak with the voice of the Church. Such messages have a great potential for increasing their pain and despair.

Leaders play an especially important role. Parents and husbands are authority figures, and abusive authority figures may make it seem virtually impossible for someone who has been sexually abused to seek help from yet another authority figure. But I have had several survivors of sexual abuse tell me that the consistent concern of a priesthood leader—even when he did not fully understand the issue or what was happening—was literally what kept them from suicide. Blessings and respectful listening are very important. They validate to a survivor that he or she is not making it up and does not have to go through the healing process alone.

My friend shared one specific way in which leaders can perform a very real service for survivors in that situation. She pointed out that "self-doubt" is "one of the inescapable results" of enduring abuse:

> That is why it is so painful when others stand at the pulpit and doubt you, too. . . . I think the reassurance [of receiving a blessing from a priesthood leader] spared me any further delay from the "hopeful" doubt that the work ahead of me didn't need to be done. With the blessing, I had permission to undertake the cure.
>
> That is one enormous contribution Church leaders can make. Give permission to take the cure. Release the victims from having to continue to take care of their victimizers. If you wish to challenge the victims of child abuse [do not challenge the reality of their memories or accuse them of being responsible for what happened to them. Rather,] challenge them to take responsibility for their own fate, while expressing sympathy for the painful undertaking this will be. And always hold out the promise [of

the Savior] that "I am with you even to the end." Who can do this better than those who are his witnesses?

Another woman who had survived years of sexual abuse from her father spoke to me of "the dreadful task of healing." I think of the Savior, who shuddered because of the suffering, who suffered and bled at every pore, and drew back from the bitter cup, hoping that it was not necessary. He shrank away. But it *was* necessary. He says, "And I partook and finished my preparations unto the children of men" (D&C 19:19). "Children of men" is a stock phrase in the scriptures that means "all human beings" or "the human family," but in this context I hope you will also hear it as a literal phrase, as the little children who have been betrayed and injured at the hands of men and women who were entrusted with their care. Christ finished his preparations for these children. The time of their physical torment may be over, but the time of their spiritual torment is great. Christ also adds, very significantly, "Glory be to the Father."

For him, accepting and fulfilling the Atonement was a dreadful task. But because he did it, we too can lift the dreadful cup to our lips. The scriptures tell us, "He descended below all things, in that he comprehended all things, that he might be in all and through all things, the light of truth; which truth shineth. This is the light of Christ" (D&C 88:6–7). It may seem inconceivable that the light of Christ is irradiating and illuminating the horrifying images and memories associated with sexual abuse, but such is his promise. If this is your situation, cling to that promise. Cling to the light. Let it grow stronger.

The sixth message I want to share is that healing from sexual abuse is a very long and very painful process. According to one study that included LDS women, being able to reach the ultimate step of forgiving the perpetrator and moving on took an average of fifteen years.[4] Many women and men who have been sexually abused respond in ways that they cannot control—with irrational fears, in compulsive behaviors, even in repeated transgressions.

Very often, they are so filled with guilt and self-loathing that repentance seems impossible for them.

Let me borrow an image from a sensitive bishop who works hard to help members of his ward who have been sexually abused. He urges leaders, family, and friends to realize that their loved one or ward member has been injured, just as if he or she had broken a leg that had never been set properly. Even though the person can walk and may have forgotten about the injury, true healing and true strength cannot return until the injury is acknowledged, the bone rebroken, and the leg set correctly. Please realize that someone who has been sexually abused has been deprived of part of her or his free agency. The individual cannot get it back except through the long and difficult process of healing from sexual abuse.

If you are willing to make a commitment to be a friend during this process, make a long-term commitment. Often, even when we acknowledge a problem, we want it fixed quickly. We think a few visits to a therapist, a few priesthood blessings, a few tears shed, a few hugs should make everything all right. Not so. The process of healing from incest hasn't made it into the lesson manuals yet, and it may be more complex than I realize, different for each survivor; but let me share with you again what my friend says:

> It is hard to answer questions that one hasn't been asked, to explain to people who already think they know, to talk to people who do not talk to you. It is especially hard when their talking to you is an attempt to make the subject go away. I want it to go away, too. I thought it would go away after I woke up screaming in the night, or after it made me so afraid I would throw up over and over, or after I recovered the three-year-old and then the six-year-old parts of myself, or after I wrote the letter to my father or after . . . or after . . . The pain ebbs and flows.
>
> . . . I am in so much pain that I will do anything to pass through this as efficiently as possible. . . . A lake cannot repent of its pollutants; it can only submit to being dredged and flushed

of its debris and poisons. I am learning that the pain is not an end in itself, but it leads me to what I am to learn. With each lesson, I get more of my life back.

The closing words of her most recent priesthood blessing assured her

> that Christ not only sorrows at my suffering but suffers with me as I suffer. I am amazed at the love He offers me. I also lose what hope I had of escaping my pain any other way than by experiencing it. I want it to be otherwise. Then, I remember Alma's great testimony that Christ will descend below all things that he may succor his people according to their infirmities. . . . I remember my own experience of being with someone who is suffering, knowing that it is their fate and that all I can offer is to suffer with them. Though I would take it away or explain it away or find someone else who could, the Spirit tells me that it cannot be done and that I must stand there *in* the pain, with them in the suffering.

The seventh point I want to make involves the perpetrator. I realize that women also physically and sexually abuse children. What I say applies to them as well; but in most cases of sexual abuse involving women, girls, or boys, the perpetrator is male. As women, we know the victims and hear their stories, but we also know perpetrators. Most abusers have mothers, wives, daughters, and sisters. Yet the secrecy with which we shroud the victim is nothing to the secrecy with which we shroud the perpetrator. When the abuse is incest, that means that a wife and a mother either does not know or chooses not to know what her husband is doing to her child. She may love him and choose to not know what is happening because the knowledge is too painful, because she feels too helpless, because there is too much to lose. Please remember the words of the Savior, "And whosoever shall offend one of these little ones that believe in me, it is better for him that a millstone were hanged about his neck, and he were cast into the sea" (Mark 9:42).

If you know a perpetrator, and if you love him, or if you love his victim, set the processes in motion so that he can receive help and start on his own process of healing. He needs professional help, and he also needs ecclesiastical help. My friend was born into an LDS family that had been active in the Church for generations on both sides. That lineage did not make her father pure. It did not make her mother brave. It did not protect my friend.

I implore you not to shield perpetrators out of a mistaken sense of love. I have never seen any study suggesting that those who sexually abuse children will alter their behavior without direct intervention. We must believe this dismal message: No child in a neighborhood is safe from a sexual abuser. No child or grandchild in a family is safe.

In many ways, the whole topic of sexual abuse is strange to me. I feel unskilled in thinking about or in knowing how to help someone who is a survivor. I am one of the other two women, not the third. I think of my father, of his steadfast willingness to work his life away as a laborer on a plantation in Hawaii to provide for his parents, for my mother, for me and my brothers. I think of his quiet pride in me, and the determination he and my mother had that I would get an education even when that meant sending me away from them, even when it meant sending me beyond the economic and social level they had reached. I think about my husband, who lived his life for others in the purest expression of Christlike love I have ever known. I think about my two sons, strong and gentle and loving. My heart is filled with gratitude to the point of overflowing for these men in my lives.

Then I think about other daughters, who are brutally taught that they exist as instruments to serve the twisted needs of their fathers. I think about sons who are abused until they grow up thinking that all fathers torture their sons. I think of wives who live with the threat of physical abuse from their husbands, or who turn their heads away from the tears of their daughters, or other mothers who see their sons grow up to become abusive husbands. I am filled with sorrow.

My eighth message is that we can do much to stop the abuse before it starts by holding the men and women in our lives to gospel standards. I have heard the disgusting report that some incestuous fathers justify their vile behavior by saying they are simply carrying out the Church's instructions to make sex education a topic that is handled in the home. We can refuse to accept rationalizations and twisted logic. We can label such behavior for the sin that it is. We can raise sons and daughters who do not make disparaging remarks about others or think they can bully anyone else just because they are stronger. We can teach children to feel ownership of their own bodies and to trust their feelings. We can insist that our sons respect the young women they date. We can raise daughters who have a sense of themselves as daughters of God too strong to submit to abusive treatment from their husbands.

But perhaps most importantly, we can be adults who accept fully our divine identity as children of a loving Heavenly Father. We can accept and be ennobled by the eternal sacrifice of Christ's atonement—not for someone else but for us, ourselves. We can refuse to accept abuse, to make excuses for an abuser, or to turn our heads away from those who have suffered abuse. We can refuse to keep the guilty secrets of abusive men and women in our families who are damaging and destroying innocence.

I have written of "us" and "them," as though all of us are the fortunate two or the fortunate nine, and the one statistical victim of abuse is someone else, a woman or man who is a statistic in another state, a person who is comfortably distant so that we do not have to deal with his or her pain. This is not the impression I want to leave. We are all here together in this Church, we are all here together in this problem, and we can all be part of the solution.

How is it possible to rebuild trust that has been betrayed? When the fabric of our lives is ripped and wrenched, what will make it whole? Let me use the analogy of a piece of lace or a crocheted doily. They begin with a long, straight thread or string, which becomes complex and beautiful when it touches other parts and other strings. But all of them are fragile. They can be shredded, unraveled, and torn. But we need to remember that there *is* a pattern. Even if it is damaged, it can be rewoven. Also, each part supports the other parts and is connected to them. You cannot pick one string out without destroying the whole pattern. I am part of the pattern. The bishop who sits with the injured members of the ward while they face their injury and begin healing is part of the pattern. My friend who discovered the abuse buried deep in memories of her childhood is part of the pattern. You are part of this pattern. And the Savior is part of this pattern. I like to think of the Savior's love as filling the spaces in the lace where there is no thread—because there wouldn't be a pattern if there weren't spaces. I think of him as the intersections where the threads come together, making something special happen where they touch and connect. We can be part of this network of service and support. We can be part of the Savior's pattern.

How can you build and keep that image in your mind? Something that may help you is to keep close at hand or in your mind a quotation that you can turn to when you are in great need of comfort. One such quotation that I like is "Abide with Me" (*Hymns*, no. 166). I love the whole song, but the second verse has had particular comfort for me:

> Swift to its close ebbs out life's little day.
> Earth's joys grow dim; its glories pass away.
> Change and decay in all around I see;
> O thou who changest not, abide with me.

The promise of the sacrament prayer, that we may "always have his spirit to be with [us]" is another promise of great power and consolation. Hymn number 115, "Come, Ye Disconsolate," acknowledges pain but also promises love and hope. The first verse says:

> Come, ye disconsolate, where'er ye languish;
> Come to the mercy seat, fervently kneel.
> Here bring your wounded hearts; here tell your
> anguish.

Then it promises:

> Earth has no sorrow that heaven cannot heal.

These words breathe a spirit of comfort and consolation to me. I hope they do the same for you, and that you can find others that speak the same strength from the Savior, the same never-failing support and love. When times are hard for you, and when you struggle with emotions that you wish you didn't have, will you think of them again? Draw deeply from their strength.

I realize that this is a painful and serious topic. When there is already a great deal of pain in your life, you, like the congregation of Jacob in the Book of Mormon, may wish instead "to hear the pleasing word of God, yea, the word which healeth the wounded soul" (Jacob 2:8).

But there is healing in the gospel and in the unfailing love of our Father in Heaven. How do we rebuild our trust in the Lord and in other human beings when a human being has so seriously violated that trust? Again, I am far from being experienced in these matters. Please, if you have a need, seek the assistance of professionals and leaders you can trust. But let me share with you some thoughts on this topic.

First, accept that you will have very conflicting emotions. It is normal that you should. Psalm 55 seems to me to be something like a dialogue between the hurt and injured self and the self that trusts in the Lord. First, the troubled and pained voice speaks:

> Listen to my prayer, O God, do not ignore my plea;
> Hear me and answer me. My thoughts trouble me and I am
> distraught at the voice of the enemy, at the stares of the wicked;
> for they bring down suffering upon me. . . .

This seems to me to be the very antithesis of the Savior's reassuring promise, "Let not your hearts be troubled." In a situation of betrayal and violated trust, even our memories bring down suffering upon us. The troubled voice continues:

> My heart is in anguish within me; the terrors of death assail me. Fear and trembling have beset me; horror has overwhelmed me.
> I said, Oh, that I had the wings of a dove! I would fly away and be at rest—I would flee far away . . . to my place of shelter. . . .

Then the sense of betrayal comes out sharply:

> If an enemy were insulting me, I could endure it; if a foe were raising himself against me, I could hide from him.
> But it is you, a [person] like myself, my companion, my close friend, with whom I once enjoyed sweet fellowship as we walked with the throng at the house of God . . .
> [This person] attacks his friends [and children]; he violates his covenant . . . his words are more soothing than oil, yet they are drawn swords.

We can understand this. Because of this betrayal comes rage, violent anger, even a desire for revenge. Listen to the voice of the Psalmist as he prays in anger and despair:

> Let death take my enemies by surprise; let them go down alive to the grave. . . . Bring down the wicked into the pit of corruption; bloodthirsty and deceitful men will not live out half their days.

But then, ah, then comes the voice of promise and reassurance:

> But I call to God, and the Lord saves me.
> Evening, morning and noon I cry out in distress, and he hears my voice.
> He ransoms me unharmed from the battle waged against me, even though many oppose me.

> Cast thy burden on the Lord, and he shall sustain thee; he
> shall never suffer the righteous to be moved. . . . Thou, O God, I
> will trust in thee. (Psalm 55, NIV and KJV)

Accept that you will deal with much emotional turbulence, with anger and pain, with desires for revenge, with a desire to flee away. Accept that the process of having the corruption drained away from you is a long and painful process. Trust in the Lord throughout that process.

Second, find others whom you can trust. I think it is very important that you seek out your bishop or another priesthood leader when you feel you can, and share this burden. It may be hard to talk to a man if a man was your abuser—if so, find a trusted woman leader to talk to who can accompany you when you are ready to go to your priesthood leader. In material prepared with the support of the Brigham Young University Women's Research Institute, we read:

> Victims need to be believed, they need to be listened to, they
> need to be relieved of any inappropriate guilt about their role in
> the abuse. Many women reported the strength they felt as their
> bishops and therapists worked together. This arrangement
> allows bishops to concentrate on the spiritual and physical wel-
> fare of their ward members, while the trained professional
> works with the victim to resolve emotional issues. One of the
> women was so anxious and frightened about going to her
> bishop that she wouldn't let him shut the door of his office dur-
> ing their first conversation. But when he heard her story, he
> "cried with me," she said, "and that is when I started trusting
> him. . . . He is the first man I ever remember trusting. I gave my
> therapist permission to talk with him . . . to better understand
> how he could best help me."

Another woman reported that her bishop was also initially baffled about how to help her, but he "took the time to go out and get educated." He still keeps in touch with her, even though she has moved to another state.[5]

Third, do not try to rush or short-circuit the forgiveness process, but continue to work toward it as you can. Wendy Ulrich, a psychologist in private practice, talks about the need to balance both justice and mercy during the process of coming to forgiveness. She writes:

> The principle of justice requires an honest appraisal of our current symptoms and the realities of our pain. . . . To forgive prematurely can close doors to the important realities that pain . . . can open. . . . Justice . . . requires that we not assume responsibility for sins we have not committed, that we not assume power to control decisions we cannot control, and that we not exonerate others' actions when they are dangerous and destructive. To attempt to be merciful in the absence of justice is to deny the characteristics which make God God.
>
> The princip[le] of mercy follows the princip[le] of justice, but cannot rob it. . . . Mercy allows peace to come to the forgiver as she enlarges her understanding of all contributors, takes action on her own behalf, and extends to others the mercy she would claim for herself through the atonement of Christ. The forgiver leaves to God the sorting out of responsibility and intentions, acknowledging others' circumstances and agency, and accepting any and all good consequences that have come from her relationship, just as she has acknowledged the evil.[6]

I think these thoughts by Donna Lee Bowen, who was associate director of the Women's Research Institute at BYU, are relevant. She wrote them after she had gone through a difficult divorce that was emotionally and spiritually wrenching for her. She writes:

> I saw a world of turmoil not calm, a world of tears rather than joy, a world of endurance rather than triumph. I was

overwhelmed at the trials men, as well as women, suffered at each other's hands.

. . . Meekness and forbearance and forgiveness are qualities not easily acquired. In addition, these traits are not valued in today's world, which teaches assertiveness and how to stick up for ourselves. None of these former qualities, of course, imply not realizing our self-worth and defending it. Rather, to my mind, they demand our knowing our place in God's system and holding firmly to it.

Through our absolute need for free agency, we are left to make our own choices, including if and to what extent we wish to involve God in our lives.

Once I turned to God to give me strength, recognizing my own inability to affect another's behavior and realizing my total ability to determine my own behavior and my own course of action, I began to feel a sense of liberation, freedom born of working within a discipline and an order. I established order in my life and, by placing myself under God's care, avoided the dark chasm which threatened to engulf me.[7]

We need to believe what Donna Lee is talking about. We still have our agency, no matter what other people do to us, even if we must work hard to regain parts of it that have been taken away. Our Heavenly Father's spirit is constantly available to us. He sorrows with us and is with us in our pain when abuse occurs. He is there when we start to make the first steps back. His love is steadfast. We may feel betrayed by our family, our church, our society, and even by God; but God does not betray us. His love is never changing. I want to share with you one of the lesser-known psalms, and I want you to speak the words in your own mind, to imagine that this is *your* psalm, spoken in gratitude and praise to the Lord:

The Lord is my rock, and my fortress, and my deliverer;

... In him will I trust; he is my shield and the horn of my salvation, my high tower, and my refuge, my savior; thou savest me from violence.

... When the waves of death compassed me, the floods of the ungodly made me afraid;

The sorrows of hell compassed me about; the snares of death [captured] me;

In my distress I called upon the Lord, and cried to my God: and he did hear my voice out of his temple, and my cry did enter into his ears.

Then the earth shook and trembled; the foundations of heaven moved and shook, because he was wroth. ...

He drew me out of many waters;

He delivered me from my strong enemy, and from them that hated me: ...

He delivered me because he delighted in me. ...

Thou art my lamp, O Lord: ... thou has also given me the shield of thy salvation: and thy gentleness hath made me great. ...

Thou has girded me with strength to battle. ...

The Lord liveth; and blessed be my rock; and exalted by the God of the rock of my salvation. (2 Samuel 22:2–3, 5–8, 17, 29, 36, 40, 47)

Perhaps these are not words that are in your heart yet. I pray that someday they may be. Let the words of other scriptures sink deep into your heart. Hear his voice saying: "Come unto me, all ye that labour and are heavy laden, and I will give you rest" (Matthew 11:18). He knows the burdens with which you struggle. He understands your heartbreak, your self-doubt, the anger, and the despair. Perhaps when he says, "Come unto me," all you feel is paralysis. When you feel you cannot go to him, remember that he is already with you. Remember his words from Hebrews 13:

I will never leave thee, nor forsake thee.

So that we may boldly say, The Lord is my helper, and I will not fear what [human beings] shall do unto me. . . .

Jesus Christ the same yesterday, and to day, and for ever. (Hebrews 13:5–6, 8)

In Second Kings, the Savior speaks gently to a sorrowing person: "I have heard thy prayer, I have seen thy tears: behold, I will heal thee. . . . go up unto the house of the Lord" (2 Kings 20:5). Think of those words as if they were spoken to you. And listen to this promise of the end times, as though it were your vision:

And I John . . . heard a great voice out of heaven saying, Behold, the tabernacle of God is [among human beings], and he will dwell with them, and they shall be his people, and God himself shall be with them, and be their God.

And God shall wipe away all tears from their eyes; and there shall be no more death, neither sorrow, nor crying, neither shall there be any more pain: for the former things are passed away. (Revelation 21:2–4)

Believe that assurance. I implore you to turn to the Savior. I testify to you that when the scriptures tell us he descended below all things, it means that he understands, knows, and accepts the pain of sexual abuse as well as other kinds of innocent suffering. He is there, with you, in that suffering.

I tell you that I love you, both men and women. For those of you who have been spared this scourge of abuse, I ask you to open the circles of your brotherhood and sisterhood and include those whose trust has been betrayed by those who should have been their protectors. Open your hearts to them. Let them open their hearts to you. This is a burden that is grievous to be borne. May we shoulder it together, not merely adjust it upon the backs of those who have borne it so long alone. May we love each other with a pure, unselfish, active love, as the Savior has loved us. May our troubled hearts find the peace we seek with him.

GOOD MEASURE, PRESSED DOWN, AND RUNNING OVER

One of my favorite scriptures is in the Sermon on the Mount where Jesus tells his disciples, "Give, and it shall be given unto you; good measure, pressed down, and shaken together, and running over" (Luke 6:38). It's a wonderful thing to know that this is how the Savior longs to give us his peace and mercy and love: not a skimpy and hastily filled measure but a container that is overflowing—one that has been pressed down, shaken down, with more and more poured in until it overflows.

I have a visual aid that I love to use when I'm talking about this concept. You'll just have to imagine it here as I describe it. Picture a quart canning jar. Let's say that I'm filling it with walnuts. I pour in as many as I can, and it's as full of walnuts as it can get, but there are still spaces around the nuts.

So next I pour in some popcorn kernels. The amazing thing is that I can actually get a full cup of popcorn into a jar that's already "full." I can press in as many kernels as I can by hand, but what does Jesus say? He says, "pressed down and shaken together." So when I shake the jar, I can make room for even more popcorn!

Well, you might think that the jar is completely full now, but it's not so. I can pour sugar into the jar—and almost two cups will fit around the walnuts and the popcorn!

You know, Jesus says that he doesn't stop there. He runs the measure over. I don't ever do that when I do this little demonstration, because I don't want to get the podium all sticky. But remember, Jesus doesn't stop when it's full. He presses. He shakes down. And then he overflows.

Let's back up and look at the context in which Jesus explains this principle to his disciples. He says:

> Love ye your enemies, and do good, and lend, hoping for nothing again; and your reward shall be great, and ye shall be the children of the Highest: for he is kind unto the unthankful and to the evil.
>
> Be ye therefore merciful, as your Father also is merciful.
>
> Judge not, and ye shall not be judged: condemn not, and ye shall not be condemned: forgive, and ye shall be forgiven:
>
> Give, and it shall be given unto you; good measure, pressed down, and shaken together, and running over. . . . For with the same measure that ye mete withal it shall be measured to you again. (Luke 6:35–38)

In other words, if we measure out our love to others in teaspoons, God will use teaspoons to measure love to us. If we use a bushel basket to give mercy to others, God will be merciful to us in the same measure. But if we judge and condemn others by the bucketful, so will God judge us. There's no question in my mind which measure I want God to use with me, so I think I need to find ways to increase the measure of my love and mercy and generosity to others.

We managed to fill our quart jar with three different substances that get along really well. I'd like to focus on three measures that I think we can all benefit from using abundantly. The first is not judging others. The second quality is forgiveness. And the third is love.

Now, I don't know that we can say that walnuts represent one of these traits and popcorn represents another. Maybe we can say that forgiveness is like popcorn, since it has a way of breaking hard little shells and turning seemingly hard, dead kernels into something beautiful and fluffy and white and surprising—something that you would have never guessed. And I think I'd like to compare love to the sugar, since it has a way of slipping into even the tiniest cracks and making everything sweeter than it was before.

But now that I think about it, maybe there *is* one way in which not judging shares a characteristic with walnuts. Not judging is an act of security and self-confidence, like a walnut protected by its shell. A person who is tolerant and accepting of others, a person who feels no need to judge others, knows what he or she believes and does not feel threatened or attacked because other people believe differently. A tolerant person can listen to all kinds of things and say, "That's very interesting. I think I understand what you mean." This person doesn't feel that his or her own beliefs are so fragile or sandy that they can be washed away by the first sign of a different opinion.

Not Judging

Let me talk a little first about not judging. One of Jesus's most telling parables was of the publican and the Pharisee. The scriptures say that he deliberately told this parable to those among his listeners who "trusted in themselves that they were righteous, and despised others." It can be wonderful to be sure that we are doing well. I think we should all aspire to stand with confidence and trust before the Lord. But even this wonderful characterististic can be poisoned if we use our righteousness as the basis for despising others. Jesus said:

Two men went up into the temple to pray; the one a Pharisee, and the other a publican.

119

The Pharisee stood and prayed thus with himself, God, I thank thee, that I am not as other men are, extortioners, unjust, adulterers, or even as this publican.

I fast twice in the week, I give tithes of all that I possess.

And the publican, standing afar off, would not lift up so much as his eyes unto heaven, but smote upon his breast, saying, God be merciful to me a sinner.

I tell you, [said Jesus], this man went down to his house justified rather than the other: for every one that exalteth himself shall be abased; and he that humbleth himself shall be exalted. (Luke 18:9–14)

Let's look at the Pharisee's life. He was really doing a lot of things right. It's great that he fasted twice a week. It's terrific that he wasn't an adulterer. It was wonderful that he knew it was wrong to extort money from others or to behave unjustly. And it was a good trait for him to conscientiously tithe everything he possessed. But because he used all of these good traits as a platform from which to judge the publican harshly and despise him, he was not "justified," meaning that he was not right with God. He was doing a lot of things right. But he was doing something wrong—something very important. He was failing to deal lovingly and charitably with his fellow human beings.

I don't want anyone to misunderstand what I'm going to say next. The First Presidency has made its opposition to same-sex marriages very clear; as a member of the Church, I support them fully in their position. But I want to stress that we can be opposed to a piece of legislation or to a practice and still behave with courtesy and decency toward those who hold other opinions. I would not want anyone to use the First Presidency's stand as an excuse for being hateful or disrespectful toward others.

When I was a member of the Relief Society general presidency, I had the opportunity of speaking privately with many men and women, mostly women, who struggled with feelings of homosexuality. It's been wonderful for me to learn to separate the worth of the individual from any particular behavior, and to feel how deeply and how keenly God loves each individual. I don't have to approve of any particular behavior, but I also don't have to judge people. I know that God loves them. By not judging, I can feel that love for them in my own heart.

It is very likely that every person in the Church knows some-one—a family member or a friend—who is gay, lesbian, or bisexual. I also think it is very likely that many people do not *know* that they know a homosexual or bisexual person because that person is afraid to reveal that part of himself or herself for fear of being rejected, punished, or excluded. I think there is much we do not understand about how such conditions come to be, or what resources for change are truly helpful. In the meantime, nothing has suspended the commandment of Jesus to love one another and to bear one another's burdens.

At the time of Jesus, it was forbidden to touch a leper or a corpse or a menstruating woman because it would contaminate the person who did so. I don't imagine the corpse minded much one way or the other, do you? But I think the women and the lepers bore an immense burden of private pain by this type of public shunning. I think we have no idea how strong and ingrained those taboos were at the time. We simply have nothing comparable.

But Jesus set a new example. He praised the faith of the woman with the issue of blood who touched him, rather than chastising or punishing her for defiling him. He was on his way to heal the daughter of Jairus, you will recall, when he was inter-rupted by that miracle. By the time he and Jairus reached the home, the little girl had died. Here was a corpse—something else he wasn't supposed to touch. But he didn't even hesitate in taking her by the hand, and his touch raised her to life (see Luke 8). And when a leper prayed, "Lord, if thou wilt, thou canst make me clean," even before Jesus spoke a word, he "put forth his hand, and touched him." Then he said, "I will; be thou clean" (Matthew 8:1–3). I can't help thinking that the sheer physical fact of a loving touch was as healing to this person, whom no one had willingly touched for years, as the words of compassion and the act of healing must have been.

I think the point I'm making is clear. As with every time of controversy, I think there is a great potential for division, for anger, and even for hatred. It would hurt me to have Mormons thought of as people who are "against," people who hate, people who call names and ostracize. Can you seek out a friend who disagrees with you on this issue and share a meal together in respect and love? Can you redouble your kindness to the gays and lesbians whom you know, as a witness to them of the love of Christ and his power to transform the human heart?

As members of the Church, we have a clear position on the issue of same-sex marriages. It is right that we should defend this position vigorously. But as members of the Church *of Jesus Christ*, we also have a clear position on the worth and value of each human soul. Let us also defend that position with equal energy, for it is the pure love of Christ, or charity, which Moroni tells us we should pray for with all energy of soul.

Francois de Fenelon wrote: "Charity does not require of us that we should not see the faults of others, but that we should avoid all needless and voluntary observance of them, and that we should not be blind to their good qualities when we are so sharp-sighted to their bad ones."[1]

So that's perhaps the walnuts in our quart jar: not judging others—having the serenity and confidence in ourselves and our own opinions that we can listen to others with respect and compassion instead of feeling so insecure that we must attack and judge them to prove that we are right.

Forgiveness

The second point I want to mention, perhaps corresponding to the popcorn, is the wonderful principle of forgiveness. The Lord is endlessly willing to forgive. He is eager to forgive us. And we should be equally eager to forgive others. The Lord told the Nephite people:

> And [they] that will hear my voice shall be my sheep; and [them] shall ye receive into the church, and [them] I also receive.
>
> . . . And whomsoever ye receive shall believe in my name; and him [or her] will I freely forgive.
>
> For it is *I* that taketh upon me the sins of the world; for it is *I* that hath created them; and it is *I* that granteth unto him that believeth unto the end a place at my right hand. (Mosiah 26:21–23; italics added)

This message is a very liberating one. To me, the Savior is saying, This is my job, not your job. If someone has made a mistake, drop it. Don't harp on it. Don't rub it in. Don't scold or nag. Don't make the person grovel. All of these things set up barriers to love. Forgive quickly. Forgive freely. Forgive generously. Let the love flow through you and around you, drawing you both together.

Jesus offers free forgiveness to all. He has taken upon himself all the sins of the world, including our own sins, so who are we to withhold forgiveness from someone else? He does not withhold forgiveness, teasing us along or tormenting us. Look at Alma the Younger after he was visited by an angel. He was in the chains of hell, experiencing bitter and "exquisite" suffering. As soon as he called on the name of Jesus, he was released from that bondage. He was filled with joy. He was transformed into a disciple of Christ, a lover of the good, a powerful preacher of righteousness. The Savior did not bargain with him or set conditions. He did not say, "Well, we'll see how you do. Maybe if you go on a mission to the Lamanites and persuade those sons of Mosiah to go with you, I'll forgive you. Maybe if you don't do anything wrong for the next forty years, I'll forgive you. Just check back in with me and see how you're doing, but you have to prove you're worthy of my forgiveness before I'll give it to you." No, Jesus forgave him at once—and *because* of the power of that experience, Alma did all the wonderful things he was able to do for the rest of his life. He wasn't trying to prove that he deserved forgiveness. He knew that he had been forgiven, and that knowledge gave him the strength and love and joy to lead a changed life.

Remember how King Benjamin's people, at the end of his sermon, fell to their knees and cried out, "O have mercy, and apply the atoning blood of Christ that we may receive forgiveness of our sins." At once, immediately, in the very next verse, "the Spirit of the Lord came upon them, and they were filled with joy, having received a remission of their sins, and having peace of conscience, because of the exceeding faith which they had in Jesus Christ" (Mosiah 4:2–3). True, King Benjamin then gave them some beautiful instructions about how to *retain* this remission of their sins, but the forgiveness was there instantaneously, immediately, without teasing or tormenting or threats from the Savior.

The act of forgiveness is an explosive act. It explodes the hard, narrow little shells that we surround ourselves with, hoping to protect ourselves. It transforms us into creatures who have received forgiveness and can therefore pass it on to others. Of all the qualities that we measure to others and that will be measured to us, I hope that forgiveness and mercy are among those for which we have full measures, pressed down, shaken together, and overflowing.

Love

Now, the third characteristic that I want to mention is love—those tiny granules that can slither into any crack and sweeten any mixture. There is always room for love, as we discovered in our quart jar.

There's a wonderful Korean brother, Hwang Hyon Ook, who is a worker at the temple in Seoul. He rises before dawn every day to carry ten gallons of fresh water from a mountain spring to the annex of the temple. He does this unseen, delivering the water even before the other ordinance workers reach the temple. He also "gathers discarded and broken umbrellas—taking a stem from one, material from another, and restructuring them" into working umbrellas, which he leaves at the umbrella stand in the temple with little tags urging people to take one if they need it for one of Korea's frequent showers. He also makes a point of inviting patrons from other countries to his home where his wife, Lee Kyong Ki, cooks delicious Korean specialties for them. He says, "Don't love by mouth. Love by behave."[2] I love that pidgin English translation of the gospel. It communicates the essence of the gospel exactly! Don't love by mouth. Love by behave.

I recently received a photograph of nineteen smiling women from the midwestern United States at their Relief Society birthday party. I'd sent them a short videotaped message of greeting for their party, and they had found this way of including me in their celebration. I've never met these women, but as I looked at their faces, so alive and alert, I could feel their spirit of sisterhood. Three were gray-haired. Three were holding little babies. And there were lots of women in between. There were about thirty-five active sisters in the ward, and the president had sent me just a sentence about each one: retired teacher, recently reactivated; mother of five, works part-time; mother of five, travels thirty-five miles to church; chronically ill but always has a positive attitude; temple worker, knits beautiful booties for all the babies; mother of ten, faithful visiting teacher; mother of five, currently going through a divorce; recently reactivated, husband does not attend, works for an insurance company; difficult marriage yet always a sweet smile and attitude; single mother, now engaged and preparing for a temple wedding. . . . And more. Each one of those women had a situation that was challenging to deal with, but each one was there, in the circle of sisterhood, smiling for that photograph. I could tell that this was a ward that loved "by behave."

Christ comes to us in various guises. Mother Teresa reminded her Sisters of Charity that the poorest beggar, the most loathsome beggar is sacred because he is Christ in disguise to them. Each Christmas season irresistibly reminds us of the innkeeper who refused an anxious father and a mother enduring the onset of labor because he did not discern in their need his opportunity to make room for the infant Christ. The apostles on the Sea of Galilee did not believe the evidence of their eyes when they first saw Jesus and thought it was a ghost. Perhaps there are elements of our past haunting us, and our first response is terror because these memories frighten us. Perhaps we cannot see in a homeless man the homeless wanderer of Galilee. Perhaps we cannot see, in the youth wearing the extreme hairstyle and the T-shirt with the ugly slogan, the preacher who dismayed lawyers and Pharisees because he wasn't very conventional in his ideas.

How does Christ come to us? What guise of inconvenience, of helplessness, of anxiety or fear temporarily masks him from our view? Sometimes we cannot see clearly, and in those times we must listen especially hard—listen to the voice that we recognize from our premortal allegiance to his cause, the voice of love, the voice of power, the voice of salvation and strength that says, "It is I; be not afraid."

Jesus Christ teaches us not to judge, offers his forgiveness even before we offer our repentance, and surrounds us with his love—love pressed down, love shaken together, and love overflowing any measure we can possibly offer in this life or the next. I pray that we may follow his way.

10

DELIVERED FROM BONDAGE

I'd like to consider with you an incident from the Book of Mormon in which the people of Zeniff had returned from the land of Zarahemla to the land of Nephi, which by then was in possession of the Lamanites, and they fell into bondage to the Lamanites. They had tried unsuccessfully to free themselves by fighting three times, but they were "surrounded . . . on every side" by the Lamanites and were conquered each time with a great loss of life. They had gone to war in the first place because they felt that their oppressions were intolerable to be borne, for the Lamanites "would smite them on their cheeks, and exercise authority over them; and . . . put heavy burdens upon their backs, and drive them as they would a dumb ass" (Mosiah 21:3). The Nephites' resentment of the unfairness and the humiliation was natural; but it was only after the third defeat that "they did humble themselves even in the depths of humility; and they did cry mightily to God; yea, even all the day long did they cry unto their God that he would deliver them out of their afflictions" (Mosiah 21:14).

Deliverance finally came to this group of Nephites, who were known as the people of Limhi, after the name of their king, who was the grandson of Zeniff. This deliverance seemed to come in six stages. First, the Lord "began to soften the hearts of the

Lamanites that they began to ease their burdens." Second, the Nephites "began to prosper by degrees in the land, and began to raise grain more abundantly, and flocks, and herds, that they did not suffer with hunger." Third, "the people of Limhi kept together in a body as much as it was possible" and each man did "impart to the support of the widows and their children, that they might not perish with hunger." Fourth, the Lord sent Ammon to them, who assured them that their kinfolk were alive in the land of Zarahemla and would welcome them when they could escape. Fifth, Ammon and King Limhi "began to consult with the people how they should deliver themselves . . . and even they did cause that all the people should gather themselves together; and this they did that they might have the voice of the people concerning the matter." Sixth, as a result of this consultation, someone thought of getting the guards drunk and slipping away. (See Mosiah 21:15–22:8.)

Now, in the spirit of Nephi, who likened all scripture unto himself, I'd like to suggest some ways that we can set forth on the Lord's errand to seek release from our bondage and help to free others.

Let me talk a little about the kinds of latter-day bondage that can oppress and depress us, yes, even adults and yes, even teenagers. Then let me suggest ways of learning from each other and of seeking freedom from bondage.

Latter-day Bondage

I have learned much from people who have been willing to share their life circumstances with me. I have gradually become aware that we talk about adversity in the Church, and we even hear people bear their testimonies that they are grateful for their afflictions, but the reality is that only certain adversities seem "okay" to talk about. Only certain types of problems are respectable. The ward will rally around and help us only if our problem is a certain type of problem.

There is immediate support and encouragement if someone in the family falls ill, or if a woman is having a difficult pregnancy, or if you're in a car accident, or if your house burns down. Everyone knows what to do. Everyone wants to do something. These are what I call acceptable problems. They're all the sort of accidents that could happen to anyone, so they're no-fault afflictions.

But there are many other situations, some of them far more trying and emotionally grinding, in which the sympathy is not as ready, the willingness to help is more restrained, and sometimes people avoid the person who is suffering. Sometimes that person feels ashamed or tries to hide the situation, feeling that no one will understand. And often, no one *does* understand, so the sufferer feels even more isolated and even less willing to talk about the situation.

Please consider these situations. Is someone in your family or someone you know experiencing this kind of situation?

• A temple marriage is breaking up after ten, fifteen, twenty, even thirty years because either the husband or the wife is having an affair.

• Your teenager or a teenager in a family close to you is on drugs. His or her grades have dropped through the bottom of the barrel. He or she sneaks out of the house at night or has been caught shoplifting. He or she is prone to reckless, violent behavior. If he doesn't kill himself, he may kill someone else.

• You have a husband or brother or sister, a son or a daughter who is homosexual, or you know someone whose beloved child is struggling with same-sex attraction.

• You or someone you know is enmeshed with the reality of long-term mental illness. Sometimes it can be controlled with medication, sometimes it can't, or the person is too unstable to take his or her medication reliably.

• You or someone you know has been raped.

• You or someone you know is addicted: perhaps to alcohol, perhaps to cigarettes, perhaps to prescription drugs, perhaps to an unhealthy behavior like gambling or sexual addiction. Sometimes the compulsive behavior takes the form of an eating disorder, like compulsive overeating or anorexia or bulimia.

• You or someone close to you has been depressed enough to attempt suicide.

• Someone you know is being sexually abused. Often this person is a child who has no means of defending himself or herself.

• Someone you know is an adult survivor of childhood sexual abuse.

• Someone you know is a perpetrator of sexual or physical abuse.

Now, fortunately, some of these problems are in transition. Twenty years ago, divorce, though far from uncommon, was a problem that often put you outside the circle of acceptability even though it was not your fault. Fifteen years ago, wife battering was a secret, unmentionable problem. Ten years ago, incest was an unspeakable problem. Five years ago, it was impossible to talk about having and loving a homosexual son or daughter. I wonder what problems are still unspeakable today that we will look back on in ten or fifteen years and wonder how many hearts broke silently and secretly because there was no one to care, no one to help.

Thanks to the courage of survivors of all of these situations, the terrible bondage of silence is being eased. There are models for other survivors. There are professionals who have the training to help. But within the Church there is still much shame, much guilt, much feeling that, "If I were more righteous, I wouldn't have this problem." Sometimes, members of the Church whose experience has been limited and has shielded them from some of these terrible problems feel that they can judge and condemn others who have these problems. In such an environment, no sharing can take place, no help can be asked for, and usually no help is offered.

Are not these situations a description of bondage? Are they not a description of burdens that are heavy to be borne? I realize that privacy is an issue in many situations—that the sufferer needs to maintain dignity by maintaining silence, at least for a time. And even the most loving people cannot force someone to confide in them. Denial is also a barrier, when a person feels that he or she will not or cannot face a terrible reality and instead puts energy into pretending that everything is all right. I'm not asking you to be snoopy or nosy, and I'm not suggesting that people indiscriminately spill all of their problems, their family's problems, and especially their neighbors' problems in testimony meeting. But I *am* suggesting that you look very hard and very carefully at this phenomenon I'm talking about.

Do you maintain a list of problems that it's okay to have and another list of problems that it's not okay to have? How do you behave toward people on the first list? How do you behave toward people on the second list? If there's a difference, do you find yourself judging and feeling superior because you don't have a particular problem? You may just be lucky, you know. Or the Lord in his infinite wisdom and mercy may know that there are some problems you are too weak to bear and is sparing you from them. Or he may be testing the depth of compassion in your heart for the sufferers, hoping that you will find the love and willingness to serve that will lead you to ease the burdens of those who are less fortunate than you, even when they cannot be delivered from their afflictions.

This is the first point: that bondage in the latter days takes many forms and can be just as real as the literal bondage that the people of Limhi suffered.

Praying for Ease, Staying Together

I want to ask you very sincerely and very humbly, now, to think with me of the next three steps that ultimately led the people of Limhi to deliverance. You remember that when the people were absolutely in the depths of humility and cried to the Lord for deliverance, three things happened: they prayed for deliverance, they strengthened themselves, and they stuck together.

When the people prayed, the Lord first "began to soften the hearts of the Lamanites that they began to ease their burdens." Second, the Nephites "began to prosper by degrees in the land, and began to raise grain more abundantly, and flocks, and herds, that they did not suffer with hunger." Third, "the people of Limhi kept together in a body as much as it was possible" and each man did "impart to the support of the widows and their children, that they might not perish with hunger" (Mosiah 21:15–17).

Now, in the case of the problems I've asked you to think about, these steps also have counterparts. If you are the one who is experiencing the problem, you can pray for an easing of the burden, even if you cannot be delivered from it. And this step is particularly applicable if you know about a problem someone else is experiencing. You may not know how to solve someone's problem. You may not know how to help that person solve her own problem. There may not be a way for the problem to be solved. There may not even be a way to talk about the problem and to share your sympathy directly with that person. But you can pray for her deliverance. You can remember her in your morning and evening prayers and lift your heart to the Lord during the day, in love and compassion and the desire that she will be delivered.

Being able to pray with sincerity of heart about a problem breaks down the walls of denial and evasion. When you're praying on the inside about, say, an addiction to a prescription drug, you can't very well maintain the illusion on the outside that you don't have a problem. Another important effect is that such a sincere prayer is an invitation for intervention. You are much less likely to reject help when it comes, even in an odd disguise. And if you are praying about the needs of someone else, then I think you are much more open to the whisperings of the Spirit about something that would help than you would be if you were secretly saying (to paraphrase King Benjamin), "This woman has brought upon herself her misery; therefore I will stay my hand, and will not give unto her of my food, nor impart unto her of my substance that she may not suffer, for her punishments are just" (see Mosiah

4:17). Or, to put it in more modern terms, "I would never dress the way she does, so I'll never have to worry about being raped," or, "I'd never let my children make the kinds of decisions they do, so my children will never try drugs or be sexually active."

Then there's the next thing that happens. The Nephites "began to prosper by degrees in the land," so that their physical suffering from hunger eased. In other words, they became stronger. They became better, over time, at learning to meet their own needs. Their work and their efforts made a difference in the quality of their daily life.

When you are struggling with a long-term problem, whether mental, emotional, economic, or spiritual, it is very easy to become discouraged at the length of the road, heartsick at the pain you are obliged to undergo, and exhausted from the constant effort. There needs to be a way to keep track of small landmarks and to celebrate small victories that are signposts on the way to progress. A diary is a good way of seeing that you *are* making progress, day by day, step by step, even when the steps are small. A good friend who can remind you what things were like a month ago or even a year ago can be invaluable. Take time to savor these signs and be grateful.

Now, the next thing that happened is what I really want to stress. Remember that "the people of Limhi kept together in a body as much as it was possible" and each man did "impart to the support of the widows and their children, that they might not perish with hunger." This is so important. They strengthened themselves—not so they could *separate* themselves from others who were suffering, but so they could *succor* those who were in need. They stayed together. The humiliations and the burdens and being treated like animals were not things they kept secret from each other, but things they shared together. They could be *for* each other when the Lamanites were *against* them, individually and collectively. They could support and encourage and sympathize and understand each other.

I want to share with you a poem written by a woman who

shared it with me to explain how grateful she was to receive understanding and compassion from a few who understood her trials:

> There was once a time
> When the Lord touched stones
> with His finger,
> And made them shine brightly,
> that His people might not
> cross the great waters
> in complete darkness.
> The Lord touched these stones,
> And made them shine
> Because of the faith
> of one man,
> Who loved Him
> and knew God would not
> leave them in darkness.
> The Lord has also
> Touched people
> With His finger,
> And made them shine brightly,
> That some of us might not
> cross the great waters
> in complete darkness.
> The Lord touched these people
> And gave them love,
> because of the need
> Of one person,
> Who loved God,
> And knew that God would not
> Leave her in darkness alone.[1]

I hope you can tell how important it was to this woman to know that she was not alone, and that the love of those who were able to accept and help her was a manifestation of the love of the Lord.

I want to tell you another story, one that has become part of the history of the Lansing Michigan Stake where I visited recently. I think mental illness is a problem that we often don't understand. It's a particularly frightening problem because we have to understand problems and shape solutions with our minds, and when our minds aren't working right, our ability to either identify the problem or select an appropriate solution is severely limited. There is so much ignorance and fear still, even at the close of the twentieth century, about mental illness. Families are ashamed. Individuals don't know how to explain mental illness. Friends and relatives keep hoping it will go away and find themselves running out of patience when loved ones seem incapable of helping themselves in very simple, common-sense ways.

Jennifer Johnson, the mother of a schizophrenic son and a member of the board of directors of the Utah Alliance for the Mentally Ill, has pointed out that "mental illness touches all of us. Severe mental illness, such as major depression, bipolar disorder, schizophrenia, obsessive compulsive disorder or panic disorder affects one in five families in their lifetime. One in six people will suffer clinical depression. Of these, one in six will attempt suicide. One in eight will succeed. This makes clinical depression as fatal as heart disease and some forms of cancer."[2]

I consider this story from Michigan to be a success story, a story of how charity did not fail in this circumstance. This story begins:

> Mildred Miller . . . passed quietly away in her sleep Sunday evening, February 16, 1992. She was living in the Cameron Adult Foster Care Home in the Hanover area. Mildred was a well known and highly thought of member of the ward. Her unique personality and child-like faith and bearing made her worthy of special note in this ward history. No one who ever attended the Jackson Ward would fail to note and be impressed

with Mildred and remember her. . . . She was a gifted organist [who] provided the music for almost every meeting and function since she became a member of the Church in the late 1940s. . . . Mildred [also] composed music and lyrics, and also wrote some poetry. She was also an excellent typist and put together the ward sacrament meeting program for many years. She also did a lot of typing for people, including the bishops, who could always count on her to help them with their confidential correspondence. She was very reliable in those matters. Mildred will be remembered as one who lived by the guidance of the Holy Ghost. She knew him intimately and relied on him more than most do in her daily walk. She was the only member of her family [who] was a member of the Church. . . .

Mildred suffered from a form of schizophrenia which required medication to control. She always felt it was a drug that she would do better without. However, withdrawal from the controlling drug resulted in a loss of contact with reality, requiring hospitalization to correct. In her later years Mildred became less consistent in the use of her medication, requiring her to live in an adult foster care home. She never lost her love for the Savior, for others and for the Holy Ghost, even during her times of illness. Up to the time of her death she attended church regularly when rides were available. She was in apparent good health and never complained of any discomfort the day of her passing. . . . She leaves a place no one will ever likely be able to fill.[3]

How sweet it is to know that Mildred had a place—a valued, beloved, and respected place—in a circle of sisters who included her as someone who was also on the Lord's errand.

Church history records a beautiful story in late July 1839, when the Saints were trying to settle Nauvoo. Many of them were very ill because of malaria, and Joseph Smith went throughout the settlement blessing the sick. He crossed over the river to Montrose,

Iowa, directly opposite Nauvoo, where many of the Saints were also suffering, and healed them. Then this incident happened:

> After healing the sick in Montrose, all the company followed Joseph to the bank of the river, where he was going to take the boat to return home. While waiting for the boat, a man from the West [evidently not a member of the Church], who had seen that the sick and dying were healed, asked Joseph if he would not go to his house and heal two of his children who were very sick. They were twins and were three months old. Joseph told the man he could not go, but he would send some one to heal them. He told Elder Woodruff to go with the man and heal his children. At the same time he took from his pocket a silk bandanna handkerchief, and gave to Brother Woodruff, telling him to wipe the faces of the children with it, and they should be healed; and remarked at the same time: "As long as you keep that handkerchief it shall remain a league between you and me." Elder Woodruff did as he was commanded, and the children were healed, and he keeps the handkerchief to this day.[4]

Over the past few years, as a gesture of love and support for me in my calling, many dear sisters have given me beautiful handkerchiefs. Each one is different, but each is beautifully made. They came to me from sisters whom I did not even know but who were acting out of love. From time to time I give one away, just so that someone else can feel a connection with those distant members of the Church and be strengthened by their love.

There is nothing magical or miraculous about these handkerchiefs, but there is something miraculous about love—about the love of the gospel that found expression in this gift of love made visible.

The thing I like about handkerchiefs is that they are very versatile. They can dry tears. They can wipe away the sweat of someone who has been working very hard. They can stanch the blood from a wound. In short, they exist to meet a need—a real, physical need. And that, in my opinion, is where the errand of the Lord takes us: among real, mortal, human beings who have the real needs—some of them not very pretty and many of them not very respectable.

Learn from the Afflicted

The next point I want to make is this: the members of Jackson Ward accepted the gifts that Mildred Miller had to offer. They did not patronize her or think that she had nothing to share because she was mentally ill. They did not take the position that they were the givers and that Mildred was the receiver. They found ways to both give and receive where she was concerned. We talk about learning from our adversities and our afflictions, but we are often unwilling to learn from those who are afflicted. So my plea is that we find ways to learn from the afflicted and to accept their gifts.

I was greatly touched by the fact that Ammon and King Limhi "began to consult with the people how they should deliver themselves . . . and even they did cause that all the people should gather themselves together; and this they did that they might have the voice of the people concerning the matter" (Mosiah 22:1).

It shouldn't be a novel, innovative idea to ask the people who need help what kind of help they need. It shouldn't be an amazing new idea to ask people who are involved in a problem how to get out of the problem. But the fact is that this very seldom happens. We have the feeling that, "I'm smarter than you because I don't have this problem," or, "I'm more competent than you or I'm more righteous than you, so I will tell you how to fix your problem."

What is often dispensed in situations like that is pretty good *general* advice, such as pray, read the scriptures, and talk to the bishop; but the problem is that it *is* general advice. It's not *specific* advice. The person trying to fix the problem hasn't listened long enough to understand the problem before launching into a solution.

What I'm asking is that we listen and learn from each other. Survivors of abuse have a great deal to teach all of us about healthy relationships, self-esteem, and protecting our boundaries. If we never listen, though, how can we learn? People who have been in financial difficulties and poverty have a great deal to teach us about money management. People who suffer from chronic ill health have much to teach us, and so do people who suffer from chronic mental illness.

Remember when Joseph Smith was in Liberty Jail, suffering great torment of both body and mind as his people were driven from Missouri during the terrible winter of 1838–39? The Lord's comfort and consolation to him was that "all these things shall give thee experience, and shall be for thy good" (D&C 122:7). The Lord wasn't just talking about being unjustly imprisoned or not knowing how his family was doing, either. The Lord drew a picture of even more extreme fear, privation, and suffering: "If thou shouldst be cast into the pit, or into the hands of murderers, and the sentence of death passed upon thee; if thou be cast into the deep; if the billowing surge conspire against thee; if fierce winds become thine enemy; if the heavens gather blackness, and all the elements combine to hedge up the way; and above all, if the very jaws of hell shall gape open the mouth wide after thee, know thou, my son, that all these things shall give thee experience, and shall be for thy good."

In other words, experience is precious and valuable for its own sake, whether it's desirable experience or undesirable experience, whether it's good or bad, whether it's positive or terrifyingly negative. This is a different view of experience! But if any and all experience can be for our own good, then nothing is excluded—not the most frightening, most unjust, most painful experiences we can think of. And if we can learn from our own experiences, then we can also learn from the experiences of each other.

Who knows but what a silent member of your ward right now is enduring an experience that will literally save your life if you can learn from him or her? The Lord promised:

> For there are many gifts, and to every [man and woman] is given a gift by the Spirit of God.
>
> To some is given one, and to some is given another, that all may be profited thereby. (D&C 46:11–12)

What are the gifts of your sisters and brothers? What are the gifts you have to offer them from the treasure house of your experience? Please open your heart to learning, not only from the adversities and afflictions that you yourself suffer but also from those who are afflicted and those who suffer.

I think that we often keep stones rolled across our hearts so that the fountains of faith and compassion are shut up within us. Our faith is so fragile that we think we literally cannot survive the adversities of mortality. So we hide ourselves from suffering and misery, fearing that they will destroy us if we acknowledge their existence.

The message of the gospel is not that we will *stay* out of trouble but that we can *get* out of trouble. The message of the gospel is not that we will be comfortable but that we will be able to give comfort. The message of the gospel is not that we are blessed by accumulating possessions but that we are blessed by sharing possessions. The message of the gospel is not that there is something wrong with us if we fail and suffer and make mistakes but that there is something wrong with us if we do not grow closer to the Savior as we fail and suffer and make mistakes. The purpose of the gospel is not to eliminate evil but to deliver us from evil. The Lord promised the people of Alma when they were in bondage:

> Lift up your heads and be of good comfort, for I . . . will covenant with my people and deliver them out of bondage.
>
> And I will also ease the burdens which are put upon your shoulders, that even you cannot feel them . . . and this will I do that ye may stand as witnesses for me hereafter, and that ye may know of a surety that I, the Lord God, do visit my people in their afflictions. (Mosiah 24:13–14)

Please remember the lessons of the people of Limhi. Deliverance begins by recognizing our bondage and acknowledging that it is real, that it hurts and hampers us. With sincere prayer, let us go before the Lord, without denial or excuses or claims of superiority. Let us confess that we are in bondage. Second, let us pray that our burdens and those of our sisters and brothers may be eased, even if they cannot be lifted. Third, let us make every effort to strengthen ourselves so that we can begin to nourish ourselves and suffer less. Fourth, let us stick together in one body, united in the Lord's errand, and generously share whatever we have to give. And fifth, let us recognize and value the gifts of each and every person, instead of dividing ourselves into the persons who are so needy that they must always be receivers and those who are so superior that they must always be givers.

In our own day, the Lord gave Joseph Smith this inspiring message:

> Let the mountains shout for joy, and all ye valleys cry aloud; and all ye seas and dry lands tell the wonders of your Eternal King! And ye rivers, and brooks, and rills, flow down with gladness. Let the woods and all the trees of the field praise the Lord; and ye solid rocks weep for joy! And let the sun, moon, and the morning stars sing together, and let all the sons [and daughters] of God shout for joy! . . . Shall we not go on in so great a cause? . . . On, on to the victory! Let your hearts rejoice, and be exceedingly glad, . . . for the prisoners shall go free. (D&C 128:23, 22)

Jesus Christ has paid the price to free us from every bondage that afflicts us. Stronger than denial, stronger than addiction, stronger than the suffering of terrible memories is his love for us and his desire that we be free. He calls us to rejoice in that freedom and to go forth on his errand to free others.

CHRIST AND CULTURE

As an American of Japanese ancestry born in Hawaii who lives on the mainland, and as a convert to Mormonism from Buddhism, I'm a firm believer in diversity, in the injection of new flowers into old gardens, in springs rising from many sources to swell the rivers and run to the sea. I love diversity. I'm comfortable with it. I celebrate it and learn from it. Let me share with you two letters from children to God that deal with this theme. The first one is from eight-year-old Amanda. It reads:

> Dear God,
> I live in Maine. I have a lot of friends here. People here are great.
> Some people say we talk funny. That makes me mad. They should talk. They are from Boston.
> Love,
> Amanda
> P.S. My mothers friends live in Boston

The second letter is from ten-year-old Andy. It reads:

God,

I know a kid at school. His name is Tom Chen. He is Chinese. Most of us are not. Boy you like to have variety.

Love,

Andy[1]

God *does* like variety, and I believe that to the extent that we try to be like him, we will also find new ways to enjoy and appreciate and notice diversity. Perhaps the easiest place to start is with the beautiful diversity of nature. Brother Ted Gibbons talks about his own discoveries:

Christopher, my nine-year-old son, came home from the summer fields with closely cupped hands and announced that he had caught a grasshopper with blue wings. I was skeptical. In my own youth, roaming the foothills and farmlands of Cache Valley [in northern Utah], I had seen grasshoppers with red, black, yellow, orange, and transparent wings, but never one with blue wings. "No, not blue wings," I said. "There aren't any."

He regarded me smugly for a moment, without speaking, and then opened his hands. Bright, deep, metallic blue—*real* blue—flashed in the afternoon sun. I stared after it in amazement, then caught my breath, glanced upward, and said very, very softly, "Thanks."

It came to me powerfully then, as it often has, that the beauty and variety of God's creation are evidences of God's love for his children. . . .

Is it even conceivable that the *only* purpose of this diversity is to maintain some precarious ecological balance? Are grasshoppers with blue wings necessary to preserve the earth in its orbit and the biosphere in its function? And even if grasshoppers are necessary, would not the red- and orange- and black-winged ones suffice? I confess that I do not know. I am not a scientist, not a zoologist, certainly not a God. But I am a child of

God with eyes and a heart. I know that grasshoppers with blue wings are surprisingly beautiful, and I know that God made them and that he loves me. The testimony of the relationship of that love and that beauty is enough.[2]

Let me share some thoughts with you about three questions: First, what do the scriptures tell us about culture in the gospel context? Second, how should we deal with cultural differences? And third, is there another step we need to take to truly implement the gospel message of equality and inclusiveness?

Culture in the Scriptures

I know that you know and love the great foundational scriptures of equality in the gospel, but let's review a few of them together.

Let's begin with Acts, chapter 17, verses 26 through 28, where Paul is explaining to the Athenians that all human beings are related to each other because God is the father of us all:

> And hath made of one blood all nations of men for to dwell on all the face of the earth, and hath determined the times before appointed, and the bounds of their habitation;
> That they should seek the Lord, if haply they might feel after him, and find him, though he be not far from every one of us:
> For in him we live, and move, and have our being; as certain also of your own poets have said, For we are also his offspring.

Another foundational scripture of equality in the gospel appears in Ephesians, where Paul repeats his beautiful vision of the unity of the Saints:

> There is one body, and one Spirit, even as ye are called in one hope of your calling;
> One Lord, one faith, one baptism,

One God and Father of all, who is above all, and through all, and in you all.

But unto every one of us is given grace according to the measure of the gift of Christ. (Ephesians 4:4–6)

And now, from the book of Colossians, "Where there is neither Greek nor Jew, circumcision nor uncircumcision, Barbarian, Scythian, bond nor free: but Christ is all, and in all" (Colossians 3:11).

I've saved for last my very favorite scripture on equality, a beautiful description of Jesus Christ's love and care for all of us: "For none of these iniquities come of the Lord; for he doeth that which is good among the children of men; and he doeth nothing save it be plain unto the children of men; and he inviteth them all to come unto him and partake of his goodness; and he denieth none that come unto him, black and white, bond and free, male and female; and he remembereth the heathen; and all are alike unto God, both Jew and Gentile" (2 Nephi 26:33).

It thrills me to the soul to read the testimony of the scriptures about our kinship to all other human beings and about the essential equality we find in the gospel. This is an ideal. I don't think that very many of us have achieved it yet, but it is a beautiful goal to strive for.

I'd like to share one more passage of scripture that I think will lead us into the discussion of how to deal with differences in culture: "For it shall come to pass in that day, that every [one] shall hear the fulness of the gospel in his own tongue, and in [her] own language, through those who are ordained unto this power, by the administration of the Comforter, shed forth upon them for the revelation of Jesus Christ" (D&C 90:11).

One leader, after quoting this verse, made a very profound and thoughtful comment. He said: "I do not think I am treating this text irresponsibly to suggest that we might well include the language of children, of youth, of the poor, of the affluent, of the educated and uneducated, and of any other group whose language is their gateway to hearing and understanding. Although the in-house vocabulary of [Mormonism] may fall easily from our lips, we will do well to remember that such language may serve as a barrier rather than a gateway. Many of us, then, will need to become sensitive to populations who are as yet relatively untouched by our witness."[3]

Marian Wright Edelman, a powerful advocate in the United States for children, is fond of observing: "When Christ told His disciples to let the little children 'come unto me,' He did not say rich children or white children or smart children or nondisabled children. He said, 'Let the children come unto me.' And so it must be."[4]

Will we learn to look beyond the simple barriers of culture, nation, and class to see that we are all precious and valuable to God? I believe we must.

Dealing with Cultural Differences

Now, let's talk about the practical problems of dealing with cultural differences. It is easy for us to relate to Brother Gibbons's joy in the beauty and diversity of the natural world, but often we find that diversity among individuals and cultures scares us. It seems unnatural, wrong, even bad. In one culture, parents may frequently slap or spank their children but would never think of sending them to a different room out of the family circle. In another culture, parents would never strike their children but will isolate them in their rooms for long periods of time. Is one system right and one wrong? I believe that both methods can be effective forms of discipline, but that both methods can also be abusive, and a great deal depends on the motivation of the parents.

The scriptures were written out of a very specific culture and a very specific time period. Many of the rules laid down for their cultures simply don't apply to us anymore. For instance, the Old Testament forbids the eating of pork. If we felt that rule applied to us, could we ever eat kalua pig at a luau? As another example, the

New Testament says that it is shameful for a woman's hair to be uncovered in church. Well, just look around any Church meeting and see if you think that still applies!

Instead of focusing on these rules that no longer make sense in our own culture, we focus on the principles behind them: eat healthy food and dress modestly. The parts of the scriptures that have remained constant, their messages still new for us today, are the timeless principles, coupled with the stories that show people struggling to make right decisions and living the consequences of their decisions.

Both the New Testament and the Doctrine and Covenants talk about the importance for members of the Church to be "of one heart and of one soul" or of "one mind." (Acts 4:32; D&C 45:65–66). Sometimes we think this means that we have to look alike, sound alike, talk alike, dress alike, and have the same number of children. I think what it really means, above all, is that we need to love the Savior with all our hearts. At that point, we will have the "mind of Christ" (1 Corinthians 2:16) to unite us in soul with others. As we think about situations and problems, the frustratingly complex ethical and moral dilemmas will become clearer and simpler because we will know what Jesus would do in a given case, and we can do what he would do, just as he was able to do what the Father would have done in his place. I think that rules confuse, principles clarify.

What does this mean for us? Let me use an example from my own life. My family is Buddhist. My mother and my brothers are still Buddhist. I am the only Christian and the only Latter-day Saint among my family. My mother respects my religious beliefs. Because I have the fulness of the gospel, does this mean that I should not respect *her* religious beliefs? No.

As you probably know, much of the practice of Buddhism takes place in the home with daily prayers and small offerings of food and flowers before a household shrine. It is a time to acknowledge the existence of God and to feel a connection with and concern for the dead in the family. Do I acknowledge the existence of God in my life? I certainly do. Do I feel a connection with and a concern for the dead? I certainly do. Do I believe in prayer? Absolutely. Am I thankful for the bounties of the earth with which the Lord has blessed us? No question about it. So can I pray with my mother at her household shrine when I visit her? Of course I can. My prayers are addressed to my Father in Heaven, not to Buddha, and I understand that the sealing ordinances of the temple link families together eternally, but it seems to me that both rituals turn the hearts of the children toward their parents in a beautiful way, and I believe that God has found a way to teach this principle in at least three different cultures: in the Old Testament culture of Malachi, the prophet who tells us about turning the hearts; in the culture of Buddhism; and in the modern Latter-day Saint culture.

Perhaps when you are struggling with ways to make traditional culture and the gospel culture come together in a way that helps you as an individual and blesses your family, you could ask yourself the same questions:

First, what is the principle behind this traditional practice?

Second, do I believe this principle?

Third, how can I show my support for this principle and participate in this practice without violating a gospel standard?

Let me give you another example. In the family of my husband, Ed, Sundays were a time for the entire family to gather at the home of the widowed mother, to talk, to laugh, to play cards, to gamble a little—never very much—to eat a big meal, to play the guitar and sing, and to drink a few beers. After we got married, we were living on Maui near Ed's mother, so I was included as part of the family in these Sunday gatherings. Because I went to Sunday School in the mornings and sacrament meeting in the evenings, it meant that Ed and I came a little later than some of the other siblings and in-laws and left a little earlier. I always gave him his choice about going earlier or staying later, but he decided it was important for us to be together, so his family adapted to this slight change in schedule and still made us welcome.

Because I was a Mormon, I would not drink coffee, and I had never drunk beer, but that was no big deal. There were plenty of other things to drink. So that was not a difficulty. But ten months after we were married, Ed studied the gospel and joined the Church. My mother-in-law was not pleased. Mormons were not as respectable as Congregationalists (that was the church Ed had been raised in), and besides that, she thought that a wife should adopt the religion of the husband—not the other way around. Also, Ed stopped gambling during the card games, passed up the coffee at dinner, and drank water instead of beer. These were differences that his brother and sister noticed and teased him about, but he just smiled and took the teasing in good part. Thus, even though Ed's mother disapproved of his conversion, Ed stayed focused on the principle behind the family gatherings—that these were times to be together and involved in each other's lives, to show that we loved each other and enjoyed being together.

But what would have happened if we had stayed away? Or gone and delivered long lectures about the evils of gambling or about the importance of keeping the Word of Wisdom? This behavior would have violated the principle of family unity that we were trying to sustain and uphold. It was no trouble to take hot water instead of tea. And best of all, Ed's brother also later joined the Church.

So this is the first point I would like you to remember. Before you dismiss any cultural practice, think about the principle behind it, decide if this principle is one you also believe, and see if you can find a way to participate in it in a way that honors that principle.

The New Tribalism

Now, I want to flip the problem over and look at the other side of it. I want to raise the possibility that we may erase our old tribes of nations and culture only to replace them with a new tribe—the tribalism of religious exclusivity based on our membership in the Church.

What do I mean by new tribalism? How is it possible to go too far in feeling brotherhood and sisterhood within our wards and stakes? Is it wrong to be able to erase national and political enmities, some of which have endured for many centuries, among groups by passing over the bridge of the gospel into a true ability to see each other as children of God and as each other's eternal brothers and sisters? No, it is not wrong. But it can *become* wrong if our ability to see another as a brother or sister stops at the door of the ward meetinghouse, and if we save our love and our friendship and our acceptance only for other Mormons.

I want to warn us all against this new tribalism, a way of seeing the world that still divides people into "us" and "them." Yes, it is wonderful progress for a Japanese person and a Korean person to transcend the tribes of their nations, with those traditional enmities, as they both find themselves reborn in their acceptance of the gospel. They have taken down one of the walls around each of them that kept them safe but also kept them confined. However, it is no advantage if they just use the same stones to build another wall in a new place.

It is wonderful when a Tongan sister and a Samoan sister and a Tahitian sister can all serve together in a Primary presidency or a Relief Society presidency, drawing on the strengths in their own cultures to find creative and loving ways to serve the sisters. However, if they can ignore other needs within their ward boundaries because the house with the neglected children is not a Mormon home, or the woman who is being beaten by her husband has not been baptized, or the pregnant fourteen-year-old doesn't want to talk to LDS Social Services, then there is a new wall. And instead of belonging to a Tongan or a Samoan or a Tahitian tribe, they now belong to a Mormon tribe.

Perhaps it will help to think of ourselves as growing like a tree, from the center out, in concentric rings of concern and acceptance for others. It is right and appropriate that the first circle of concern should be for ourselves. If we do not have a strong and healthy relationship to our Heavenly Father, if we do not have our own individual testimonies of the Savior, then we are a tree without heartwood. We are brittle. We will snap easily. Others cannot lean on us for support.

The next circle is our family, those who have given us life and the stories that connect us to the past. This is the bond of blood. We do not choose these families—our parents, our grandparents, our brothers and sisters and aunts and uncles. We love them because we belong together. We love them because we spend time together. We love them because we share space and food and stories about our lives.

The next circle is the family we choose and make. This is the circle where we choose to marry and bring children into the world. We get to choose our spouses but not our children—as you may have noticed! And for some, marriage doesn't happen, and for other couples, children do not come. But the circle is still one of choice. We choose to stay involved with our families or to get involved in new ways with them.

And whether married or single, all of us choose the circle of friends, ranging all the way from soul brothers and sisters who are as close to us as members of our genetic families, to acquaintances that we associate with for a few weeks or a few years until work, moving, ward boundaries, or different interests imperceptibly drift us apart. For most of us, other members of the Church are in this category. They become a sort of ready-made family as we move from place to place. We share so much because we are all Latter-day Saints.

You remember that very powerful lesson Jesus taught the people when he was encircled about by a multitude and his mother and brothers came to see him. When he learned that they were there, people expected him to call them in or go out to them. Instead he said, "Whosoever shall do the will of my Father which is in heaven, the same is my brother, and sister, and mother" (Matthew 12:46–50). Does this mean that we should abandon our families for the service of God? Is it really God's will that we should ignore and not recognize our families? Not at all. In Jesus' culture, where the family was of such preeminent importance that few other social bonds even registered, he was saying, "Enlarge your circle. Include in your familial love and esteem people who are outside your family but who believe the same way. Faith is a bond that can create a family feeling too." Don't you think this is the real reason we call each "brother" and "sister"?

But should our concern stop there? Should we not care about others who believe differently? If that were true, then Paul would never have become the apostle to the Gentiles, and Peter would never have had the vision that taking the gospel to the Gentiles was God's will.

Most of us have a circle of love for created nature—the sea, the forests, the mountains, the animals. Most of us have special places to which we are attached by memories and affection or a special sense of beauty.

Most of us also have circles of love and concern where we have relationships with people we don't actually know personally—the leaders of our Church, the leaders of our country, inspirational figures like Mother Teresa, tragic figures like Princess Diana, or sports heroes. I think our circles should keep expanding, that we should never draw lines that would put anyone or anything in creation outside our area of concern.

Please do not misunderstand me. It is appropriate that we think clearly about where our first priorities of concern and responsibility lie. I think most of us do this instinctively. Any mother can pick the sound of her baby crying out of a dozen infants. Any brother can look over a whole field of soccer players and instantly identify which nine-year-old is his sister, even though the uniforms are all alike.

But we need to be able to say: "I know you. I love you. We belong together in certain ways" without also sending the opposite message: "I don't know you. I hate you. I will try to keep you away from me and maybe I will even try to destroy you." It is right for the Church to stress the importance of motherhood and fatherhood, but it is not right to exclude or shun those who have not experienced the blessings of parenthood. It is right for the Church to stress the importance of education without communicating that the uneducated are despicable. It is right that our missionaries should try to bring the beauties of the gospel to all, but it is not right for them to feel contempt or patronization toward other religions.

Differences are neither right nor wrong—they are just differences. But so often we try to attach a value to the difference. Men are different from women. Does this mean they are better than women? Some are. Some aren't. Filipinos are different from Chinese. Does this mean they are better citizens? Depends on the person. Republicans are different from Democrats. Does this mean that they make better politicians? Some do. Some don't.

Think about that word *better*. I remember learning a little poem in grade school to teach us about comparative adjectives. It went like this:

> Good, better, best.
> Never let it rest
> Until the good is better
> And the better is the best.

When we start thinking, "Being the elders' quorum president is good, but being the bishop would be better," then it's very easy to think, "And being the stake president would be the best!" Then we start aspiring, judging, comparing ourselves to others, feeling bad about ourselves if we think they are ahead of us on some scale that we have arbitrarily chosen to honor, feeling proud if we are ahead of them on some scale. It is much better to say, "It is good to be a visiting teacher. It is good to be the bishop. It is good to be the Relief Society president." I think the only time we should use "better" is when, as President Hinckley counseled us, "We should all try to do a little better than we have." Did you notice that he included himself? And how can we tell if we *are* doing better?

Only by comparison with our past, not by comparison with anyone else's accomplishments.

Yes, some differences will make an eternal difference. Ultimately, the time will come in the history of this earth "that at the name of Jesus every knee [shall] bow . . . [and] every tongue . . . confess that Jesus Christ is Lord, to the glory of God the Father" (Philippians 2:10–11). But does that mean we should walk around with a two-by-four whacking our neighbors behind the knees to be sure that they will bow at the right time? Not at all.

When I talk about avoiding judgment and accepting differences, I am not talking about the difference between good and evil. Some things are bad all of the time or almost all of the time. Murder is always evil. Adultery is never good. If there are benefits from getting drunk, I don't know what they are. So I am not talking about the difference between good and evil behavior. All societies and all cultures have ways of controlling the powerful impulses toward violence or indiscriminate sexual expression or total self-indulgence that tear individuals, families, and societies apart. I think that there *are* lines between good and evil, and that these boundaries should be diligently observed. But when it comes to good-better-best, particularly as regards our own behavior, we should concentrate on that—not on other people's behavior. And we should never, ever try to make ourselves look good or feel good by making other people look bad or feel bad.

I believe the Savior counseled us, "Judge not, that ye be not judged" (Matthew 7:1), not just because he was passing on a piece of good advice but because in his infinite mercy he was lifting an enormous burden from our backs. Judging is so serious a task in the Church that only one person in a congregation of two or three hundred is designated a judge, by ordination and bestowal of special keys, and then he is given counselors to advise him. And even then, most bishops will tell you that they still make mistakes in judgment. It is a great blessing to be commanded not to judge!

Remember that the gospel is pointing us toward a time when we can see others—all others—truly as God sees us, as one blood, one flesh, brothers and sisters. God is literally the father of us all. In Christ the divisions and the divisiveness—between men and women, between different national groups, between different economic circumstances—are done away with, and all are alike unto him. Even those who don't know him are known and loved by him.

This acceptance must be truly universal. If the gospel gives us tools with which to take down the walls of national or cultural differences between ourselves and someone of a different nationality, let's not just build a new wall to encircle our new Mormon tribe.

And in conclusion, I ask that we may follow the admonition of Paul to the Colossians, that these blessings will also be our own:

> Put on therefore, as the elect of God, holy and beloved, . . . mercies, kindness, humbleness of mind, meekness, longsuffering;
>
> Forbearing one another, and forgiving to another . . . even as Christ forgave you. . . .
>
> And above all things put on charity, which is the bond of perfectness.
>
> And let the peace of God rule in your hearts, . . . And be ye thankful . . . (Colossians 3:12–15)

12

STONES

The scriptures are full of interesting references to stones. Jacob slept at Bethel with a stone for a pillow and had his remarkable night vision of angels ascending and descending, bearing blessings to humankind. The Book of Mormon is the keystone of our religion. David plucked five smooth stones from the stream bed as he walked out to meet his giant. Elijah's altar of undressed stones was totally consumed by lightning from heaven, together with the carcass of the bull and the barrels of water that Elijah had drenched it with. Stones are something we get to throw at someone else only if we are without sin.

I have a brooch with a lovely shimmering pattern that was a gift to me from Amelia McConkie, wife of Elder Bruce R. McConkie. We had become well acquainted with them while Ed and I were serving in Japan and Elder McConkie was assigned to supervise our mission. He was something of a rock hound and loved collecting stones and polishing them. Sister McConkie said she had only one or two left from those he had finished before he died, but she wanted me to have it. And she reminded me that on the day he died, when she was sitting with him, she asked, "Is there a message you have for me or for the family, Bruce? Is there anything left undone? Is there something we need to know?" And he answered, "Carry on."

As I pondered the scriptures that urge us to build on a sure foundation of the rock of the gospel and to base ourselves on the rock of revelation in our Church, I was intrigued by the image of Elder McConkie, whose tallness always seemed simply enormous to someone as short as me, seeing the possibility in ordinary dusty stones, and putting them in the tumbler that gently turns the rocks over and over, letting them roll and tumble and fall against each other. It is the very motion of coming into contact with each other, over and over, that gently smoothes and polishes and brings out the beauty in these stones.

You've seen polished stones in piles at souvenir shops. You can buy them by the stone or by the handful or even in some cases by the pound. Would you get yourself a little polished stone like that to remind you of some of the important principles we're going to discuss here? I want you to think about how it was polished and about the role of adversity in your own life. I'd like it to remind you that something as simple as a stone can be an effective weapon against even a terrifying giant. And I'd like you to think about Jesus Christ as the chief cornerstone of the Church and also as the chief cornerstone of your personal faith. So let's talk about faith during adversity, faith for courage to right wrongs, and faith in the Lord Jesus Christ.

Adversity

President Howard W. Hunter certainly seemed to have more than his share of adversity in mortality, but he reminded us that adversity can also be a connection to God:

> Jesus was not spared grief and pain and anguish and buffet-
> ing. No tongue can speak the unutterable burden he carried, nor
> have we the wisdom to understand the prophet Isaiah's
> description of him as "a man of sorrows" (Isa. 53:3). His ship

was tossed most of his life, and, at least to mortal eyes, it crashed fatally on the rocky coast of Calvary. We are asked not to look on life with mortal eyes; with spiritual vision we know something quite different was happening upon the cross.

Peace was on the lips and in the heart of the Savior no matter how fiercely the tempest was raging. May it so be with us—in our own hearts, in our own homes, in our nation or the world, and even in the buffetings faced from time to time by the Church. We should not expect to get through life individually or collectively without some opposition.[1]

As President Hunter tells us, we cannot anticipate a life free from adversity, confusion, discouragement or doubts. The Savior warned the people of Joseph Smith's time: "Be not deceived, but continue in steadfastness, looking forth for the heavens to be shaken, and the earth to tremble and to reel to and fro as a drunken man, and for the valleys to be exalted, and for the mountains to be made low, and for the rough places to become smooth—and all this when the angel shall sound his trumpet" (D&C 49:23). This doesn't sound like anything we'd look forward to—but if we're not willing to look steadfastly on the heavens as they shake, we may not recognize that the sound we hear in our ears is the trumpet of annunciation.

I had a powerful experience of vicarious adversity when I visited the Holocaust Memorial Museum in Washington, D.C. You may know that visitors to that museum are each given the card of an individual who died in one of the concentration camps, in keeping with their theme: "For the dead and the living we must bear witness." This was a motto that sounded very familiar to my Mormon ears. I had prisoner number #1586, a number assigned to a man named Israel Cendorf, who bore that number tattooed in blue on his inner wrist. He had been born on May 19, 1902, in Lodz, Poland. According to the information that was provided, he was born into a religious Hasidic family, who hoped he would become a rabbi. But Israel rebelled and apprenticed himself to a of the love and respect due to each human being as a child of our Heavenly Father. It was wonderful to learn this information about this beloved former Hawaiian missionary.

Can your little stone remind you that even a simple stone can be an effective weapon in the hands of a righteous person who knows the difference between right and wrong?

Faith in Jesus Christ

We've talked about how a stone can represent adversity and how a stone can represent the courage to act for the right. Now let's think of Christ as the cornerstone of our personal faith.

The greatest hunger in the world is not for food or water but for a knowledge of our beloved Savior. We long to enter into an eternal relationship with him that will remove the barriers between ourselves and our own hearts, as well as the barriers between ourselves and others. I think often of Mother Teresa, who explained how, in 1976, at the invitation of the president of Mexico, she sent sisters from her order to open a house in that country. She wrote:

> Our sisters, as is the custom in our society, walk and walk until their legs ache to see which is the worst place, where the need is greatest to begin from.
>
> In Mexico, the poverty of the people was very great. . . . To the sisters' surprise, nobody asked for clothes, for medicine, for food. Nothing except, "Teach us the word of God."
>
> It struck me so much! These people are hungry for God: "Teach us the word of God."[3]

We are among the most fortunate people who have ever lived, because we have the gospel. We know who the Savior is. We have felt his eternal and abundant love. We rejoice in the gift of the Holy Ghost. Through the shifting fogs of mortality, we have caught glimpses of the nobility of our eternal selves and the gloriousness of other human souls. Listen to these testimonies of the Savior by some prophets of this dispensation:

printer when he was sixteen. He read constantly, deepening his sympathy with the workers' struggle, and he soon began to write his own revolutionary songs. His first book of poems, *The Red Agenda*, was warmly received. Then in 1933, the year Hitler became chancellor of Germany, Israel moved to Paris. But the city was racked by unemployment, and Jewish immigrants were in constant danger of being deported. To support his family, Israel peddled wood from door to door. He continued writing. He joined the Writers' Union and wrote for the New Press.

The Nazis occupied Paris in June 1940. Israel worked for eleven months with the antifascist underground, then was arrested and deported to Pithiviers, a transit camp of 2,000 Jews. There he helped organize the underground, set up cultural evenings, and continued writing. He would go from shack to shack, reading his poems to the other prisoners. One poem, "Our Courage Is Not Broken," was sung as the camp's anthem. "Our courage is not shackled/ Life is marvelously beautiful . . . " In May 1942 he was put on a transport to Auschwitz.

That's where he died. But many prisoners from Pithiviers sang his song "Our Courage Is Not Broken" on their way to the gas chambers.

I felt honored to bear his name as I passed through the memorial museum. I felt uplifted by the courage that he expressed in that song. A great evil fell upon him and his people, but he did not give in to that evil.

Not all adversity is evil. Not all of it is purposeful malice directed at us as individuals. Some of it is just the normal accidents, the ill health, the bad luck that accompanies being alive. But adversity always hurts. And it always requires strength to deal with it. So seek in yourself for that rocklike strength to endure adversity.

Courage

The second quality of a rock that I want you to remember is symbolized by the five smooth stones that David chose from the stream he crossed on the way to reach Goliath. There are many giants who seek to harm us, giants who damage our society. We need more Davids who are willing to go forth with their smooth stones to defeat these evils.

I am reminded of a good friend of mine, Grant Burns, who has been willing to make such a difference. Grant had learned lessons in tolerance and accepting diversity as a Mormon missionary in Hawaii, and he provided crucial leadership in modeling that respect for others. When Ed and I could not buy a home in Salt Lake City because restrictive housing covenants and so-called gentlemen's agreements excluded Japanese people in those years after World War II, Grant and his wife, Marion, sold us the lot on which they had planned to build their dream home. He accepted the challenge to behave in a Christian way regardless of ethnic diversity. He made a moral choice. And as a result, he made a very positive and welcome change in our lives. We hold his name in honorable remembrance and always will.

Just recently he wrote me a letter telling me some incidents that he had never before shared with us. I learned that he had befriended Ed and me not because we were special, or because he had a soft place in his heart for Japanese people, but because he was truly filled with the love of Christ and was not willing to see wrong done to any child of our Heavenly Father. He wrote:

> I was Assistant Planning Director of Salt Lake City from 1951 to October 1959. In this position, I was able to help alleviate some problems related to race prejudice, particularly towards the blacks. One day, Rev. Harry W. Williams, a black pastor of the AME Methodist church came to see me with a request for help in getting permission for black children to swim in municipal swimming pools. This was out of my jurisdiction; but I was so appalled, I went to work on it. I discussed the matter with Mayor Earl J. Glade. He, too, was disturbed by this problem and had the city attorney research city ordinances and regulations. There were no regulations prohibiting persons of any race to

> participate in swimming or in any other city activity, so Mayor Glade took the matter before the City Commission, who issued a directive to the Department of Recreation to change their policies. This changed nothing.
>
> When Rev. Williams reported this fact to me, I wrote an ordinance establishing nondiscrimination as the rule of the City and penalties for discrimination in city-owned facilities. Mayor Glade and the City Commission adopted it. I thought this would solve the problem; but again, black children were denied. I then took several black children to the Liberty Park pool. I was armed with a copy of the ordinance, a pad of writing paper, and a pen. Again the children were refused entrance. I asked the names of all city employees involved and started writing them down as I produced the ordinance. I warned them that I would take this act of insubordination directly to the City Commission and advised them to look for new employment. Their attitude changed. The children were admitted, then and thereafter.
>
> Another act of discrimination I assisted in solving involved the principal of the old South High School and a very nice black girl—a straight-A student, age seventeen, who had been elected senior class president by her peers. The principal, however, denied her the right to be so recognized. I went to the principal who explained that he had received a number of calls of prote from parents and school board members and he considered action the wisest thing to do. I asked him which he would fer—favorable recognition from those few or recognitio bigot from the public at large. I told him of the ordinance discrimination adopted by the city and, while it might r him directly, I knew a number of news reporters w probably write some interesting, if not flattering, n about the principal of Salt Lake City's largest high sc discrimination against one deserving black girl. H that this was not his intent, he had made a mista rectify it immediately. He did, and that was the

Grant Burns is an ordinary man with an

Lorenzo Snow testified: "The spirit of God descended upon me, completely enveloping my whole person . . . dispelling forever, so long as reason and memory last, all possibility of doubt or fear in relation to the fact handed down to us historically that the 'babe of Bethlehem' is truly the Son of God."

President George Albert Smith witnessed: "I have been buoyed up and, as it were, lifted out of myself and given power not my own to teach the glorious truths proclaimed by the Redeemer of the world. I have not seen Him face to face but have . . . felt His presence in a way not to be mistaken. I know that my Redeemer lives."

President Spencer W. Kimball testified, "In quiet, restrained, divine dignity he stood when they cast their spittle in his face. He remained composed. They pushed him around. Not an angry word escaped his lips. They slapped his face and beat his body. Yet he stood resolute, unintimidated. . . . He had said, 'Love your enemies.' Now he showed how much one can love his enemies. He was dying on the cross for those who had nailed him there."[4]

The prophets have testified of Jesus, but their testimonies are no more eloquent, no surer, and no more devoted than the testimonies of many brothers and sisters in the Church. I know Latter-day Saints all over the world. I know their faith. I know their love. I have seen the works that they have built upon the cornerstone of faith in our Lord and Savior. I add my testimony to theirs. I know he loves us. I know he hears our prayers. I know he reaches out to us.

In conclusion, I want to share one more stone with you. It is the tower or altar of stones erected by Esau and Jacob after they were reconciled as brothers and made this small monument to commemorate their pledges of love and support for each other. They called it Mizpah, which means *watchtower* in Hebrew. It signifies, "The Lord watch between me and thee, when we are absent one from another" (Genesis 31:49).

May the Lord watch between us, may he bless you, and may you continue to bless others, reaching beyond adversity, striving with courage, and building upon the cornerstone of Jesus Christ.

BEHOLD THY HANDMAIDEN: THE ANSWER OF FAITH

The phrase "Behold thy handmaiden" is taken from the story of the annunciation to Mary, the mother of Jesus, and it is the second recorded speech in the New Testament from her. The first is her question to Gabriel: "How shall this be, seeing I know not a man?" He gives her a simple, factual answer: "The Holy Ghost shall come upon thee, and the power of the Highest shall overshadow thee: therefore also that holy thing which shall be born of thee shall be called the Son of God" (Luke 1:34–35).

Even though he has answered her question, he is explaining something to her that has never happened before to anyone in the whole history of the world. This particular set of facts, even if she accepts them, might not necessarily be meaningful to her. So he draws on something that is at the same time broader and deeper, something less specific than the technique of how a child may be conceived without a mortal father, but more specific because it is something Mary has experience with—her faith in God. The angel continues: "And, behold, thy cousin Elisabeth, she hath also conceived a son in her old age: and this is the sixth month with her, who was called barren. For with God nothing shall be impossible" (Luke 1:36–37).

Mary responds to this statement because it is an appeal to her faith. She knows that it is impossible for a woman as old as Elisabeth, who has been barren for her entire life, to conceive a child, so she has faith that one miracle has already occurred. She, like the angel and like Elisabeth, believes that "with God nothing shall be impossible," and out of that faith, she answers the angel, "Behold the handmaid of the Lord; be it unto me according to thy word" (Luke 1:38).

Mary's example teaches us much about giving the answer of faith when things happen that we don't understand, about trusting in the Lord when things happen that try us and challenge our faith, about having confidence in his goodness at seasons of loss and sorrow.

We are so used to thinking of the annunciation as the beginning of the joyous celebration of Christmas that we focus on Mary's joy, which I'm sure she felt, and on the great gladness of the Savior's birth. We are not used to thinking of this season as a time of loss for Mary. But it was a loss. She was a righteous young woman, but she was bound to lose her reputation among her family and friends and those who knew her in Nazareth. What else could they think, when they saw her pregnant, but that she had been unchaste? The last line in the annunciation is, "And the angel departed from her" (v. 38). In other words, the angel didn't take the rabbi aside for a quiet chat about this very special young woman he had in town. He didn't whisper to the chief merchants that Mary was going to be remembered till the end of time, while their names would barely survive their own generation. The angel was not there at the well when Mary went for water, after she came back from visiting Elisabeth, her body already rounded with a sixth-month pregnancy. He didn't explain to the other women, shocked and scandalized and whispering to each other behind their hands, that Mary was the chosen vessel of the Lord. Nobody explained to the girls younger than Mary that she was the living embodiment of faith.

Furthermore, *Mary* didn't explain it either. She obviously didn't explain it even to Joseph, because Joseph was the one person to whom the angel did come, to tell him that his faith in Mary was not misplaced. So, yes, I think we have to admit that despite the joy this was also a season of loss and mourning.

Life usually hands us mixtures of good and evil, of joy and sorrow. Think of the sorrow of Mary again as she stood at the cross, watching the slow, tortured dying of the beloved body to which she had given birth. That sorrow was as much a part of the experience as the joy of the resurrection.

Let me share with you something about my own season of sorrow. On the second Saturday in March 1992, just after the Relief Society sesquicentennial broadcast, my beloved husband, Ed, was stricken down with a massive cardiac arrest from which he never regained consciousness. He died a few days later, just shortly before Easter. So that season of the year is always bittersweet for me. I love the coming of spring with its visible reawakening from winter sleep. I love the promise of the resurrection, which we celebrate each year. And the sweetness of that promise is intensified by the bitter loss and deep sorrow.

In December, just a few days before Christmas, I sat in a chapel in Newport Beach, California, with my son Bob and his wife, Chris, watching my six-year-old grandson and his cousin sing in a Primary chorus at a funeral. The woman in the casket was Matthew's other grandmother, Gayle Wynn, the mother of my daughter-in-law. Her son, her bishop, and three friends—all people who knew her well—paid her wonderful, personal tributes, celebrating her life and mourning her death of cancer. The Primary chorus was a reminder of how much she loved children, and how willingly she had given her time to the youth of the ward and stake.

The song that Matthew was singing was a lovely two-part

Primary song written and composed by Janice Kapp Perry, "A Child's Prayer." Let me share the words with you:

> Heavenly Father, are you really there?
> And do you hear and answer ev'ry child's prayer?
> Some say that heaven is far away,
> But I feel it close around me as I pray.
> Heavenly Father, I remember now
> Something that Jesus told disciples long ago:
> "Suffer the children to come to me."
> Father, in prayer I'm coming now to thee.

And then the reassuring answer:

> Pray, he is there; Speak, he is list'ning.
> You are his child; His love now surrounds you.
> He hears your prayer; He loves the children.
> Of such is the kingdom, the kingdom of heav'n.[1]

As I went through the hours surrounding the funeral with my son and daughter-in-law, I felt surrounded and comforted by that love. I knew that our prayers were being heard. But I didn't know about Bob and Chris. Their sorrow may have been too fresh, too keen, for the quieter answers of faith to be heard. The day of the funeral was a dark and cloudy one. As we gathered around the grave, a wind began to blow, and the rain began just as we finished. It was drumming on our cars as we drove away.

Christmas was coming: the first Christmas without their mother for Chris and her two brothers and two sisters, the first Christmas without his Gayle for Bob Wynn. There was great strength in that family, and deep expressions of love, but there were also many tears shed.

This is the third death in their family that six-year-old Matthew and three-year-old Andrew had experienced. First was the death of their beloved Bapa, Grandpa Ed, in March of 1992.

Chris had not been able to attend Ed's funeral because she was only a few days away from giving birth to their third son. It was a terrible blow when that baby died just two days before birth. And now Nana Gayle had died.

In his lovely, concerned way, little Matthew, struggling to bring order to his world, slipped his hand into mine as we sat together having a quiet moment in the Wynn home before the funeral. "Bapa Ed is dead," he began.

"Yes," I said.

"And now Nana Gayle is dead," he continued.

"Yes."

"And they are together? Bapa Ed is taking care of Nana Gayle?" he asked, looking at me anxiously.

"I don't know if she needs to be taken care of," I answered, trying to speak in his own terms but to be as clear as I could. "But we know that when people die, people who love them meet them. It was a happy reunion between them, because you know how much they liked each other. And you know that Bapa Ed will do everything he can for Nana Gayle if she needs anything."

He brightened up. "Well, then," he said in a practical way, "maybe you can marry Bapa Bob and take care of each other."

We can laugh lovingly at a little boy's limited understanding, but I think we also laugh because we recognize in us the same hunger that he had—to understand, to have things make sense and be orderly, to sense that things are progressing according to a plan. Mortality is often so jagged, interrupted, and disrupted. And often, just as Matthew could not see a larger pattern, we struggle to find meaning and assurance in our lives.

Like Mary, we sometimes ask a technical question—something on the order of this: "I love my husband. My greatest joy has always been to be with him. Now he is gone. How will I ever feel peaceful and happy again?" There are technical answers: "Time will ease the pain. The jagged edges of memory that hurt every time you do something alone that the two of you used to do together will soften. You will find strength to carry on." These answers have never been particularly comforting because, like Mary receiving her technical answer of how her baby would be conceived, we don't understand how it is possible. At times like this, we need the answer of faith. We need to remember from a broader, deeper context that God is a God of miracles, that with him nothing is impossible.

People close to our family, who know of the multiple sorrows that have come repeatedly to us, have expressed concern about me. "This has to be hard, Chieko," they say. "Are you all right? Are you getting close to the limit of what you can take?"

It was a question that I had not asked myself, but when I did, I knew the answer. The death of a loved one is never easy, but the great principle even here is at work. I have great trust in the Lord—great trust in his hands of love and mercy holding me up. I seek his consolation quickly, and it is always there.

When I lost Ed, a great source of strength was the knowledge that kept ringing in my heart, "I don't have to do this by myself." You don't have to do it by yourself either—neither death nor illness nor any of the trials that face you. "When ye shall search for me with all your heart," the Lord told Jeremiah, "ye shall . . . find me" (Jeremiah 29:13). "Trust in me," says the Savior. "A hair of [your] head shall not fall to the ground unnoticed" (D&C 84:116). "The very hairs of your head are all numbered. Fear not therefore: ye are of more value than many sparrows" (Luke 12:7).

Losing Ed was the hardest thing in my life. I accepted Ed's death, my faith was strong, and I had the love and support of my sons and many, many friends; but I was bewildered and disoriented by grief. I groped for the hand of the Savior. I went back again and again in prayer, asking for strength for each new day, asking for comfort, asking for patience, asking for the ability to serve others rather than be absorbed by my own sorrow. Each of those prayers was answered in the measure I needed. I could feel myself becoming stronger every day. I could feel my ability to endure in patience growing. When my moments of sorrow and loneliness and weeping came, I could accept them. I took great comfort from the promise, "This too shall pass."

I still grieve, but my grief is not compounded by a lack of knowledge of God's plan or by my inability to cope with it. My sons have been concerned and close. We have the best neighbors in the world. No one could be more loving and helpful than our bishop. My sisters in the gospel have been a never-failing source of strength and support.

But I missed Ed in such little ways. It really wasn't much of a burden to pick up the clothes at the dry-cleaner's, but it seemed a heavy, heavy burden, because Ed had always done it before; now it was a reminder that we were no longer a team. When our water softener developed a malfunction just a few weeks after his death, it was not hard to pick up the phone and call the repair service, but it seemed like a monumental task because Ed wasn't there to talk it over with. I didn't know anything about water softeners—and I don't actually know if Ed did either, but I kept thinking, "It would be so much easier if he were here. He would know whether it needed to be replaced or whether it's something that can be easily fixed." When I realized that I honestly didn't know whether Ed really *did* know anything about water heaters, it helped me keep things in perspective.

My trust in the Lord has grown immensely. I kept thinking of that question about whether I was close to my limit, and I realized that, despite my moments of sorrow, I felt strong. I tried to think of a comparison. In some ways, it's like a balloon with a capacity that simply keeps expanding. The mouth of the balloon is always the same size, meaning that we're still mortal persons with real limitations, but our souls are stretched by the experiences of mortality. That's not a perfect example, of course, because balloons can't keep on stretching forever. They pop! And I don't think many of us really know the infinite capacity of our souls.

Perhaps a better example is learning how to use my computer. The first time I tried to save a document, I had to have my manual right there. I turned to the right page. I read all the instructions. I went through the steps very slowly, reading each one as I went. I read each instruction line and thought about what it meant and thought about what I wanted to happen. It probably took me five minutes just to save one document! Now I hit the keys quickly, without even looking at them, without even thinking about them. I can think what I want to have happen, and my hands perform the functions automatically. That's not a good example, either, in some ways, because dealing with grief is never thoughtless or automatic. But I can feel now that it is familiar. I know what I am supposed to do.

As I listened to Chris, my daughter-in-law, weep for her mother and pour out her feelings of loss, I knew there was nothing I or anyone else could say that would magically make everything all right. Grieving is a process. It's okay to experience that process. To deny the bitterness of the sorrow is to deny some of the sweetness of the comfort when it comes.

I hope you will forgive me if what I've shared in these pages has seemed too personal or if the burden you are struggling with is so heavy that my expression of sorrow has intensified your own. I am temporarily separated from my companion, but he was a good and loving man who tried in every waking moment of every day to live a Christlike life. I have not "lost" Ed. I know exactly where he is.

Yes, there is sorrow, but my sorrow is sweet compared to the grief of women I talk with every day who have truly lost their companions. There are husbands who have betrayed marriage vows, who have betrayed their responsibilities of fatherhood, who have abused and neglected and injured their children. There are husbands who have broken temple covenants, who have turned out to be dishonest. In such cases, a woman grieves not only for the loss of her husband but also for the loss of her marriage.

Children who have rejected parental values and turned to unrighteous ways cause a special kind of pain and grieving. Life is full of losses. Women grieve for the loss of their health, for the loss of financial security, for the loss of dreams of marriage as years pass without bringing a companion into their lives, for the loss of the dream of children as years of infertility accumulate.

How can we give the answer of faith when adversity seems likely to overwhelm us? Let me share five ways that have helped me.

First, as I've already said, we need to acknowledge the emotional reality of what is happening to us. It's all right to grieve. It's all right to experience suffering.

But, second, we also need to use our minds. Even if we don't believe it, we need to tell ourselves: "I don't know how it will happen, but I know that time will help me deal with this." We need to set limits and goals for ourselves. I read in a magazine article that one woman, experiencing a shattering divorce, would allow herself to cry when she needed to, but she'd set the timer for ten minutes because she needed to feel that she was stronger than her grief. For her, that was a way of saying that she had a right to grieve but also that she was strong enough to make decisions, not just let the suffering she was undergoing make all decisions for her.

Third, we need to understand the plan of salvation. It may not seem very comforting at times of pain and loss to think about the plan of salvation. It may seem too intellectual, too remote, and too theoretical to be very comforting. But each of us makes sense of our experience in a context. It is wise and truly comforting to see that context as a purposeful and loving plan—and especially as something that we chose.

Francine Bennion, a wise student of the scriptures and of life, explained her perspective in a BYU/Relief Society women's conference. She said:

> We don't know if there were several possibilities of which we have no record, but I doubt there was a never-never land where we could have been happy children without responsibility forever. Apparently there was a point at which we had to grow up or choose not to. Our scriptures suggest that there were

unavoidable decisions to be made consciously and responsibly by all inhabitants in the premortal council, as in Eden. We could not be mere observers, only thinking about the decision, only imagining what might happen if we made it, only talking about the meaning of it all. . . .

. . . We wanted life, however high the cost. We suffer because we were willing to pay the cost of *being* and of being here with others in their ignorance and inexperience as well as our own. We suffer because we are willing to pay the costs of living with laws of nature, which operate quite consistently whether or not we understand them or can manage them. We suffer because, like Christ in the desert, we apparently did not say we would come only if God would change our stones to bread in time of hunger. We were willing to *know* hunger. Like Christ in the desert, we did not ask God to let us try falling or being bruised only on condition that He catch us before we touch ground to save us from real hurt. We were willing to *know* hurt. Like Christ, we did not agree to come only if God would make everyone bow to us and respect us, or admire us and understand us. Like Christ, we came to be ourselves, addressing and creating reality. We are finding out who we are and who we can become regardless of the environment or circumstances . . .

Then Francine tells this illuminating experience of watching a little boy in sacrament meeting one day.

He had a quiet book open to a page with colored shapes—a purple square, an orange circle, red rectangle, green triangle, and on top of these, attached with Velcro, matching shapes and colors. The boy was clearly inexperienced. He pulled off all the shapes, then stuck a purple square on a green triangle, pulled his father's knee, and beamed up at him in utter delight because he had put a purple square on a green triangle, and it stayed there. The father looked down, saw the mistake, shook his head, and turned back to the speaker. The boy pulled the purple square off the green triangle, stuck it on an orange circle, pulled his father's knee, and beamed up at him in utter joy and delight. The father looked down, saw the mistake, shook his head, and turned back to the speaker. The boy pulled off the purple square and put it on a purple square, *discovered* the match, pulled his father's knee and beamed up at him in utter delight. The father nodded and turned back to the speaker, and the boy began to experiment with the removable green triangle.

Of course, this is not a perfect metaphor for our suffering . . . but it suggests much to me. . . . The boy was learning about shapes and colors, not just about being a good boy and pleasing his father by matching the right shapes and colors. Shapes and colors, useful though they be, were part of more comprehensive matters he was learning: he *can* learn, ignorance or mistakes need not be indelible, he is becoming himself, he is not the circumference of everyone else's universe, there is delight in discovery and invention, some "utter" joys are better than others, and so forth. The learning was his own, and he was taking part in creating as well as discovering that which he learned.[2]

I've quoted this very long statement because it explains so well that suffering is part of the plan. We chose it. We wanted to know it. We understood, in the premortal world, a lesson so powerful that Eve could remember and articulate it even in the moment of terror and shame and uncertainty after she and Adam had partaken of the forbidden fruit. She knew that it was better to pass through sorrow than to remain ignorant of either joy *or* sorrow.

Fourth, we can work toward acceptance. I do think we should struggle for understanding just as hard as we can. It's not showing a lack of faith to say, "I don't understand this. Tell me how. Explain why." But at the same time, we also need to remind ourselves—sometimes right out loud—that, as the Lord explained to Isaiah: "My thoughts are not your thoughts, neither are your ways my ways. . . . For as the heavens are higher than the earth, so are my ways higher than your ways, and my thoughts than your thoughts" (Isaiah 55:8–9).

We need to accept and be patient with our lack of understanding. It's a superb and glowing faith to say, "I don't understand this and I don't like it very much, but I accept it. Show me how to live with it, how to deal with it." The limitations of mortality are so real and so personal that I'm sure one of the things we're going to do in the next life is laugh and laugh.

You've undoubtedly heard the saying, "Let go—and let God." To me it means, "Let go of your way of seeing things. Let go of your way of fixing things. Trust me. Let me do more than fix it. Let me make it wonderful and new for you."

Fifth, we need to actively seek the presence of the Holy Ghost and the spirit of Jesus Christ. We are promised this blessing in each sacrament prayer every Sabbath day. This spirit is a promised presence in our lives, not a rare and exotic visitor. It is a comfortable, reassuring companion, not a confusing and upsetting party-crasher. I know that you know the ways in which we can be worthy of this spirit, and the ways in which we can prepare ourselves to receive it, but I want to urge you to concentrate also on welcoming it. Sometimes we're so busy serving, going to the temple, reading the scriptures, and preparing, preparing, preparing, that we forget to welcome the guest. I'm talking about simply being aware that the Spirit is with us, interacting with that Spirit so that prayers become almost conversations, and recognizing the feelings of that presence.

I testify to you that the answer of faith is a viable one, even in the most difficult of circumstances, because it does not depend on us—on our strength to endure or on our willpower or on the depth of our intellectual understanding or on the wealth of resources we can accumulate. No, it depends on God, whose strength is omnipotence and who has the will to walk beside us in love, sharing our burden, and whose understanding is that of eternity. Many waters cannot quench his love.

He could part the Red Sea before us or calm the angry storm

that besets us, but these would be small miracles for the God of nature. Instead, he chooses to do something harder. He wants to transform human nature into divine nature. And thus, when our Red Sea blocks our way and when the stormy sea threatens to overwhelm us, he enters the water with us, holding us in the hands of love, supporting us with arms of mercy.

If I could call Ed back, I would. And it would be wrong. If we could all eliminate our problems, we would. And it would be wrong. But we need to learn to do something better and, therefore, harder. The Apostle Paul explains it this way: "And be not conformed to this world: but be ye transformed by the renewing of your mind, that ye may prove what is that good, and acceptable, and perfect, will of God" (Romans 12:2).

May our faith also be renewed and transformed—not just that we will see again those we love, but that we will, in this life, be transformed day by day, that our faith will increase, that we will understand the means by which miracles happen, and that our faith in the Lord of miracles, who is our Savior, will increase until it is strong enough to burst the bands of spiritual death and bring us again into his presence, even now, even in this life.

CHANGE, CHOICE, CHALLENGE, AND THE COCKROACH

My experience with cockroaches goes back to childhood. In Hawaii, on the big island where I grew up, ours were shiny black and small, about as long as a fingernail. Another species we found in the house was a tiny, tiny variety, about the size of a housefly. They inhabited the kitchen, and sometimes we found them in the bedrooms. My mother had no tolerance at all for cockroaches. She was constantly cleaning and scrubbing. She was the fastest woman in the world with a flyswatter when she saw a cockroach. She would smack them into kingdom come, pick up their little corpses by the antennae, drop them in the garbage, and then run and wash her hands. I didn't care too much for cockroaches myself.

Then in Japan where my husband and I lived for three years, the cockroaches were brown and huge—sometimes as big as my thumb—and they would either jump or fly, I wasn't sure which, with their wings vibrating against the chitin of their shells with a rattling sound. When I'd go down to the kitchen, I would reach around the corner, turn on the light, and wait a second while they sprang away from it. They were not just on the floor but on the walls and the ceilings, even in the cupboards. I developed an obsession about cleaning that made my mother look sloppy. We fumigated every few months and sprayed everything in sight every day. Leaving food out on the counter was a major sin. And because I wouldn't take a chance that a cockroach might have walked across a plate, I washed everything I used for cooking and serving food, every time I used it.

Why talk about cockroaches, of all things, in association with change, choice, and challenge? Because there are three facts about cockroaches that make them the mascot of the other three C's. First, cockroaches know a lot about change. There are more than two thousand species in the world today. Second, cockroaches are very successful in meeting challenges. They have survived basically unchanged for three hundred million years and are among the oldest insect groups in the world. And third, they have perfected the art of making great choices as a species: they strike the perfect balance between being adaptable enough to survive—even thrive—and retaining what it is that makes them cockroaches and not something else. So let's talk about these three principles: change, choice, and challenge.

Change

First, cockroaches know a lot about change. It's interesting to me that the most common of the pest varieties are known by national names. We have the American cockroach, the Oriental cockroach, the Asian cockroach (yes, these are actually two different varieties), the Australian cockroach, the German cockroach, and the brown-banded cockroach.

The female Oriental cockroach is wingless as an adult, while the American cockroach has well-developed wings. The Asian cockroach has shown a great adaptability by developing an *attraction* to artificial light. In human terms, this would be something like the president of IBM developing an expertise in a very trendy phenomenon like roller blading or snow surfing. But the point I want to make is that the ability to change is one of the reasons for the success of cockroaches.

I think any successful leader must ask himself or herself: How do I *really* feel about people who are different from me? How do I *really* feel about ideas that are different from mine? How do I feel about leadership styles that vary *greatly* from my own? How do I feel about personal values that even *contradict* my own?

You'll notice that I've used the same verb in each sentence: *Feel.* I haven't asked what you *do* about these differences, how you negotiate or compromise, how you communicate about them, or how you work them out. I'm asking about feelings, because sooner or later life will hand you the opportunity to show in your behavior how you feel in your heart.

For example, suppose you are a Caucasian male. You have been carefully trained not to make sexist or racist remarks about women and minority ethnic groups. This is good. This is wonderful. But if you still believe, even in a tiny corner of your heart, that women are basically irrational or that Hispanics are basically lazy or that African Americans are basically irresponsible—or whatever other stereotype you may harbor—then sooner or later you will act on that belief. So I'm asking you to examine your heart.

I want to tell you that we cannot change and we cannot learn from change unless we value it. Thomas R. Dewar said, "Minds are like parachutes: they only function when open."[1] But how do we keep an open mind? When we see a difference, it's almost automatic to place a label on it or to judge it. Let's take an easy example. Suppose you're working with a colleague whose idea of a great weekend is to start partying Friday night after work and keep it up all weekend. It might be easy to say: "That's a dysfunctional lifestyle, and this person is really stupid to find pleasure in an activity that's so addictive, so dangerous to himself and others, and so expensive." Think how many judgments there are in that sentence! Such judgments have one advantage. They set a clear boundary for you about what you consider to be acceptable and healthy as a lifestyle. That boundary may be important for governing your own behavior.

But suppose your goal is to help your colleague change, because you're genuinely concerned about his health, his family life, and his finances. The boundary can become a barrier over which it's very difficult for you to reach. My experience as a teacher and a principal is that people change best in an atmosphere of high expectations and very high support. Think about both parts. The high expectations are easy to communicate. You've done it through the labeling and the judging and the boundary setting. But how do you communicate high support?

I'd suggest that you do it through honestly acknowledging your colleague's drinking, saying how you feel about it, expressing your faith in his ability to change, and expressing your willingness to help. Notice that I said "acknowledge." That's different from those other two "A" words: *accepting* his drinking as a good thing or *adopting* that lifestyle as your own. If he invites you to come take a drink, say honestly, "You know, I don't drink. I never have, and I hope I never will. I really wish you didn't either. I like working with you, and I worry about you bingeing every weekend." There are a couple of other things you can say, too. You can say, "I don't understand very well what goes on when you drink. Would you like to tell me about it sometime?" Or you can invite, "If you'd ever like to talk about it, I'd really be glad to listen."

Now, I said that was an easy example. It is. Weekend bingeing is, I suppose, a form of diversity, but it's obviously not a very desirable one. It's hard to think of it as setting up a values conflict for you or learning something that might change your own lifestyle. I hope that you also see how learning from a binge drinker will enrich and deepen your human understanding.

But what do you do when your new supervisor is a woman? Or when the trainee whose progress you've been monitoring with a great deal of pride and interest comes out to you about his gayness? Or when one of the people in your carpool must use a wheelchair for mobility and has to carry oxygen? I suggest that you can do the same thing. You can acknowledge that difference and acknowledge where your own boundary is, if it involves a value for you. You can maintain a distinction between acknowledging the difference and putting a label or a judgment on it. You can ask for that person's help in understanding his or her situation. You can avoid making judgments.

When it comes to ideas, I've always enjoyed Wilson Mizner's credo. He said, "I respect faith, but doubt is what gets you an education."[2] It's crucially important to be able to turn a different idea around, examining it three-dimensionally in the context of your own intellectual field and values system, cataloging the differences and noting the points of contrast, but not bringing them into conflict until the process is complete. Reasonable, healthy, needed change cannot occur if we aren't willing to go through this process. If we hurry through the process, we may end up junking a very valuable idea without seeing its value; or we may prematurely decide our own system is flawed and throw out parts of it that we will later discover were not only bathwater but the baby as well.

I'd like to tell you a story about a real character in the field of jurisprudence. Some of you may be acquainted with him: Monroe McKay. Monroe McKay is the only BYU graduate to hold both the position of appellate judge and also the position of chief judge in a federal court. (He was appointed the chief judge of the U.S. Court of Appeals for the 10th Circuit.) He grew up in Huntsville, Utah, next to his cousins, the David McKay family. Judge McKay was thirteen when his father, James Gunn McKay, died of cancer, leaving his mother, Elizabeth Peterson McKay, with eight children, ranging in age from under one to fifteen. The day James died, his wife burst into tears in her father's arms, then screamed, "'What am I going to do?' Finally, he replied, 'You'll do what you have always done, you will do what you have to do,' and that's exactly what she did."

The family lived in such poverty that when the children

heard that the "only man in Huntsville who had any money" had a fancy for their mother, the children immediately began dreaming of what life would soon be like for them.

. . . She finally sat [the children] down and with a certain sense of finality, explained, "I am not going to marry Mr. So-and-so. He is a good man, but he has his way of doing things, and we have ours. And if I were to marry him, we would have to change our ways, and that will not be." She never told us this man's ways were wrong or that ours were right, only that they were different from each other.

Judge McKay commented, "I think it was from Mother that I learned to respect others' ways of living. . . . I tell people that she was not perfect; she simply did the best she could in that day. She didn't do the best that *you* wanted her to do or that she wanted to do, but she did the best *she* could and that was good enough." This woman, incidentally, was named Utah Mother of the Year in 1969.

He struggled to get an education, and probably he got lots of cockroach messages about how it would be a fine thing if he just stayed in Huntsville and worked as a hired hand on one of the farms there. But he had higher aspirations for himself. Because he needed to be so strong, he's been something of a maverick all of his life on the bench. He's a man of very strong views and admits that some people see him as "inflexible." He explains:

I know that I am personally accountable for both my views and my behavior, and it doesn't worry me that I have to answer for them. Now, if you ask, "Are you comfortable that these views are absolutely correct?" the answer is no. I'm not comfortable that in the end my judgment will be judged acceptable, but I'm comfortable to be struggling with that. I am also comfortable with experimenting with ideas and then revising them. Because I assert things so strongly, people view me as sometimes inflexible; but my life has been a series of revisions in the way I think about these things.

One of those strong opinions is about changing our minds and respecting the process of change. He believes that one of the most important aspects of that change is that we need people who think differently from us. It's not just that it's nice to tolerate them or even that it's our responsibility to tolerate them. We *need* them. He said, "The Bill of Rights was never written for the majority—it was written for the 'obnoxious,' the minority." He's a Mormon, and I was fascinated to read his views about Mormon history and about the trouble some Mormons have with respecting diversity. He said:

> There were three kinds of sermons when I was a kid: "Live the Word of Wisdom," "Pay your tithing," and "They're coming to get us." But what have we learned from that [persistent persecution complex]? . . . Remember that [Mormons to their neighbors in Illinois and Missouri and to the nation at large during the Utah period] were adulterers. We were blasphemers, we were dangerous communalists. I used to think the Missourians had horns. But now I see that they were people just like those who live here . . . who react exactly like the Missourians did when someone who is gay or is a Hare Krishna moves in.

The problem, he says, is that Latter-day Saints have forgotten that they too were once a "tiny, obnoxious, little group"—who should have been protected by the Bill of Rights.

"You don't need [the Bill of Rights] for the majority," Judge McKay comments.

> They get the legislation they need and want. Cops don't come in and kick in doors [in rich, white neighborhoods—he actually said Edgemont, and some of you BYU graduates may know where that is] but they may in southwest Provo. They do in black neighborhoods. So, the Bill of Rights was written only for the minorities and the obnoxious.

And . . . what we sometimes forget is that the obnoxious may be right.[3]

When you are tempted to discard someone's opinion or lifestyle or contribution, or to reject the possibility of needed change—in short, when you act like my mother with the fly-swatter when she saw a cockroach—I'm asking you to remember Judge McKay. The obnoxious may be right. We need to hear before we can evaluate. We need to acknowledge before we can respect. And we need to value before we can learn.

Challenges

The second point I want to make is that cockroaches are very successful when it comes to meeting challenges. They have survived for three hundred million years and are among the oldest insect groups in the world.

Cockroaches don't run very many opinion polls. It doesn't bother them very much that people don't like them, even though they do have something of a bad press. I was surprised to learn that most cockroaches are outdoor insects, living under logs, stones, bark, and in palm fronds, or as tenants in ant and termite nests. In fact, fewer than 1 percent of cockroach species are considered pests.

It's nice to be liked. It's nice to be appreciated. It's nice to be valued. In the discussion of change, I concentrated on some of the situations in which you have the choice of liking, appreciating, or valuing. Now, let's look at the other perspective. What do you do when people don't like you, don't value you, and definitely don't appreciate you?

I think we should listen carefully to their message. It's always a challenge to listen to a message that's hard to hear, but they may be telling us something we need to hear. Maybe you *aren't* a good listener. Maybe you *are* bossy.

And maybe you're not. But until you listen to the message,

you won't know whether it's directed at you personally or whether it's a stereotype that's being applied to you unfairly because you're a member of a group somebody doesn't like, such as a lawyer, an environmentalist, a woman, or a Mormon.

Try to separate messages about you as an individual from those directed toward you as a representative of a group. Do your best. Work hard and work well. I stress this because if you're not pulling your own weight on a team, nothing else matters very much. Not all jobs are fun and challenging. Not all parts of a job are enjoyable. Have the discipline to stick with it. George Macdonald, a Scots minister, once commented, "When a man's duty looks like an enemy, dragging him into dark mountains, he has no less to go with it than when, like a friend with loving face, it offers to lead him along green pastures by the river side."[4] Be a responsible worker. That's not a glamorous challenge, but it's perhaps the most important one.

But there will still be times when you will *not* change someone's mind. What then? Let your clean conscience deflect many blows that fall on you. Edward H. Chapin said: "Never does the human soul appear so strong and noble as when it forgoes revenge and dares to forgive an injury."[5] Even more important, when we can forgive others, it means that we can go forward into our futures unencumbered by a lot of emotional baggage.

So the second lesson of the cockroach is to deal with challenges creatively—not to give up when we find ourselves an unpopular minority, but to listen to the messages, change when it's appropriate, have nothing to reproach ourselves for when it's not, work hard, do our best, and forgive those who misunderstand and misjudge us.

Choices

The third lesson of the cockroach is this: cockroaches as a species have perfected the art of making great choices: they are adaptable enough to survive—and even thrive—and yet they retain whatever it is that makes them cockroaches and not trilobites or spiders. Cockroaches are three hundred million years old. If we're going by exalted genealogy, all of us would have to bow to the cockroach. But cockroaches don't spend any time reciting their ancestry or claiming special privileges on the basis of past achievements. Each cockroach fully expects to get out and hustle its own living. Furthermore, cockroaches are among the fastest running insects. They don't sit around waiting for their dinners to walk up to them on silver platters. Cockroaches are humble.

So let's talk about the choice of humility that leaders need to make. I once saw a little poster that might be relevant. It reads:

There are two things I know for sure:
1. There is a God.
2. You're not him.

Now, some people think that not all leaders have assimilated that message. Let me illustrate what the conscious choice of humility can do in terms of leadership, drawn from the experience of writer Robert Fulghum. He says that whenever anyone ends a lecture or a long meeting with the invitation, "Are there any questions?" he thinks that most people have one of two questions: "Can we leave now?" and "What was this meeting for?" But his impulse is always to ask, "What is the meaning of life?" Sometimes he *does* ask that question. But only once, he said, did he get a real answer. And it's an answer that applies to everything we've talked about—to a willingness to listen and learn, to forgiveness, to persistence even in holding an unpopular position, and to knowing who you are and what you are about so that you stick with your principles even while you adapt to circumstances.

Robert Fulghum was attending a conference in the village of Gonia on the island of Crete. On a rocky bay stood an institute dedicated to peace, especially to better relations between Germans and Cretans. Significantly, the site overlooks a small airstrip where Nazi paratroopers invaded Crete during World War II. Terrible atrocities were committed there, and hatred between the two peoples reigned.

Fulghum writes:

> Against this heavy curtain of history, in this place where the stone of hatred is hard and thick, the existence of an institute devoted to healing the wounds of war is a fragile paradox. How has it come to be here? The answer is a man. Alexander Papaderos.
>
> A doctor of philosophy, teacher, politician, resident of Athens but a son of this soil. At war's end he came to believe that the Germans and Cretans had much to give one another—much to learn from one another. . . . For if they could forgive each other and construct a creative relationship, then any people could.

And so the institute was created, and Papaderos himself became a living legend, the embodiment of intelligence and courage and humanity. Fulghum attended a summer session at the institute, and on the last morning, after Papaderos had finished his last lecture, he asked, "Are there any questions?"

Fulghum asked, "Dr. Papaderos, what is the meaning of life?" People laughed and started to gather up their papers, but Papaderos

> held up his hand and stilled the room and looked at me for a long time, asking with his eyes if I was serious and seeing from my eyes that I was. "I will answer your question," [he said.]
>
> Taking his wallet out of his hip pocket, he . . . brought out a very small round mirror, about the size of a quarter, [and said]: . . .
>
> "When I was a small child, during the war, we were very poor and we lived in a remote village. One day on the road, I found the broken pieces of a mirror. A German motorcycle had been wrecked in that place.
>
> "I tried to find all the pieces and put them together but it was

187

not possible, so I kept only the largest piece. This one. And by scratching it on a stone, I made it round. I began to play with it as a toy and became fascinated by the fact that I could reflect light into dark places where the sun could never shine—in deep holes and crevices and dark closets. It became a game for me to get light into the most inaccessible places I could find.

"I kept the little mirror; and as I went about my growing up, I would take it out in idle moments and continue the challenge of the game. As I became a man, I grew to understand that this was not just a child's game but a metaphor for what I might do with my life. I came to understand that I am not the light or the source of the light. But light—truth, understanding, knowledge—is there, and it will only shine in many dark places if I reflect it.

"I am a fragment of a mirror whose whole design and shape I do not know. Nevertheless, with what I have, I can reflect light into dark places of this world—into the black places in the hearts of men—and change some things in some people. Perhaps others may see and do likewise. This is what I am about. This is the meaning of my life."

And then, says Robert Fulghum, Alexander Papaderos carefully slanted his tiny mirror, caught the sun's rays, and sent them dancing across the room, glittering on Fulghum's hands.[6]

We face a turbulent future, one in which the hunger for leadership will rise to famine proportions. We will have to walk through some very dark places and see into still darker places. Make the choice to be a light-bringer to dark places. Have the humility to reflect the greater light rather than to rely only on your own resources.

Service

Now I'd like to make a fourth point, one that a cockroach may not have a very strong connection to—service. (Although you probably didn't know that cockroaches devour other insects that are even more repulsive, like bedbugs.) Leadership is service. Leaders are servants.

When I was an elementary-school principal, there was a lot of attention paid to what we called "administrative styles." I read the studies, but I knew what kind of leader I wanted to be. I wanted to be a leader like Jesus. I never talked about this goal at school, but it was the powerful ideal behind my behavior.

What kind of leader was Jesus? He didn't pull rank. He didn't demand special privileges. In fact, he said some pretty severe things about the leaders who wanted the best places in the synagogue and wanted people to step aside for them in the marketplace. As a teacher, I always felt that I was a servant. Max de Pree defines leadership not in terms of giving orders or staying in charge, but in terms that should sound very familiar to us. He says: "The first responsibility of a leader is to define reality. The last is to say thank you. In between the two, the leader must become a servant and a debtor." Isn't that wonderful?

So I saw myself as a servant. When I was a teacher, I served the children, I served the parents, and I served the other teachers. When I became a principal, the scope of my service increased. In addition to serving all the children and parents—rather than primarily those in my classroom—I also served all of the teachers, the superintendent, my supervisor, and my colleagues who were also principals. My horizons of service got broader and broader.

I had seen enough of people in "leadership positions" to understand the problems that could develop when they thought people should serve them instead of the other way around. They caused a great deal of turmoil. They interfered inappropriately with people. They demanded constant feedback. They nurtured cliques of insiders and outsiders. They became suspicious of any information that didn't come to them from an "approved" source. I didn't want to be that kind of leader. I could really understand what Jesus meant when he instructed that the greatest among us should be the "servant" (Luke 22:24).

What else about Jesus? He didn't have an office. He didn't barricade himself behind a desk. He went to the people. He didn't wait for people to approach him, he sought them out; and because he was on the road, opportunities came to him. He was constantly on the move—in Mary's and Martha's home, on the road, in the synagogues, in the marketplace, on the shores of the Sea of Galilee, *on* the Sea of Galilee. He was a leader in motion. He went where the people were. So I decided to be a roving leader too.

I went to school at six-thirty or seven every morning and did most of my office work and got my day organized. The teachers arrived by seven-thirty, and that's when I left my office. I walked around our building and just said "Hi!" to each one and visited with them for a couple of minutes. At eight o'clock, when the buses started to arrive, I went out to meet the children. I knew the name of every child in the school, and I said hello to a good share of them every day. I mingled with them on the playground before they went in; and if anyone seemed to be having a problem, I took a minute to talk to him or her then.

Then, when school started at eight-thirty, I made the rounds again. I visited every classroom, slipping in and out if the teacher was talking, pausing to help a teacher with a group now and then, or just observing. If the children were doing desk work, I walked by and looked at their projects, making comments and offering suggestions and praise.

Then I'd walk through the music room, stop in the cafeteria kitchen, visit the gym, and see the custodian. There wasn't a person in that school who couldn't run into me within a day without even trying. Every morning I'd make a formal observation visit to one classroom; in the afternoon, I'd do another one. Then I'd come straight back to my office, write a positive little note about something I'd seen, and ask the teacher if he or she could meet with me for a conference later that day. (I'd see them slip into the office as soon as they could after my visit so they could read the notes. You know, adults are as hungry for real praise as children.) Then that same day, I'd give them feedback about their classes, mention anything I'd observed that I wanted to bring to their attention, and consult with them about their questions. That means I saw every teacher in action every three weeks.

After the teachers left at four-thirty, I spent until six o'clock doing more administrative work. So, before seven-thirty in the morning and after four-thirty in the afternoon, I was an administrator. The rest of the day I spent in ministering. My leadership style was one that specialized in many, many, face-to-face, informal communications. And no matter what the subject we were discussing might be, I always tried to communicate another message, too. "I like you. I trust you. I respect your professional commitment and achievement. You're an important part of the team."

Now, was it worth it? Definitely, yes. I wasn't interested in being the biggest frog in the pond. I was interested in having the healthiest, happiest pond possible. I didn't want to be served. I wanted to serve. Furthermore, this style was the most efficient way to save time that I ever found. It prevented dozens of problems and solved still others when they were still little. I didn't have any crises when I was a principal. Emergencies just didn't happen—not because I was so great at solving them but because the way we all worked together didn't accommodate a crisis mode. I was interested in being a problem-*preventing* principal. If a teacher needed something, he or she had at least two chances a day to say, "Can I talk to you for a minute?" By investing two minutes then, I saved two hours later. What's more, the two minutes came with a lot of positive feelings, whereas the two hours would have come with a lot of emotional turmoil.

And I taught my teachers the same principle. "If you see something happening with one of the children," I would say, "call the parents that very day, and say, 'I noticed something happening with Jason today. I'm not sure if it's going to be a problem, but this is what I saw'—and then describe the situation." Then the teacher would say, "I'd like you to watch and see if you observe the same things at home. I'll be back in touch if I see some progression in this pattern." That way, the parent was prepared if a

191

more serious problem developed—and 95 percent of them didn't develop because that dual attention at home and at school often solved the problem painlessly. As a result, our parents trusted the teachers, were genuinely grateful for their interest in the children, and were so supportive of the school that many problems other principals might have struggled with simply never developed.

I encouraged the teachers to call parents, praised them when they did, followed up on what the parents had said—and made it easy for the teachers by having telephones in their area lounges so that it was not an enormous project to make these calls. And that's a point worth making, too: Be sure that your people have what they need to do their job—in addition to your excellent advice. Defining ourselves as servants eliminates more problems than you'll ever imagine.

I was delighted when I read that the managers of excellent organizations often exercise "management by wandering around," meaning that the president or the CEO or the various supervisors spend a lot of time out of their offices, dropping in on people, visiting at the drinking fountains, looking over people's shoulders at projects on their screens. I was pleased because I thought *I'd* invented this technique.

Max de Pree says, "Efficiency is doing the thing right, but effectiveness is doing the right *thing*." It seems clear to me that defining ourselves as servants and teaching people around us to see the same way is one of the most important ways we have of showing people that we value them.

Let me close with a final thought from A. C. Carlson: "Good work is never done in cold blood; heat is needed to forge anything. Every great achievement is the story of a flaming heart."[7] I hope for all of us a future illuminated by the vision of a flaming heart.

15

UNSPONSORED SERVICE: THE *KIGATSUKU* SPIRIT

Some time ago, I was in my office a little before lunch when one of the secretaries walked in and said, "Oh, Chieko, your Explorer has a flat tire!"

"Oh, my goodness!" I exclaimed, "it must have been leaking on the way in to work. What should I do?"

"Oh, just call the Motor Pool," she said. "They know how to fix flat tires, surely."

So I called the Motor Pool, and the woman who answered the telephone was very gracious. She said, "Oh, yes, that will be fine. Of course we can take care of it."

When I got back from a luncheon appointment, there was Gary Babb waiting in the foyer outside my office. He introduced himself and said, "You know, we have a policy restricting whom Motor Pool personnel can assist with car problems, so they really couldn't assign anyone to fix your flat."

"Oh," I said, "well, I can certainly understand that. I guess you couldn't fix cars for everybody who works in the Church Office Building."

But that wasn't what he had come to tell me. He was

continuing, "I'm off-duty now, and I'd really like to help you change your tire."

I wondered if this wouldn't make him late to classes or to another job, and I exclaimed, "Oh, I don't want to take your time."

"Oh, no," he said, "I'm just so grateful that I can help you out. I'm so happy to do it for you."

I could tell he really meant it, so I very thankfully gave him my key, and he went off and changed the tire, then came back and reported that the job was done. It took him less than half an hour, and it gave me such peace of mind.

I call Gary Babb my Good Samaritan, even though this wasn't an emergency. I wasn't bleeding by the side of the road. I also wasn't stranded by the roadside surrounded by strangers or in a place that wasn't safe for a woman to be changing a tire alone. I had insurance. I could have called any number of garages in the downtown area. My son Ken also works downtown. Even Helen Pehrson, Sister Elaine Jack's secretary, who is about my size, said, "Oh, pooh, I can change it for you."

But Gary still rescued me—not because my need was so great but because his heart was so great. He saw a need—even though it was not a very urgent or pressing need—and he met it with real pleasure in being able to perform a service. I predict that Gary Babb will be a very happy man throughout his entire life because of his quick eye, his generous heart, and his willing hands. And I know God will bless him for his service.

Gary has the attitude that I call *kigatsuku.* This is an important Japanese word that means self-motivated goodness. A person who is *kigatsuku* is someone who seeks out good to do. He or she has an inner spirit to act without being told what to do. It's exactly the spirit that is captured in Doctrine and Covenants 58:27–28, where the Lord told Joseph Smith:

> Verily I say, men [and women] should be anxiously engaged in a good cause, and do many things of their own free will, and bring to pass much righteousness;

For the power is in them, wherein they are agents unto themselves. And inasmuch as men [and women] do good they shall in nowise lose their reward.

Well, a *kigatsuku* person knows that doing good is, in itself, the greatest reward of all. Mother Teresa told the women who worked with her as Sisters of Charity:

> Be kind and merciful. Let no one ever come to you without coming away better and happier. Be the living expression of God's kindness: kindness in your face, kindness in your eyes, kindness in your smile, kindness in your warm greeting. In the slums we are the light of God's kindness to the poor. To children, to the poor, to all who suffer and are lonely, give always a happy smile. Give them not only your care, but also your heart.[1]

We're obviously not working in the slums of Calcutta with the poor, but the same principle applies. In our kindness, in our heartfelt service, we can reflect God's love just as clearly as those Sisters of Charity carry his message to the poor of Calcutta.

Kindness isn't a flashy or a glamorous trait. Sometimes, as parents, Ed and I wondered if our children were learning this important value. Let me tell you about one of our proudest moments as parents. It came when one of our sons told us that he'd been in trouble at school.

Our family was in Japan, where Ed was serving as president of the Japan Okinawa Mission. Our two boys were teenagers then, attending the international school so that they could continue their studies during our three years there. We weren't rich, of course, but most of the students who attended that school had very wealthy parents. There was a lot of money, a lot of worldliness, and a lot of glamour attached to some of the events and people at that school. The students dressed in the latest fashions, arrived at school in fancy chauffeur-driven cars, and followed the latest trends.

This was during the late 1960s, and our two boys decided to let their hair grow a little longer, following the styles made popular by the Beatles. They explained to us that they looked too conspicuous at school because they were so different from the other boys. You may remember that there was a great deal of concern about dress standards and appearance at BYU (I believe there still is), and that hair length was one of those items that attracted a lot of concern. Some of the Church members in Japan knew it. They knew that drugs were available at our sons' school, and they were concerned about the association of long hair with drugs. I remember that Ed and I talked it over, prayed about it, and talked with the boys about it. It seemed quite important to them to not look unnecessarily conspicuous at school, and that seemed reasonable to us. After all, if they were Mormons and keeping standards like honesty, the Word of Wisdom, and chastity, there were plenty of ways in which they couldn't avoid being conspicuous. We didn't want to make things unnecessarily hard for them.

Ed finally put his finger on the crux of the situation: "Chick," he said, "if we want the boys to cut their hair because we're worried about the members' worries, then that's *our* problem." I saw his point immediately. We weren't worried about the boys. We were worried about the members. So we told our sons that the most important thing for us was that they were worthy to administer the sacrament, and we asked them to keep their hair neat and shampooed. And Ed had a kind way of listening to members who commented about the boys' hair and then saying, "They have their free agency," in a way that reminded the members that they also had agency and invited them to consider how they were using it.

But we still watched a little, wondered a little, and prayed a lot for the strength of our sons in an environment where they had many opportunities to do things that did not accord with gospel principles. That's all background for the point I wanted to make about kindness.

One night at the supper table, Ken said, "I got a demerit today at school"—which meant that he had cut class or been disrespectful to a teacher. As a schoolteacher, I had a whole range of responses to this little announcement. Ed and I looked at each other, and then Ed asked gently, "What did you get the demerit for?"

And then Ken told us this story that made us very proud as parents. One of the girls in his class had been under a great deal of strain and personal tension. Ken saw this and made it a point to speak to her during lunch. He became aware that she was very disturbed, so he walked with her in a quiet cemetery that bordered on the school grounds, where they could be uninterrupted. He listened to her, without judging her or giving her advice. She trusted him and poured out her soul to him, then stopped and begged, "You mustn't tell anyone what I'm saying. Promise me you won't tell anyone." Ken promised, and the girl continued, the talk relieving her frustration and confusion. The bell rang for class, but Ken would not leave her. They continued to walk and talk. Finally she brought herself to the point of admitting that she was on the verge of committing suicide. Ken had had a strong premonition that something was very wrong, and this confirmed his feeling. He remained with her for the rest of the afternoon, continuing to listen, to express support, and to help her clarify her thinking and her options. By being able to speak her worst nightmare, this young woman was able to dissipate her fears and diminish her frustrations. By the end of the school day, she felt much better.

They parted and went their separate ways back into the school building. No one had seen them in the cemetery, but the assistant principal saw Ken in the building, knew he had been absent from class, and grilled him about where he had been. Ken knew that the man was just doing his job, and that his responsibility for the students meant that he needed to be concerned, but Ken also knew that he was bound by his promise. So he said respectfully to the assistant principal, "Yes, I was not in class, but I can tell you that I did not leave the school area and that I was doing nothing wrong. I cannot tell you more than that." He was respectful but firm and would not answer the principal's questions. Frustrated, the principal imposed the penalty of the demerit, which Ken admitted that he had earned by missing class, and which required Ken to make up the work. More importantly, it went on his record as a permanent black mark.

Ed and I exchanged glances again across the table, and I saw great pride and gratitude in Ed's eyes for a son whose heart was so tender and true. "The demerit is not important, Ken," Ed said.

We asked, of course, about how the girl felt and whether she was still in any danger. Ken felt that she was really at peace at that point and did not need any professional help. We asked if there was anything we could do or if she needed a place to stay for a few days. Ken said he would ask her, but that he truly felt she was back in charge of her life. We did not even suggest that he tell us what her problem was. We knew he would not break her confidence, even with us, his parents.

That incident confirmed for us where Ken's heart was. We knew how important it was to him to do well at school, but to see him unhesitatingly choose to meet a human need, regardless of the consequences to himself, was one of our proudest moments as parents. We rejoiced in Ken's kindness and thanked the Lord for his *kigatsuku* spirit. At that moment, the length of his hair seemed totally unimportant, compared to the size of his heart.

There are rules for courtesy and rules for protocol, but kindness doesn't go by rules. Kindness isn't really one of those things that can be commanded. It has to spring out of an interior desire. Sometimes kindness may be a more accurate marker of the Christianness of an individual than more conspicuous things like observing the Word of Wisdom or attending meetings. Kindness can't be sponsored or commanded or regulated. It's deliberate and spontaneous at the same time.

Do you remember the apostle Paul's harrowing voyage to Rome under guard, when the ship he was on encountered the violent winter winds that drove them on the rocks off Melita?

And the soldiers' counsel was to kill the prisoners, lest any of them should swim out, and escape.

But the centurion, willing to save Paul, kept them from their purpose; and commanded that they which could swim should cast themselves first into the sea, and get to land: [That was one act of kindness.]

And the rest, some on boards, and some on broken pieces of the ship. And so it came to pass, that they escaped all safe to land.

And when they were escaped, then they knew that the island was called Melita.

And the barbarous people shewed us no little kindness: for they kindled a fire, and received us every one, because of the present rain, and because of the cold. (Acts 27:42–28:2)

If you've ever been cold and wet clear through, in shock from having escaped with your life after being in danger, then you will know how Paul felt. These people's kindly intentions must have warmed his heart as much as the fire warmed his body. And surely the irony hadn't escaped him that the Romans, who represented the most civilized nation on earth, were suggesting wholesale executions while the "barbarians" were showing kindness. The memory of their kindness has endured in the Bible for nearly two thousand years.

Perhaps Paul had this incident in mind when he wrote to the Hebrews, "Be not forgetful to entertain strangers: for thereby some have entertained angels unawares" (Hebrews 13:2). When Paul was in Rome, the scriptures tell us that he lived under house arrest in a rented house for two years and welcomed all of the people who came to visit him. He was a prisoner. He had nothing. What kind of hospitality could he offer? And what must his attitude have been? Was he angry and resentful? No, he was filled with kindness. Probably some came out of compassion, while others came out of curiosity, or maybe even with a cruel desire to taunt him in his captivity. Paul saw each encounter as an opportunity to give the one thing that his captors could not take away—his testimony of Jesus Christ. Whoever walked in the door—Christian, Jew, Roman, pagan—was someone upon whom he thirsted to bestow the great gift of eternal life—he, a prisoner, with nothing, as we would think.

What does it take to be kind? Really, not very much. Rachel Crabb, a member of another Christian faith, writes:

> Recently I finally got around to inviting a couple from our home church over for Sunday lunch. Sandy and Mike are young college graduates with promising careers and an adorable new baby. They are busy people and had not yet gotten involved in our church. I was ashamed to discover that although they'd been members of our church for nearly three years, ours was the first personal invitation they had received from anyone in our congregation. . . .
>
> Paul's instructions in Romans 12:9–13 emphasize that this ministry of love in action belongs not just to elders, but should be a trademark of all believers. . . .
>
> The emphasis in our practice of hospitality should be on how we give of ourselves to minister to others—not how we perform to entertain others. The Bible commands us to carry out this ministry [of hospitality and kindness]; it does not set up requirements for housing or meals. We do not need a large, beautifully decorated, immaculately tidy house in order to invite others into our home. "Breaking bread" with others does not require serving filet mignon or lobster tails. The issue is not spending money, but spending our time—not giving things, but giving ourselves.
>
> Focus on people, not preparations. In the Lord's hands, a few loaves and fishes go a long way.[2]

We never know the results of an act of kindness. I was very touched with the 1993 *Ensign* account of the Tabernacle Choir's tour of Israel. LaRene Gaunt writes:

Four choir members and two spouses [took] a taxi to the Hadassa-Hebrew University Medical Centre in Kadesh to see the famous Chagall windows portraying the Twelve Tribes of Israel. "All of Jerusalem is talking about your choir," said Yocheved, the receptionist. But when asked if she would be attending the final concert that night, she stammered that "complications" would not allow it.

After the six left, they realized that the "complications" meant that she did not have the money for a ticket. Quickly, they returned, and one of the spouses gave her his concert ticket. Her joyful response was spontaneous; and during the concert that evening, she was moved to tears. She embraced each of her new friends after the concert and said, "I didn't have any way to repay you for your kindness. I did not even know your names, so today I planted a tree at the Hadassah Hospital in the name of the Mormon Tabernacle Choir. It will continue to live and grow, and the next time you can come to Jerusalem, you can see your tree. Your being here has brought us joy and peace.[3]

Remember Yocheved's tree. Remember those loaves and fishes. I pray most sincerely that we may feel ourselves encircled about in the arms of our Savior, so that we, knowing of his goodness and love and acceptance, can reach out in kindness to others.

HEARTS TO THE PAST, HANDS TO THE FUTURE

Every woman of the Church, by belonging to the Relief Society and accepting its goals as her own, has become the heiress of a precious legacy of service and community involvement that is like a treasury to her. I want to tell three stories about women who are part of our past, women to remember and honor as our spiritual foremothers.

The first story is about a group of women in 1921 whose names have not been preserved but whose situation seems all too familiar in these desperate days of international refugees and ethnic slaughter. In 1919, the Muslim Turks were systematically exterminating the Armenian Christians within their borders. (Does that sound familiar?) Elder David O. McKay and his wife, Emma Ray Riggs McKay, were living in Ogden, Utah, then, where Sister McKay was president of the Fourth Ward Relief Society and Elder McKay was a young apostle. In January 1921, he recorded in his diary driving her "around the ward as she distributed her workers literature, cards, and buttons for those who contribute to the Armenian and Syrian Relief Fund."[1] Two years later, President Heber J. Grant sent Elder McKay on a tour of the world's missions.

He risked his life to go into Syria to visit some of the Armenian Saints and later recounted his horror at their terrible suffering. Do you remember when we fasted as a Church some years ago and contributed the money for relief of the famine in Ethiopia? Much the same type of fast had been held for relief of the Armenian Saints, and Elder McKay wrote to his wife: "It is not too much to say that every man or woman or child in Utah who fasted on that occasion would be willing to abstain from food for a week, or longer if necessary, could they have seen the good their money was doing."[2]

The mission president, Joseph W. Booth, reported that one branch of Armenian Saints in Aintab, Turkey, "had been wiped out" and that the survivors were "so destitute that . . . the Saints were eating grass and leaves." He evacuated those he could find to Aleppo in Syria and reorganized the branch. He also organized a Relief Society for the thirty women. Only eight of them had shoes, he noticed, but he proudly wrote that the sisters came to work meeting, barefoot and destitute as they were, "'as relief workers to help others less fortunate than themselves.' Inspired by President Booth, these sisters put on a feast for their undernourished fellow refugees and sewed clothing from the hundred yards of cloth purchased by the mission president."[3]

The second story is also about a group of women whose names I do not know, although perhaps my dear friend Mary Ellen Edmunds can tell us more. This story happened when Mary Ellen became the first welfare services missionary in Indonesia in 1976. "These Relief Society sisters, led by their president, Ibu Subowo, were giant souls in small bodies," she wrote. "Every morning before they began their cooking, each sister would hold back a spoonful of rice. They kept the rice in plastic bags that they brought to Relief Society each week. After the meeting, they would gather and prayerfully consider who needed a visit. All would then go together to visit those in need, taking the bags of rice with them to share with those who had less than they did."[4]

The third story is about an indomitable Dutch Relief Society president during World War II, Gertrude Zippro. When the German army invaded the Netherlands, she heard that they had devastated Rotterdam, where two sisters and a brother lived. Determined to go to them and see if they were all right, she pedaled her bicycle the entire sixty miles, moving against the stream of the German invading army that, she says, "roared by me on motorcycles, tanks, tractors, etc." She tells of continuing her visits to the branches, of passing through checkpoints where she was stopped and searched repeatedly. The soldiers were actually fairly free to take what they wanted from civilians. Sister Zippro's bicycle was never confiscated, although she was stopped many times. Women all over the city were raped and molested by the German army during the five long years of the occupation. Sister Zippro was not, even though she had to make most of her visits at night.

One night she was on a train that was strafed by Allied war planes. All the passengers were evacuated, and she huddled in the ditch, trying to make herself small and praying for safety, while the bombs and bullets struck the train and the dirt next to her. The train was damaged, but she was not injured, and the next week, she was out making her visits again. She told her concerned children, "Do not worry. I'll be perfectly safe."[5]

I have brought you these stories from Syria, from Indonesia, and from the Netherlands to place beside your shining legacy of Nauvoo women. These sisters are worthy successors to Emma Smith, Eliza R. Snow, Elizabeth Ann Whitney, and Zina Diantha Huntington. I don't have to remind you how all the women of the Church have drawn strength from Sarah Kimball and Margaret Cook and their simple impulse toward kindliness and their willingness to contribute what they could.

I do want to remind you that everybody has something to contribute. We need to be united, but we do not have to be the same. In our diversity are enormous gifts that we could not share with each other unless we were different. Think for a moment of that first Relief Society, as we turn our hearts to the past.

Remember that Margaret Cook was single and that Sarah Kimball was married to a nonmember. Of the first sixteen members of the Relief Society, three were teenagers and one was a woman in her fifties. Eleven were married; two were widows.[6]

In the Gospel of Mark we find a truly remarkable story about Jesus—the only time, as far as I can tell from the scriptures, when the Savior expressed any reluctance or hesitancy at all about performing an act of service for someone. And it was because she belonged to a different ethnic group.

> For a certain woman, whose young daughter had an unclean spirit, heard of him, and came and fell at his feet:
>
> The woman was a Greek, a Syrophenician by nation; and she besought him that he would cast forth the devil out of her daughter.
>
> But Jesus said unto her, Let the children first be filled: for it is not meet to take the children's bread, and to cast it unto the dogs.
>
> And she answered and said unto him, Yes, Lord: yet the dogs under the table eat of the children's crumbs.
>
> And he said unto her, For this saying go thy way; the devil is gone out of thy daughter.
>
> And when she was come to her house, she found the devil gone out, and her daughter laid upon the bed. (Mark 7:25–30)

We don't know anything about this woman except that she wasn't Jewish, and the usual interpretation of this passage is that Jesus was following his own injunction to the apostles when he sent them out on their first mission: "Go not into the way of the Gentiles . . . But go rather to the lost sheep of the house of Israel" (Matthew 10:5–6). Was Jesus comparing this woman to a dog? That doesn't seem very courteous, but the woman seems to have understood it. She wasn't insulted. What she said seems like a reminder that there are no limits on love. It overflows the table and on to the floor. There is enough and to spare. Something in her, not only her love for her daughter but also—I believe—her own innate sense of self-worth, let this woman stand up to Jesus and claim her blessing as his sister in spirit and as a member of the human family.

And even though what Jesus first said might be considered a rebuke or a reminder that her turn hadn't come, he agreed with her! He granted her the blessing that she desired.

The barefoot sisters of Aleppo, Gertrude Zippro, and Ibu Subowo of Indonesia are spiritual queens. Knowing their experiences in the past enriches our present. May we remember these wonderful women, our spiritual foremothers, as we turn our hearts to the past.

Hands to the Future

Each person alive today has an amazing opportunity to shape the future of this planet by contributing love, goodwill, and service. Each kindly deed, each loving thought creates a small reality of goodness that becomes a pinpoint of light in the blackness of the despair and violence that seem to be smothering our society. I remember a Russian proverb: "If everyone gives one thread, the poor man will have a shirt."

I'm sure there are sisters in many cities of the world who would look at us and think that we were already in heaven. But it's not that simple, and appearances don't tell the whole story. My experience with women around the world has been that they carry many burdens, often without much help.

Please, don't try to do it alone, and don't make a sister do it alone. Reach out to each other. But if you are the person struggling with the burden, let me caution you of two things. Don't just pick someone and unload on her. If you don't know her circumstances, you may be giving her something she is not prepared to handle. Recognize that no one can carry your burdens for you except the Savior. Recognize that we are here in mortality by our own free choice to have experiences with both joy and sorrow. There is a line of appropriateness between sharing your sorrow and broadcasting complaints.

If you are one who has a sensitive heart and a listening ear to offer, do not intrude on anyone's privacy, but make yourself available and offer support and love until such time as the sister is ready to share with you. Always keep confidences. Pray with and for each other. And above all, let us seek opportunities to serve. It's mostly a matter of simply tuning our hearts to listen to the promptings of the Spirit about the needs of another.

All of us know the opportunities for service within our own homes, but there's a whole world beyond our doorsteps. Glenn L. Pace, former second counselor in the Presiding Bishopric, said: "We must reach out beyond the walls of our own church. In humanitarian work, as in other areas of the gospel, we cannot become the salt of the earth if we stay in one lump in the cultural halls of our beautiful meetinghouses. We need not wait for a call or assignment from a Church leader before we become involved in activities that are best carried out on a community or individual basis."[7]

One woman who reaches out in a beautiful way is Beth McCarthy, a widow for many years. In her late fifties, she began volunteering at Odyssey House, a drug and alcohol treatment center for teens in Salt Lake City. She was struggling with loss and loneliness after her mother's death, but her volunteer work—as much as twenty hours a week—gave her "a warm sense of joy and satisfaction."

She sat in on group counseling sessions and took residents on errands—to the doctor, dentist, bus station, or airport. Occasionally, she would take them to church—to whatever denomination they wished or to her own ward. But mostly, Beth spent long hours listening to the troubled teens as they spilled out their problems, dreams, and desires. "I don't judge them. I just listen to them and love them," she says.[8]

What Beth is doing is something we can all do.

Now that I'm a senior citizen, I was very interested in a group called the Senior Gleaners, more than two thousand volunteer senior citizens in Sacramento who help feed 100,000 people. In 1991, they gleaned 18,000 tons of food that went to 125 charities, food that would otherwise have gone to waste in nearby farmers' fields. Their slogan is, "The poor we shall always have with us, but why the hungry?" This organization is not a current fad. It was organized in 1976 by thirty-seven senior citizens who were concerned about hunger in their community and placed a newspaper ad asking for volunteers to help salvage food that would otherwise go to waste. Farmers call them for a variety of reasons. Sometimes there's no market for a crop. Sometimes the automatic nut pickers shake off hundreds of nuts. Mechanical tomato pickers have to have turn-around space at the end of a row. A crop may be too ripe to ship or the wrong size or shape for the supermarket. These gleaners are so careful with the plants that farmers sometimes plant an extra row or two, just for the gleaners, to show their appreciation. They also salvage thousands of pounds of unsalable food from supermarkets—"dented cans, torn boxes, items still unsold when their freshness dates expire. You have to be at least fifty to volunteer, but many are in their eighties."[9]

That means I'm eligible! Think of the opportunities we have, if only we have the willingness to use them. Let me share with you a poem by Bertha A. Klienman that was set to music and sung by the Saints in the 1930s.

> To use the gifts Thou gavest me, while yet the day is mine,
> To help some other feet, dear Lord, their [stony] way to climb,
> To use the power day by day I may alone possess
> To stir some other heart I know to find its happiness.
> To fit myself with patience, Lord, and broad capacity,
> To bear the burdens of the day that Thou hast meant for me.
> To take each trial I must endure, with noble fortitude,
> To shape my every weakness, Lord, and handicap for good.
> To sum in service year by year, e'er yet my life is spent,
> Each noble aspiration, Lord, and every good intent—

This is my calling each new morn. I take it up each day.
This is my part in thy great plan, if I but live thy way![10]

So this is my second message. "Hands to the future" is just
another way of saying "Charity never faileth." That motto is a
glowing and powerful one. It's one that is just as true in our generation as it was for the Nauvoo generation. It's our challenge, our
opportunity to keep it bright as we pass it to the next generation.

We may feel inadequate and weak. We may feel that we have
little to give. I tell you that we cannot fail because we are in the
most powerful partnership of all, partnership with the Savior in
doing good.

I am overcome, sometimes, with gratitude and love when I
think of Jesus who is willing to love me, to help me, and to defend
me. We know that Jesus is our advocate with the Father. John
reminded the Saints of his day: "If any [one] sin, we have an advocate with the Father, Jesus Christ the righteous" (1 John 2:1). Half a
dozen times, Jesus Christ told Joseph Smith things like this: "Lift
up your hearts and be glad, for I am in your midst, and am your
advocate with the Father; and it is his good will to give you the
kingdom" (D&C 29:5; see also 32:3; 62:1; 110:4).

It is a great joy and comfort to me to know that our Savior,
who has already paid the price for my own mistakes and sins, has
promised: "I am the first and the last; I am he who liveth, I am he
who was slain; I am your advocate with the Father" (D&C 110:4).

That idea gives me confidence in moving forward. I know I
can rely on the Savior to help me, to understand me, and to love
me. I don't have to be paralyzed by fear of making a mistake, or
paralyzed by guilt when I *do* make a mistake, because the Savior's
mercy is profound. And so, in turn, I want to be an advocate for
the Savior, to stand as a witness for him in all times and in all
places.

When we think of advocacy for the Savior and for his cause,
I'm sure we think of things like serving a full-time or a stake mission, setting higher standards for ourselves, repenting, and

defending principles of the gospel in a loving way when they come under attack. But as I thought about this topic, another scripture came to mind: "Verily I say unto you, Inasmuch as ye have done it unto one of the least of these my brethren [or my sisters], ye have done it unto me" (Matthew 25:40).

This was a wonderful concept to me. I can be Christ's advocate by becoming an advocate for those who are the least among us. Think about Jesus before he emerged from his mortal disguise. Was he someone you would have reached out to serve? Jesus Christ was a homeless man. He was embarrassing to be around because he made public scenes. He refused to accept the authority of the scribes, the Pharisees, and the lawyers. He consorted with tax collectors, thieves, and prostitutes. He made extravagant claims—such as that he was the Son of God. He actually touched lepers. No wonder the respectable people of the day shunned him. But he will be our advocate for the eternities, this man who was despised and rejected in life.

He was very much too much for a great many people. Is he too much for us? Is his gospel too much for us? No, it is our joy and our glory, that we can serve him by serving the least among us. "The least of these" are all around us. Not one of us, myself included, does not have circumstances in her life where she is "one of the least." Not one of us, myself included, does not need an advocate in at least one part of our lives. Not one of us, myself included, has not been blessed and uplifted and cherished by the sensitivity and compassion and love of a friend. And, on the other hand, not one of us, myself included, is incapable of being an advocate for someone else. Not one of us, myself included, is so overcome with problems that we cannot be a nonjudgmental listener, a helpful friend, a loving sister to someone who is also in need, a defender when someone is gossiped about, an includer when someone is marginalized.

Think of the joy we will experience when we hear Christ the Lord speak for us on that great day when he is our advocate with the Father. I cannot help thinking that he experiences equally great joy when he hears us—weak, limited, and imperfect as we are—speak for the "least of these, my brethren [and my sisters]."

It is Christ who has called us out of darkness into his marvelous light. He is both means and motive for our service. We long to serve others because of the love he has blessed us with. May we be linked in heaven as we are on earth by the outpouring of love from our Savior.

LET DOWN YOUR NETS

When the Savior was ready to begin his formal ministry, one of the first things he did was seek out the people who would be close to him for the rest of his mortal life. These people were his apostles. This event is recorded in Luke, chapter 5.

It sounds almost as if it could have been a chance meeting. Jesus was standing on the shore of the Sea of Galilee talking to people who were crowding around him, closer and closer, trying to hear what he had to say. Two boats were pulled up on the beach while the fishermen were off washing their nets, so Jesus got into one of the boats—it happened to belong to Simon Peter—and asked him to push off a little from the shore. There's no indication here that Peter knew Jesus or had met him before, and he must have been tired from fishing all night, but he obliged the Master, then sat listening while Jesus spoke from the bow of the boat to the company assembled on the shore.

Then, when Jesus was through speaking, he turned to Peter and said, "Pull out further, to the deep water, and you and your partners can let down your nets for a catch."

Peter said, "Master, we worked hard all night long and caught nothing." I imagine there might have been a long pause then. Jesus didn't say anything, but I imagine him looking at Peter and Peter looking back, and some flame of faith suddenly flickering into life in Peter, because he said, "But if you say so, we'll let down the nets."

So they pulled into the deep water and cast their nets. Immediately the nets were filled with such an enormous number of fish that the nets were in danger of breaking and they had to have their partners in the other boat—who just happened to be James and John, the sons of Zebedee—come help them haul in the nets. The fish filled both boats so full that they were in danger of sinking. The scriptural account doesn't say what Jesus did while these amazed fishermen were making the catch of their life, but I imagine he watched, smiling.

And then Peter came out of his amazement and fell on his knees before Jesus and said, "I'm not worthy that you should be in my presence, Lord. I'm a sinful man." And Jesus heard the message that he was really saying and reassured him, "Don't be afraid." Then he outlined a new mission for Peter, James, and John: "From now on you will be catching men."

So they rowed back to the beach, pulled up onto the sand, and they "forsook all," the scripture says, "and followed him."

I think this is a wonderful story for two reasons, reasons that make points of contact with our own lives as disciples. The first reason is that the Savior is calling all of us to launch out into the deep. Second, the Savior's call is characterized by respecting our agency, by responding with abundance, and by involving others in sharing that abundance.

Launch Out into the Deep

Let's consider that first invitation of the Savior's: "Launch out into the deep, and let down your nets." You know, the great thing about a beach is that it's a point of transition where the sea and the land come together. With the exception of extraordinary events like *tsunami* or tidal waves, there are boundaries in this zone of transition that are marked by high tide and low tide. There's a lot of activity there. You can see people sunning themselves or playing volleyball or having barbecues. You can see crabs scuttling sideways on their fragile little legs, and sea anemones blooming in tide pools. You can see gulls following the cresting waves to see if any fish become visible for a second. In other words, you could spend your whole life on the beach and it would always be beautiful and interesting and exciting because interesting, beautiful, and exciting things are going on all the time.

But the Savior wants us to pull for the deep, to launch into the deep water, because he has treasures for us that simply don't exist and can't exist in the sand, the froth of the crashing waves, and the constant activity of the beach. Doctrine and Covenants 42:61 gives us some indications of the treasures of the deep. The Savior says, "If thou shalt ask, thou shalt receive revelation upon revelation, knowledge upon knowledge, that thou mayest know the mysteries and peaceable things—that which bringeth joy, that which bringeth life eternal."

But as Psalm 42:6 says, "deep calleth unto deep." The deeps are not just the deep knowledge of the gospel, but also the deeps in you. I hope you have a beach part of your personality where there's a lot of scrambling and laughing and sunning. But I hope there's also a part of you that leaves the shallow, sandy self and goes into the deep. There you will discover, I promise you, who you really are and who the Savior really is. You will discover your disciple self.

Perhaps our deepest hungers and our deepest needs are the hunger to love and be loved, the need to give and receive love. Truman Madsen points out in his little book *Four Essays on Love:*

> It is common to suppose that in love "opposites attract." This may be a motive of much popular writing about the transcendence of God—as if the more unlike two beings are, the greater the power of love. Love, for Joseph Smith, however, is a relationship of similars. "Intelligence cleaveth unto truth, virtue loveth virtue, light cleaveth unto light, mercy hath compassion

on mercy." Even the opposites within us must merge and harmonize before we can truly love. The "pure love of Christ," then, is Christ's love for us as well as ours for Him. Actual kinship is the core of it. . . .

There is in most of us a hidden apology for the lack of love. We tend to identify love with action, to credit ourselves with it when we do a good turn hourly, when we serve in the sheer constraint of obligation. . . . Going the second (or the first) mile grudgingly, or even habitually and numbly, is not Christ's way. Love becomes a fountain even "unto the consuming of our flesh" in the growing person—not a source of drudgery but a captivating awareness that pulls us even in our most miserable hours. Until our duty-sense merges into this "energy of heart," until love is the feeling-tone at the root of all our feelings and actions, we are still spiritual infants trying to get credit for our moral strength.[1]

We need to think about these things. We need to ask the hard gospel questions and then struggle hard for understanding. Disciples need doctrinal deeps in which to search for the glorious patterns of the gospel, but then we also need to allow respectful space for other fishers to cast their own nets. What good is served if we form understandings on doctrinal topics and then blast anyone who disagrees as someone who is weak in faith? Such approaches, in my opinion, short-circuit the process of education by closing off discussion, by giving priority to only one body of information, and by judging people who hold different points of view as unworthy of respect. What do you *learn* under such circumstances? And *how* do you learn it? And what *kind* of a learner do you make yourself into? The answers to those questions are not very appetizing. American novelist F. Scott Fitzgerald said, "The test of a first-rate intelligence is the ability to hold two opposed ideas in the mind at the same time, and still retain the ability to function. One should, for example, be able to see that things are hopeless and yet be determined to make them otherwise."[2]

215

The gospel is not an orchid that droops without the right temperature and humidity. It's like a dandelion. It can grow out of a crack between two bricks or in the most luxuriantly green lawn. It doesn't have a subtle blossom but a bright, shouting, golden one. It doesn't have a single seed that needs to be carefully transplanted by hand. It explodes into a puffball of seeds, each one equipped with a parachute that will take it far. Be a learner with dandelion faith—tough, resourceful, deep-rooted, bright-blossomed, and far-seeding.

Maybe, to get back to the image of the sea and nets, we should compare a healthy, vigorous faith with a crab—it can live in the water and on land; it has a hard shell for protection and claws for defense; it moves fast; and inside it's full of delicious, sweet meat. It doesn't need to be coddled. It's not an endangered species.

I want to tell you the story of Amanda Barnes Smith. She was a New England woman whose family moved to Ohio in the 1820s when she was a child. Soon after she was married, she and her husband became interested in the form of Baptist doctrine that an eloquent young minister named Sidney Rigdon was preaching. And when Rigdon discovered the gospel, Amanda and Warren conducted their own investigation and joined the Church. They went to Missouri with their five children and arrived at a little settlement called Haun's Mill just in time to pitch a tent before dark. Two days later, just before sunset, an armed mob descended on this little settlement of about thirty families. Amanda saw them coming and recognized that it was the same Missourians who had stopped them two days before, searched their wagon, and taken all their weapons. She grabbed at the hands of her two little daughters and ran on a lumber walkway across the mill-pond and into the woods. The Missourians shot at her—an unarmed woman, running away with two children—but she and the girls got away and hid in the woods during what must have been a horrifying half hour of gunshots, silence, and more gunshots.

When she ventured back, the first sight that greeted her eyes was her eleven-year-old son, Willard, carrying his brother, seven-year-old Alma, unconscious and dripping with blood. A Missourian had put his rifle through the cracks in the mill, pressing the muzzle to Alma's hip, and pulled the trigger. Willard told her that ten-year-old Sardius was dead. A Missourian had put the gun to his head and blown off the top of his skull, commenting, "Nits make lice." Her husband was dead. A Missourian had shot him, then, while he was dying, pulled off his boots, dragging his helpless body back and forth on the floor to get them loose. About eighteen or nineteen men and boys were killed that day, and their bodies were tipped into a dry well. The man who was putting the bodies in had traveled with the Smiths and could not bear to tip Sardius's body in among the rest, so Amanda, with Willard's help, had to do it herself.

This part of Amanda's story gets told frequently to show the barbarism of the massacre. Frequently told also is the miracle of Alma's healing. As this desperate mother, with no medical training and miles from any professional medical assistance, prayed to the Lord, a voice spoke clearly and calmly in her mind, telling her how to make a poultice that drew out the fragments of bone and prevented infection. After this, she made a second poultice out of slippery elm root and wrapped it in linen. Then she said to her little boy:

> "Alma, my child," I said, "you believe that the Lord made your hip?"
> "Yes, Mother."
> "Well, the Lord can make something there in the place of your hip. Don't you believe that he can, Alma?"
> "Do you think that the Lord can, Mother?" inquired the child, in his simplicity.
> "Yes, my son," I replied, "he has shown it all to me in a vision."
> Then I laid him comfortably on his face and said, "Now you lay like that, and don't move, and the Lord will make you another hip."

So Alma laid on his face for five weeks, [says Amanda] until
he was entirely recovered—a flexible gristle having grown in
place of the missing joint and socket, which remains to this day
a marvel to physicians.[3]

This boy grew to manhood. He walked, rode a horse, danced,
and fathered a large family. According to the testimony of his
mother, he did not even limp. Without a hip joint, he still had a hip
that functioned perfectly.

Now, here is a deep question: Why would the Lord, who willingly whispered to Amanda Smith's mind how to treat a major
wound and who healed her child, not have prevented the massacre in the first place? I suspect that the answer had something to
do with the exercise of agency on the part of both the Mormons
and the Missourians. I feel perhaps there were ways in which the
Lord could not act without infringing upon that agency. But after-
wards, when it was a matter of a newly widowed mother and a
little boy, he was free to give the comparatively small gift of medical knowledge and healing for one child that was certainly a
gigantic gift to Alma for the rest of his life.

But it's not even this experience that I wanted to focus on. It
was Amanda's experience of letting down her nets, so to speak,
that I wanted you to understand. You might think that she had
done so when she pled for the life of her son and prayed for
knowledge about how to care for him. Certainly that was a letting
down of her nets, but there were other trials of her faith ahead of
her. Because of Alma, she and her other children could not travel
and escape from the state with the other Mormons, even though
the mobbers were intent on driving out every Mormon.
Immediately after the massacre, in her words:

All the Mormons in the neighborhood had fled out of the
state, excepting a few families of the bereaved women and children who had gathered at [a nearby] house [owned by a
Mormon]. In our utter desolation what could we women do but

pray? Prayer was our only source of comfort, our Heavenly Father our only helper. None but he could save and deliver us.

One day a mobber came from the mill with the captain's fiat: "The captain says if you women don't stop your . . . praying he will send down a posse and kill every . . . one of you!" [I'm leaving out the swear words, but Amanda didn't!]

And he might as well have [killed us], as to stop us poor women praying in that hour of our great calamity. Our prayers were hushed in terror. We dared not let our voices be heard in the house in supplication. I could pray in my bed or in silence, but I could not live thus long. This godless silence was more intolerable than had been that night of the massacre.

I could bear it no longer. I pined to hear once more my own voice in petition to my Heavenly Father. I stole down into a corn-field and crawled into a [stook] of corn. It was as the temple of the Lord to me at that moment. I prayed aloud and most fervently.

When I emerged from the corn a voice spoke to me. It was a voice as plain as I ever heard one. It was no silent, strong impression of the spirit, but a voice, repeating a verse of our hymn:

> That soul who on Jesus hath leaned for repose,
> I cannot, I will not desert to its foes;
> That soul, though all hell should endeavor to shake,
> I'll never, no never, no never forsake!

From that moment I had no more fear. I felt that nothing could hurt me.[4]

And Amanda behaved fearlessly. When the mob came back to drive her out, demanding to know why she hadn't already gone, she said, "Come in and see your handiwork," and made them come in and see Alma's hip. The men went out in the yard afterward and quarreled. Finally they all left but two, and she was certain that these were the two who were appointed to kill her and the children. Instead, one of them asked, quite respectfully, if she had any meat in the house. Well, of course she didn't. There was barely any food at all anywhere. Then he asked,

> "Could you dress a fat hog if one was laid at your door?"
>
> "I think we could!" was my answer.
>
> And then they went and caught a fat hog from a herd which had belonged to a now exiled brother, killed it, dragged it to my door, and departed.
>
> These men, who had come to murder us, left on the threshold of our door a meat offering to atone for their repented intention.

The next crisis came as soon as Alma could walk. In fact, Amanda knew Alma could walk because she came back from fetching a bucket of water and found him dancing around in front of his brother and little sisters. She was anxious to leave the state immediately, but the mob had taken all of the horses and oxen. She heard that one of her horses was in the corral of the "captain" of the mob that had done the massacre. She fearlessly went to his house and demanded it back. He told her that he had impounded it and she would have to pay him for its feed, and that his wife sneered at the mobbers as "fools for not killing the women and children as well as the men—declaring that we would 'breed up a pack ten times worse than the first.'" Amanda walked into his corral and took her horse, and he never raised a hand to stop her. She heard that her other horse was at the captain's mill, so she went there and took it. He did stop her this time, but only to ask if she could use some flour. She pointed out that they hadn't had any flour for weeks. Without another word, she says:

> He then gave me about fifty pounds of flour and some beef, and filled a can with honey. The mill, and the slaughtered beeves which hung plentifully on its walls, and the stock of

flour and honey, and abundant spoil besides, had all belonged to the murdered or exiled Saints. Yet was I thus providentially, by the very murderers and mobocrats themselves, helped out of the State of Missouri.

Then she bears this testimony: "The Lord had kept his word. The soul who on Jesus had leaned for succor had not been forsaken."[5]

The point I want to make here is a simple one. The Savior calls us to go into the deeps. He wants us there because he has treasures of faith, joy, and peace to give us that will not come on the sandy shores or the shallows. He wants us there because he knows that life will take us into the depths of adversity and challenge, and that we need a faith that is equal to that challenge. And I invite you to live with the same zest for learning, the same hunger for knowledge that will sometimes keep you fishing all night but still make you willing to clean your nets and go back again in the morning.

Abundance

The second point I want to make is that the Savior's call is characterized by respect for our agency combined with abundance. Did you notice how the Savior honored Peter's agency? He didn't command him to become an apostle and follow him. He didn't command him to go into the deeps. He didn't threaten him and say, "Boy, are you going to be sorry when you see all the fish the other guys catch if you don't do what I say." He invited him to go into the deep water and then waited for Peter to make up his mind. Peter knew that Jesus wasn't a fisherman, and Peter also knew that he personally had been fishing all night without catching a thing. So he explained these facts to Jesus.

But Jesus didn't change his mind. He didn't say, "Oh, of course you'd know that there aren't any fish there." He didn't say anything at all, and that's when Peter said, "Nevertheless at thy word

I will let down the net." He had Jesus' instructions, he had his own experience, and he had, we can tell, enough faith to act on it.

And his reward was enough fish to break the net. Can you imagine making a more powerful statement to a fisherman than filling his net and his boat and his partners' boat with so many fish that they could barely wallow to land, especially when those fish were coming from a place where there hadn't been any fish for hours? No wonder the impetuous Peter threw himself to his knees and cried, "Depart from me; for I am a sinful man, O Lord."

The point I want to stress here is that Jesus answered Peter's faith with abundance. He didn't scold Peter for arguing with him. He didn't rebuke him for having weak faith, even though he would occasionally comment on this point in later settings. He opened the windows of the sea and poured fish into the net until the net could not contain them.

I want to testify to you that the Lord is waiting to pour out blessings upon you that you cannot contain. Blessings of knowledge. Blessings of wisdom. Blessings of service. Blessings of love that surpass your deepest experience of love and expand your capacity in ways that you cannot yet imagine. Another lesson from Peter's experience is this. I want to tell you that, in addition to pulling for the deep and being willing to cast your net, you need to strengthen your net to receive it and be sure there are places for your friends to stand as they help you heave it in.

One of my cherished possessions is a fisherman's net that my father, Kanenori Nishimura, made in Hawaii many years ago. It has been mine since he died thirty years ago; I asked my mother if I could have it after his death, because I loved the memory of my father standing on the rocks on the beach near our home, holding the net close-gathered in his hands and then, with a strong, graceful gesture, like a dancer, flinging the net up and out. It would unfold in flight, opening like a fan or an umbrella or a square of Chinese silk, spreading out to its full size. For me, that moment of casting the net was a supremely beautiful one. He could see where the school of fish was darting, shining silver through the surf, and cast the net so that it would fall exactly over them. The lead sinkers all around the edge of the net would keep it sinking gently and steadily to the sandy bottom, completely enclosing the fish.

Then he would jump down off the rock into water up to his thighs or sometimes deeper, and begin to gather the net from the bottom, pulling the outer edges into his hands, until he had scooped it up like a bag. He would walk up on the beach with the dripping net full of twisting fish in his arms, spread it out, and quickly toss back the fish he didn't want. He would bring home enough for our supper and for the next day, very often a fish or two for several of our neighbors who were less skillful or less lucky, and then release the rest into the sea. I can still see him walking home, the net over one shoulder and the fish in a basket in his other hand.

You know that the gospel has been compared to a net, but its way of gathering differs from my father's. The gospel brings all of us together, and we cherish each person. We don't pick over the catch, choosing some to keep and throwing some back. All of us are worth keeping. And the net does not take us out of our native element into alien air where we die. It brings us into the gospel environment where we experience some of the cherishing, the kindness, the love, the service, the instruction, and the watching over each other that give us reminders of what heaven can be like. In fact, we are the fish, the net, and the fisher simultaneously.

But I want to stress another point about the net that does hold true for our sisterhood and brotherhood. My father *made* his net with his own hands. He bought the hard-twist, double-ply twine at our local general store. Then he spent many hours in the evenings after work and on weekends, patiently working. He started a small square in what would become the middle of the net. Then he worked outward in a circle, patiently knotting the other squares of a size that he could just get his thumb through. At every corner, he made a square knot so that each square of the mesh was solid and strong. If one strand caught on a rock or ripped through because it was weak, the squares next to it would not unravel. They would hold strong and firm.

And every time my father used this net, he took care of it. When he got home, he would rinse it thoroughly in fresh water so that the salt water would not weaken and eat through the fibers. Then he would hang it on the fence, shaking out the folds carefully so that it would dry quickly and evenly. When it was dry, before he folded it up and put it away, he went over the net minutely, inspecting the mesh. If a knot seemed to be loosening or if a string was frayed, he repaired it immediately, before it became serious. A net like this would last for many years. It would stay strong because he always took care of it.

This is also what happens when we cherish each other, watching over and taking care of each other. We can't prevent rips and damage any more than my father could always keep the net away from rocks when he cast; but we can make sure that we tend and mend our own network every time we use it, particularly if there is damage.

William James, toward the end of his long and very productive life, said: "I am done with great things and big plans, great institutions, and big success. I am for those tiny, invisible loving human forces that work from individual to individual, creeping through the crannies of the world like so many rootlets, or like the capillary oozing of water, which, if given time, will rend the hardest monuments of pride."[6]

And there's one final lesson from the deeps and the nets. When Peter, James, and John brought their boats to land, full of more fish than anyone had ever seen on that beach before, they didn't say, "Great! Now we're millionaires." Jesus doesn't give a miraculous abundance of fishes to be peddled in the marketplace or turned into a vacation condominium on the Sea of Galilee. We don't know what happened to those fish, but I like to imagine that everyone in the village came running, amazed by the incredible number of fish. I think there was the biggest celebration that village had ever seen, with everyone building fires on the beach for a fish fry that they talked about for the next generation. I think everyone ate their fill, sang and danced, rejoiced in the bounty, and took some home later. And I think Jesus was right there, joining in the celebration. The abundance was not to be hoarded but to be shared. And after it was shared, the apostles left their boats on the shore and followed Jesus with the faith that they could, if he wanted them to, become fishers of men and women.

Think of the deeps that are waiting for you. Ask hard questions and look hard for answers. Remember the dandelion and the crab. Build a tough, vigorous faith, without being dogmatic. Remember Amanda Barnes Smith, finding deeps of adversity that she had never wanted and didn't know if she could cope with. Find the equivalent of a temple for you, even if it is only stalks of corn leaning together to dry. Listen for that quiet whisper, speaking to you in love and pure knowledge.

Choose to let down your nets—as a freely chosen action—in full confidence that there is abundance waiting for you. Remember my father, patiently knotting his net a square at a time, washing it daily in fresh water, and keeping it in good repair, just like Peter. Seek to reach out to each other and stand shoulder to shoulder in casting out the net in faith and bringing it up in abundance.

In the normal course of life, trouble and adversity will come to you. You will on occasion find yourself in deep waters, sometimes swimming freely and joyously, sometimes feeling slapped by the waves. There will be times when you feel, "Deep calleth unto deep [and] . . . all thy waves and thy billows are gone over me" (Psalm 42:7). Yet I promise you, many waters cannot quench love, neither can the floods drown it. Pull for the deep in faith. Let down your nets with love. And draw in the Lord's own abundance.

18

LAMPS AND TRUMPETS

Lamps and trumpets appear prominently in the story of Gideon, one of the warrior-judges of the Old Testament, and they represent for me two qualities that I think are absolutely essential for all of us as members of the Church. These two qualities are honesty and faith.

I've always loved the story of Gideon because it's so eventful and suspenseful, but at least part of why I love it so much is because I really like Gideon. Let me tell you the story of Gideon *as* a story, the way you might have heard it around a campfire for the first time.[1] You remember that Gideon lived at a time when the Israelites had forsaken God and had been delivered into the hands of Midianites, who stole their crops and cattle and defeated them in battle. It was also a time when Israel had no leader to unify all the tribes into a group that could take forceful action. All of Gideon's brothers had been killed by the Midianites. One day he was threshing wheat secretly, so that no one could steal it, when he saw a stranger standing beside him.

"You are a brave man," said the stranger. "God is with you."

Gideon didn't waste any time with the compliment. He went straight to the point. "If God is with us," he asked, "why has he delivered us to the Midianites? Why aren't there any miracles for us?"

"You will deliver your people from the Midianites," said the stranger.

Gideon remembered his manners at this point and offered the stranger hospitality, preparing meat, bread, and broth for him. The stranger told him to put the food on a rock. Then he touched the rock with the tip of his staff, and fire spurted from the rock and consumed the food. Then Gideon knew he had seen a messenger from God and, presumably, took the stranger's promise with great seriousness.

That night he obeyed an inspiration from God and boldly cast down his father's altar to Baal, replacing it with one to Jehovah upon which he offered sacrifice. For wood, he chopped down trees from a grove used for idol worship. When the people wanted to kill Gideon, his father said, "If Baal is truly a god, he can avenge himself." That gave the people something to think about.

Then, with Midianite and Amalekite armies massing in the desert for more raids, Gideon sent messengers to four of the tribes, and thirty-two thousand warriors responded. You might think that Gideon was all set, but instead he went back to the Lord again, double-checking his information, you might say. He prayed, "If you will truly save Israel by my hand, then give me this sign. I will put a fleece on the ground. If the fleece is wet from the dew the next morning and the ground around is dry, then I will know this is what you want me to do." Next morning, the ground was dry but he wrung a bowlful of water out of the fleece. Then, just to triple-check, Gideon asked the Lord to reverse the sign. This time, he wanted the fleece to be dry but the ground to be wet. And so it was.

Now Gideon was sure of the Lord, but the Lord was apparently not sure of Gideon and his army yet. They camped one valley over from the Midianites, and the Lord said, "There are too many of them. They will say that it was their own strength, not I, who gave them the victory." First he told Gideon to dismiss all who were afraid, and twenty-two thousand men left. The Lord had Gideon lead the others to the river to drink. Everyone who got down on his hands and knees and lapped water from the river was sent home, leaving only the three hundred who scooped the water up in their hand, still holding their weapons.

And there was still more. That night, the Lord sent Gideon and his servant up to the edge of the Midianite and Amalekite camp, a host so numerous that they were like "sand by the sea side." There he overheard a soldier telling a foreboding dream, and the other soldier interpreting it as Gideon's victory.

That night, Gideon divided his men into three companies. He handed every soldier a trumpet and a lamp inside a pitcher, and gave them their orders. In the middle of the night, the three companies crept up to the Midianite camp from different directions. Then Gideon and his hundred gave a great blast on their trumpets, smashed their pitchers, and let the light of their lamps shine forth. They shouted together, "The sword of the Lord, and of Gideon." Instantly, the other two companies did the same thing. The sudden trumpeting and the lights appearing all around them, along with the shouts echoing from the hills, panicked the Midianites. They thought a great army was attacking them. In the confusion, they began fighting among themselves and then began to run. The Israelites poured down the hills to pursue them into the desert, utterly demolishing the army, including the captains who had killed Gideon's brothers. For the rest of Gideon's lifetime, Israel lived at peace, free from its enemies.

Now, what does this story tell us about honesty, and what does it tell us about faith?

Honesty

Let's begin with honesty. One of the reasons I like Gideon very much is that he was very honest about his questions. The very first words he spoke weren't, "Oh, hello. Where did you come from?" or "Thank you for the compliment." The questions burst out of him from a heart apparently full of rage and sorrow: "If the Lord be with us, why then is all this befallen us? and where be all his miracles which our fathers told us of, saying Did not the Lord bring us up from Egypt? but now the Lord hath forsaken us, and delivered us into the hands of the Midianites" (Judges 6:13). These questions almost sound like accusations.

The scripture says that the stranger was an angel of the Lord, and events subsequently proved that to be correct, but obviously Gideon did not see him in glory. He saw him only as a stranger. You might think that it was fairly imprudent of Gideon to unburden his heart so promptly and even so untactfully to someone who could have been a spy or a priest's servant, who might have thought the questions lacked faith or political correctness. Obviously, neither the angel nor the Lord thought so. I think they loved him for his honesty.

Gideon did not question that the Lord existed, or that he had performed mighty works for the fathers of the Israelites, or that he was capable of still performing miracles. In other words, Gideon was a man of faith. And so it was to that faith that the angel responded, by miraculously consuming the bread, the meat, and the broth poured out on the rock. It's almost as if the Lord were saying, "Okay, Gideon. You want to know about miracles? Let's just *start* with a miracle."

And then he went on with miracle after miracle, as Isaiah said, "For precept must be upon precept, precept upon precept; line upon line, line upon line; here a little, and there a little" (Isa. 28:10); and as the Lord expanded in Second Nephi:

"For behold, thus saith the Lord God: I will give unto the children of men line upon line, precept upon precept, here a little and there a little; and blessed are those who hearken unto my precepts, and lend an ear unto my counsel, for they shall learn wisdom; for unto him that receiveth I will give more; and from them that shall say, We have enough, from them shall be taken away even that which they have" (2 Nephi 28:30).

Sometimes I think we don't create a very hospitable climate

for questions in our Sunday School classes, Relief Societies, and priesthood quorums. Sometimes we give people the very clear message that there's something wrong with them if they don't know something already, or if they don't see it the same way as the teacher or understand it to the same degree as the rest of the class. Sometimes this happens in the workplace too. The boss will snap out, "Understand?" and the clear implication is: "You'd better, or you have ten seconds to find yourself another boss." Or a discussion leader will ask the group, "Now, what are *your* ideas?" And the group members already know that their ideas had better be the same as the leader's ideas.

So people lie. They say they understand when they really don't. Or they say they agree when they really don't. Or they find one point they can agree on and swallow the four points they disagree on. Or they suppress the perfectly wonderful questions they have, because they're afraid that the questions may sound accusatory or faithless. As a result, no miracles happen. Did you realize that this is one of the messages of the lamp and the trumpet? If we don't have questions, there won't be any miracles for us. I don't know about you, but I *need* miracles in my life. I *want* miracles in my life. I hunger and thirst for miracles in my life. So I think I'd better ask questions—questions from the heart, questions that hurt, questions with answers that I'm afraid will hurt.

One characteristic of a trumpet is that it's not discreet. It's not subtle. When the Midianites heard the trumpets, they didn't just roll over and go back to sleep. They knew they'd heard something. They knew they were in trouble. They knew that this was something to deal with.

Gideon isn't the only scriptural figure associated with trumpets. The apostle Paul asked the Corinthians: "For if the trumpet give an uncertain sound, who shall prepare himself to the battle?" (1 Corinthians 14:8). He was telling them: If you have a testimony, bear it and live it. Let people know you're a Christian. Alma's longing to preach the gospel throughout all nations burst forth in his plea: "O that I were an angel, and could have the wish of mine heart, that I might go forth and speak with the trump of God, with a voice to shake the earth, and cry repentance unto every people! (Alma 29:1). The Doctrine and Covenants is full of references to the "voice of a trump" when it comes to missionary work. Here's just one, in a message sent to Oliver Cowdery: "And he shall not suppose that he can say enough in my cause; . . . And at all times, and in all places, he shall open his mouth and declare my gospel as with the voice of a trump, both day and night. And I will give unto him strength such as is not known among men" (D&C 24:10, 12). And then the next verse is interesting. It begins, "Require not miracles." Well, I guess that puts Oliver in his place. Do you suppose maybe the Lord was just humoring Gideon along because he belonged to a less sophisticated age and needed to be coaxed along toward faith, first with the miracle of the sacrificial food, and then with the miracle of his father's altar, and then just a little farther with the miracle of the fleeces?

Is this what's happening here? Absolutely not. We need miracles just as much today. And this verse to Oliver continues: "Require not miracles, . . . *except* casting out devils, healing the sick, and against poisonous serpents, and against deadly poisons" (D&C 24:13; italics added). Well, again, I don't know about you, but it's as if the Lord were saying, "I want people to develop faith in me by the Holy Ghost, so I want you to go out and preach the gospel, Oliver, but don't do any miracles—I mean, any miracles except just those simple, everyday, ordinary, run-of-the-mill miracles, of course. I mean, it's okay to cast out devils, heal the sick, be protected against poisons and snakes—but nothing flashy, you understand. Nothing spectacular that will compel belief." I think most of us would willingly settle for those miracles in our lives. And I think the story of Gideon tells us to be honest about the feelings in our hearts, and miracles will happen.

Now, being honest with God is one aspect of honesty. Being honest with yourself about what you really think and feel is another aspect. And then behaving honestly—being scrupulously honest in your dealings with the people—is also extremely important. I want to focus on it briefly, because this Church could not survive if members of the Church were not, in the main, honest people and if their honesty could not be trusted. Never play fast and loose with the truth.

I was very moved by a story that Elder S. Dilworth Young told about honesty at a point in his life where it made an enormous amount of difference to him personally. He said, "If you tell the truth always, no matter what, it will someday save your reputation and perhaps your honor."

> One time [Elder Young wrote] I turned over books to be audited by the auditor for our Boy Scout council. I was keeping the books.
>
> He called the next day and said, "Come over. I want to show you something." So I went over. What he showed me was a receipt written in my handwriting for $500 and the back deposit for that day for $300, also in my handwriting. I was $200 short.
>
> So to make a quite long story shorter, we visited the president of the council. I had said to the auditor, "I can't account for it. I don't remember." It had been a year before, and I couldn't remember a thing about it. So when we got to the president of the council, the auditor briefly told him what was wrong, and the president looked at me, and I said, "Sir, I can't account for this. But I know one thing—I didn't take the money. There is an error somewhere and I don't know what the error is. But I suppose you will want my resignation and so I shall write you one. You can do with me what you will—if you want to prosecute me, go ahead. I can't tell you more than that. I don't know."
>
> So I went home and wrote the letter and took it to him. Two days later he had a meeting of the whole finance committee of our executive board, and he surprised me. I sat there and he told them what I had told him. He said, "Dil, we know you didn't take the money. We are instructing our auditor to find out *how* the mistake occurred."
>
> The only way the auditor could figure it out was that I had

written a receipt for both the cash we received, which was $300, and the pledges we received, which was $200 perhaps. Nobody knew. I didn't know and I don't know to this day. I don't know why, but I had a reputation for being honest and truthful and it saved me. I could have been ruined on that occasion and never again would anybody ever have trusted me. But the trust went right on just the same. It never was brought up again.[2]

Be scrupulous with the truth. Don't lie to protect yourself. Don't shade the truth to protect someone else. And never ask anyone to misrepresent the truth for you. It is simply not worth it. As one executive commented, "I've learned that people who lie for you will lie to you."[3] Don't do it. Be honest, even if the truth doesn't happen to be very popular just at that particular moment. Remember Gideon and give a *certain* sound with your trumpet.

Light

And that brings us to our second point—the light that flashed from the lamps of Gideon's men. A footnote in one of the Bible versions I read specified that these lamps were torches or firebrands. Well, when you wave a firebrand in the air, particularly after it's been smoldering in a pitcher, it's going to blaze and spit sparks. The flames are going to leap and stream from it. This kind of light is alive, lively, leaping from place to place, impossible to catch or contain or suppress unless you come back to the source and do something to the lamp itself, or the firebrand burns out for lack of fuel.

John Stewart Hill said: "One person with a belief is equal to a force of ninety-nine who have only interests."[4] Well, that's our friend Gideon. You might think that Gideon may have been a little lacking in faith. Consider all those miracles he received, as though one was not enough and he had to be bolstered up and persuaded again and again. Well, I think it's very interesting that there's no chastisement from the Lord. He doesn't say, "What! Do I have to do *another* miracle for you? Why didn't you get it the first time?" In fact, he seems almost eager to pour forth blessings and miracles upon Gideon. He seems pleased by Gideon's questions, by Gideon's anxiousness to be sure that he's interpreting God's will correctly, and by Gideon's willingness to do risky, even apparently foolish things. What could be riskier than cutting an army of thirty-two thousand against an unnumbered host to a mere three hundred, after all?

If we live in Gideon's world of faith, we live in Gideon's world of miracles, too. President Howard W. Hunter called our attention to this fact in his talk at the April 1989 general conference. He said:

> The first miracle by Jesus recorded in the New Testament was the turning of water into wine at the marriage at Cana. . . . But poor, indeed, was the making of the wine in the pots of stone, compared with its original making in the beauty of the vine and the abundance of the swelling grapes. No one could explain the onetime miracle at the wedding feast, but then neither could they explain the everyday miracle of the splendor of the vineyard itself.
>
> It is most remarkable to witness one who is deaf made to hear again. But surely that great blessing is no more startling than the wondrous combination of bones and skin and nerves that let our ears receive the beautiful world of sound. Should we not stand in awe of the blessing of hearing and give glory to God for that miracle, even as we do when hearing is restored after it has been lost?
>
> Is it not the same for the return of one's sight or the utterance of our speech, or even that greatest miracle of all—the restoration of life? The original creations of the Father constitute a truly wonder-filled world. Are not the *greatest* miracles the fact that we have life and limb and sight and speech in the first place? Yes, there will always be plenty of miracles if we have eyes to see and ears to hear. . . .

President Spencer W. Kimball taught us with a book by the title *Faith Precedes the Miracle.* But there is, of course, an increase of faith that should follow the miracle as well. As a result of the many miracles in our lives, we should be more humble and more grateful, more kind and more believing. When we are personal witnesses to these wonders which God performs, it should increase our respect and love for him; it should improve the way we behave. We will live better and love more if we will remember that. We are miracles in our own right, every one of us, and the resurrected Son of God is the greatest miracle of all.[5]

The Psalmist says, "Thy word is a lamp unto my feet, and a light unto my path" (Psalm 119:105), and Proverbs says, "For the commandment is a lamp; and the law is light" (Proverbs 6:23). Jesus called himself "the light of the world" and told a parable of the wise virgins, who were prepared to provide light for the coming of the bridegroom, and the foolish virgins, who were not (see Matthew 25:1–13). Sometimes we think of light as concerning the intellect only. It's not so. Rather, this light is also a spiritual light that enables us to see the miraculous world around us more clearly. Choosing to walk by this light takes a great deal of courage, a great deal of love. When there's an army of several thousand Midianites preparing to roll over your country the next day, and you decide to stand on a hill on a dark night, break a crockery pitcher, yell something about swords, and turn on a light, it means that you're going to attract a certain amount of attention. You are not going to be inconspicuous. You are going to stand out. You have to have faith, when you do that, that the plan is going to work. And that's what miracles are all about.

Let me share with you a personal miracle. When my husband, Ed, and I were students at the University of Hawaii, he struggled with smoking. And I struggled with his struggle. He had learned in the army to smoke, but he never smoked around me. I'd told him what my standards were when it came to smoking, and I'd said that I could never marry a man who smoked. For most of his senior year, it was a problem for him—and oh, how I prayed that he would find the strength he needed to overcome this addiction. Then one day he caught the flu and went to the Veterans Administration hospital to get some medicine. The doctor confirmed that it was the flu and said, "We've got some open beds. Why don't you just stay here for the weekend? That way you can rest properly and get lots of fluids." Ed agreed. And because he was in the infirmary, of course, he wasn't allowed to smoke from Thursday night until Monday morning. A few days later, he told me, "I think the flu cured me from smoking! I haven't had a cigarette since I got out of the hospital and I haven't wanted one."

You can imagine how pleased and grateful I was! I said, "You probably don't know that I was praying really hard for you." He was surprised. "You were?" he said incredulously. "Yes, I was," I said. It was sort of a bold thing to say. Since I had told him that I wouldn't marry a man who smoked and now I was praying for him to quit, it was pretty clear what my feelings for him were. And sure enough, before the end of the school year, we were engaged. Later, Ed used to tease me by saying that the Lord had answered my prayer by making sure he caught the flu.

Now, some people might think that it was just coincidence, but I strongly felt that the Lord, who loved both of us—me, a convert from Buddhism to Mormonism, and Ed, a Congregationalist who had been a Christian all his life—had reached down in love to put Ed in an environment where the desire for nicotine simply dwindled and died away in a weekend. Yes, he could have taken the desire away while Ed was in class or walking across campus or trying to decide whether to buy another pack of cigarettes. But he chose to work in that particular way—I think so that Ed and I would be knit more closely together in love and so that Ed's new ability to live the Word of Wisdom would quite clearly be part of the love we shared for each other and for the Savior, and the faith we already had in him.

Let me share another miracle under even more trying circumstances. A missionary from another faith, kept out of Liberia for about two years because of the civil war, went back for the first time in February 1992, and was appalled at the carnage, much worse than the reports that had come out. Members of their congregation reported atrocity after atrocity: Men were forced to join the rebel troops. If they refused, they were taken and used as human shields in battle. Newspapers reported that even children were used as shields. Whole groups were killed simply because they could not speak the correct dialect. Starving people ate river mud, tree bark, grass, dogs, and rats. Women and girls were raped by looting soldiers; anyone who tried to defend them was killed. Pregnant women were slashed open, their babies ripped from their wombs. Rockets and artillery leveled buildings. Those left standing were looted and burned. Although burying the dead is a sacred duty in African society, many bodies had been left where they fell—there were just too many to bury and often family members were too weak from starvation to do so.

This missionary writes:

> To say that we were overwhelmed at what we saw and heard does not begin to express our horror and revulsion. We found it difficult to even discuss what we were seeing and experiencing with each other. In the midst of this awful situation, I began to ask myself, . . . indeed, where *is* God in all of this pain and suffering?
>
> Amazingly, the Liberian people answered this question without it ever being asked aloud. Every time we met with our members they began the meeting with a prayer of thanksgiving for God's blessings. Without hesitation, they would break into songs of celebration for what God had done for them even in all their suffering. The Holy Spirit was present in great power as we met for worship and fellowship. The people were tireless in their testimony of God's love and sustaining presence in their lives.
>
> Even though I found it difficult to understand how God could be found in such a place with so much suffering, to my

amazement and awe the people who had lived through it, those who had suffered beyond our understanding, never lost the awareness of the divine presence.

Questions about the existence of God are a luxury that perhaps only those of the developed world can afford to ask. People of the developing nations who daily struggle for survival, meaning, and hope find God in the everyday experiences of life. Their faith in God gives life meaning and purpose in a hard world.[6]

Probably very few of us have experienced one-tenth the suffering or the horrors of these Christians in Liberia, but we must all come to terms with the problem of pain in our lives—of how a loving, generous Father in Heaven permits the suffering of the innocent. Why were there no miracles for these patient, suffering Africans? At a time that seems to cry out for torchlight and lightning bolts, accompanied by crashing thunder, why is there only the quiet candlelight miracle of faith?

A young mother, Pamela H. Finlayson, shared her perspective on this topic with the Washington D.C. Stake. Pamela had joined the Church over the objections of her parents, praying for the miracle that they would understand. But the miracle didn't happen. Her parents are still so strongly opposed to the Church that they can't talk about it. After she married, their second child, a little daughter, was born prematurely, very sick and weighing barely two pounds. The doctors told her and her husband that the baby could not live. She writes:

> With all the faith of our hearts, [we] knelt and asked for a miracle. . . . We received an answer that day, but . . . it was not what we expected. Instead of hearing, "I will make her well," we heard: "I will help you through it. I will comfort you. I will give you strength."

The baby survived, but with many problems. She was on a

ventilator for months and had many surgeries to correct problems caused by a brain hemorrhage. Then their third child was born, a little boy, who became suddenly very ill with viral meningitis that infected his brain. That child, Sam, was four years old at the time Pamela gave this talk. Those four years had been terrible years:

> Sam . . . has endured dozens of surgeries and countless hospitalizations. Often it has turned out that the very things we have done to help Sam medically have worsened his condition. It's not unusual for Sam to spend six months of a given year in the hospital. He has had trouble with almost every system in his body, and he is in daily pain. Sam is now kept alive by intravenous nutrition delivered through a catheter placed into a major vein above the heart—a process which, over time, in and of itself puts his life at risk, and which keeps Sam hooked up to machines for 17 hours each day.
>
> *But* you could never know a more joyous, happy child. He is active, funny, bright, cheerful. Sam could be a child filled with fear and fraught with nightmares, but instead, there is an amazing aura of peace around him. We frequently find him giggling in his sleep.
>
> Throughout Sam's life, many, probably thousands of prayers have been offered on his behalf. He has had blessings, his name has frequented the temple rolls, our ward has fasted for him and the Primary children have prayed for him regularly and without fail in a way that has been extremely inspiring to us. Yet, physically, Sam continues to struggle.
>
> I began to worry, in fact, that the children would wonder why their prayers on behalf of Sam had not been answered.

And then Pamela bears this inspiring, faith-filled testimony:

> I prayed about this, and it was then I was able to grasp and articulate the wonderful miracle we were, in fact, experiencing. For you see, the peaceful happy spirit that Sam possesses *is* the

answer to our prayers, and it *is* a miracle—a miracle perhaps even greater than that of physical healing.

It would be easy, it seems, for the God of the Universe, the God who can part the Red Sea and raise the dead, to perform a miracle and cure a little boy. But I believe that we have witnessed something far greater and far more difficult. For instead of merely taking away the pain, God has been able to grant Sam comfort in the midst of pain, strength in the midst of physical weakness, hope in the midst of uncertainty, joy in the midst of sorrow, peace in adversity. . . .

I now acknowledge the other miracles of my life: the miracle of strength and courage that allowed me to join the Church; the miracle of comfort and support that allowed me to care for tiny Kate. I had always hoped for physical miracles—which should be prayed for and which, I believe, can and do happen—but in doing so I had ignored the glory of the spiritual miracles that were occurring in our lives.[7]

The next time you see a flashing light or hear a trumpet, remember that they call us to live the life of honesty of faith that called Gideon from his father's threshing floor to the judgeship of Israel. Make the truth your own shield. Lies will not protect you. Don't use them. And don't allow anyone else to persuade you to shade the truth.

Remember the faith that led Gideon from miracle to miracle. Remember that we live in a world of miracles and worship a God who delights to give us miracles—not often big ones, but always small tokens of his love for us. May we keep our lamps aglow, whether they send out powerful, flashing beams or a quiet, steady glow. Both of them are honest and honorable manifestations of faith. May our honesty and our faith produce our own record of miracles.

19

REJOICE WITH SINGING

The scriptures have an amazing amount to say about rejoicing, but one passage that captures my feelings perfectly is the section of the Doctrine and Covenants in which the Lord instructs Emma Smith to make a selection of hymns. And the Lord explains why this was such an important job:

> My soul delighteth in the song of the heart; yea, the song of the righteous is a prayer unto me, and it shall be answered with a blessing upon their heads.
>
> Wherefore, lift up thy heart and rejoice, and cleave unto the covenants which thou hast made. (D&C 25:12–13)

What is the Lord telling us? He is telling us that singing and prayer are, in some ways, interchangeable. He wants us to lift up our hearts, to rejoice, and to cleave to our covenants.

I'd like to focus on three ideas suggested by this scripture: first, on lifting up our hearts, second, on how the prayer of the heart can bring us closer to the Savior, and third, on cleaving to our covenants.

Lifting Up Our Hearts

The first point that I want to make is that we can lift up our hearts and rejoice because Jesus Christ is involved in our lives. We're not rats in some divine laboratory that Heavenly Father is running tests on. We are his beloved sons and daughters. He cherishes us. He cares passionately about us. The reason we know this is because of the Savior's mission. What do we know about how Heavenly Father feels about Jesus? We know that Jesus is his "beloved son, in whom [he is] well pleased." I hope that we all know the feeling of having pleased our Father in Heaven; but we're also far from perfect. There are times when we probably could not say that he is "well pleased" with us, even though I think there would never be a time when he is not also whispering to us, even in our saddest moments, "You are my beloved child."

Jesus Christ is the son that God allowed to come to earth and die for us. Not because he felt sorry for us, not because Jesus didn't happen to be doing anything else that weekend, but because *he* loved us that much, and *Jesus* loved us that much. Jesus came to earth to experience mortality; he knows what it's like for us. He knows what kind of help we need. He knows where it hurts. He knows where we get tired. He knows when we're ready to give up. And he's there with us in the pain and the fatigue and the discouragement.

He told the Saints of Joseph Smith's day:

> Verily, I say unto you that ye are chosen out of the world to declare my gospel with the sound of rejoicing, as with the voice of a trump.
>
> Lift up your hearts and be glad, [does that have a familiar sound?] for I am in your midst, and am your advocate with the Father; and it is his good will to give you the kingdom. (D&C 29:4–5)

He's not trying to pile on the trials and temptations to see if our knees will buckle. He is in our midst. He is our advocate with the Father. And the Father is not a stern judge who has to be placated and negotiated with and talked around. The Father's good will is to give us the kingdom. He wants us to have it. He's on our side too.

Jesus also told the Saints of Joseph Smith's day: "Lift up your hearts and be glad, your redemption draweth nigh. Fear not, little flock, the kingdom is yours until I come" (D&C 35:26–27).

Isn't that beautiful? He is promising that our redemption is near and coming closer. *He* is coming closer. We do not need to be afraid. We are in his kingdom already, not anxiously waiting for the big computer in the sky to machine-score our multiple-choice tests of mortality and morality to see if we can squeak by. Jesus is saying his disciples should act out of abundance—an abundance of love, an abundance of joy, an abundance of faith and trust and confidence in him and in our Heavenly Father.

Just one more of the Savior's promises to the Saints of our dispensation:

> But, behold, I, the Lord, will hasten the city in its time, and will crown the faithful with joy and with rejoicing.
>
> Behold, I am Jesus Christ, the Son of God, and I will lift them up at the last day. (D&C 52:43–44)

The upshot of all this is that there's lots of room for happiness and good cheer. The Savior loves us. He promises us joy and rejoicing. He doesn't want us to beat up on ourselves, to feel guilty, or to wallow in discouragement. The message of the gospel isn't that we're miserable sinners. It's that we're unique and beloved children of our Father in Heaven.

Furthermore, each one of us is the recipient of this divine love—not because of our faithful mother, or because of our devoted bishop, but just because of who we are. Jesus Christ didn't just die for *all* of us. He died for *each one* of us. And if you were the only person in the whole world who needed the

Atonement, Jesus would have willingly laid down his life, just for you. Is that a reason to rejoice? Oh, yes!

One of the most moving scriptural passages I know is Joseph F. Smith's beautiful vision of the redemption of the dead. He describes how he saw the throng of the dead in paradise, waiting for Christ to come preach the gospel to them after his crucifixion and before his resurrection:

> I beheld that they were filled with joy and gladness, and were rejoicing together because the day of their deliverance was at hand.
>
> They were assembled awaiting the advent of the Son of God into the spirit world, to declare their redemption from the bands of death.
>
> Their sleeping dust was to be restored unto its perfect frame, bone to his bone, and the sinews and the flesh upon them, the spirit and the body to be united never again to be divided, that they might receive a fulness of joy.
>
> While this vast multitude waited and conversed, rejoicing in the hour of their deliverance from the chains of death, the Son of God appeared, declaring liberty to the captives who had been faithful;
>
> And there he preached to them the everlasting gospel, the doctrine of the resurrection and the redemption of mankind from the fall, and from individual sins on conditions of repentance. (D&C 138:15–19)

The mission of the Savior is to free us from bondage and death and enslavement. It is to lift and exalt us. He is our Savior, and we can rejoice in him.

That's the first point I want us to remember. When the scriptures tell us to lift up our hearts, where should we lift them? We should lift them to the Savior. We should rejoice in him. We should feel his closeness to us, and we should try to increase that closeness.

The Prayer of the Heart

The second reason to rejoice that I want to discuss is the importance of prayer. Sometimes we concentrate on the externals of prayer. Sometimes when we're asked on the spur of the moment to pray in an informal meeting, like an inservice meeting or a Sunday School class, we have a moment of worry. Questions flash through our minds: Should I stand up to offer this prayer, or is it all right to sit down? I have my notebook in my hands; is it all right to just clasp my hands around it, or should I put it down so I can fold my arms? Can I remember the four parts of prayer? Can I remember all the right language to use?

In other words, sometimes our prayer is pretty flustered and anxious because we're focused on all the externals that are involved. I remember all of these feelings. After all, English was not the first language that I learned.

But if our songs are prayers to him, then I think it's also true that our prayers are songs to him, sweet music that brings him joy and rejoicing. How much better it is to pray from our hearts instead of from our minds and our worries! If we are glad for the other people who are with us, let us express that thankfulness. If the teacher expressed a concept that was comforting and enlightening to us, express that gratitude. Ask in humility for help with the things that are hard.

Hymn number 145, "Prayer Is the Soul's Sincere Desire," describes for me the kind of experiences we should have with prayer: the expression of our sincere desires, not the expression of our most polished rhetoric or our most telling logic or our most complete catalogues of wants and wishes.

Cleaving to Our Covenants

Now we come to the third point, cleaving to our covenants. When I was baptized at the age of fifteen, I understood that I was now a Christian and a Latter-day Saint, that I had made promises to God to be his witness at all times and to obey his commandments. This wasn't a commitment I made out of convenience or social pressure or because it was a nice thing to do. Being baptized was the outward form by which my love for the Lord, which had been growing gradually for four years, could manifest itself. My commitment did not waver during the years that followed as I graduated from high school, went to the University of Hawaii to become a teacher, and met a handsome hero from the 442nd named Ed Okazaki.

Ed was a very popular fellow, well-known on campus, and involved in student government and politics. Everybody liked him; even then he had the reputation of giving you the shirt off his back, if he thought you needed it. He was a Congregationalist who took his religion seriously, just as I took mine seriously.

I loved Ed, and he loved me, and we wanted to be part of each other's lives. When I knew that our relationship was moving in the direction of marriage, I talked to my parents. My father said very little. He made an observation, "Ed is a good man," and then he asked a question, "And he is not a Mormon, is he?" I said, "Yes, he is a good man, and no, he is not a Mormon. But I think he is a good Christian."

Did I think Ed would join the Church? I really did. I felt that someone with his purity of heart and his love for God would willingly accept more truth when he encountered it. He knew how important the Church was to me, but was it fair to make his conversion a condition of our marriage? Could I say, "I'll marry you if you become a Mormon?" No, absolutely not. I felt with all my soul that it would be wrong to coerce anyone into the Church in any degree, no matter how strongly I felt that he belonged there.

But what if Ed decided never to join the Church? Could I respect that decision, and could we still have a good marriage? I had to think long and hard about that, because it brought many other questions with it. Could I stay active in the Church if Ed were not a member? Yes, I could. Would I have the strength to stay active in the Church even if Ed opposed my activity? I didn't think he would. He wasn't that kind of person. But even if he did, and even if there were some callings I would have to turn down in order to keep peace at home, I felt that my commitment was unwavering and that I would find ways to attend church and serve no matter how difficult it was. How would Ed feel about the children going to church with me if he didn't?

Ed and I talked about these issues. We discussed my commitment to the Church. We discussed the religious training of our children. Ed promised that he would never interfere with my religious duties and that he would support me in creating a Mormon home for the children. I took that promise absolutely seriously, because I knew that Ed was an honorable person.

Were there any guarantees? No, there weren't. Even honorable people can change their minds, alter their opinions, or see things differently. I knew that was a risk. Did God tell me, "You're breaking a rule, but it's all right because Ed is going to join the Church and become a mission president?" No, God didn't tell me any such thing. He just confirmed that Ed was a good, kind, faithful man, a beloved son of his. I looked squarely at that risk. I searched my soul to the very bottom. I examined the strength of our love for each other and the depth of our love for God as objectively as I could. I thought about the happiness I felt being with Ed. And I knew that I wanted to marry him and spend my life with him, even though there were no guarantees about our eternity.

So we were married in the Congregationalist Church and settled down on Maui where I was teaching school and Ed was a county probation officer. We lived about a fifteen-minute walk away from church, and so on the first Sunday we were living in our little house, I got up Sunday morning, made Ed's breakfast, kissed him good-bye, and went to Relief Society and Sunday School. We brought our lunches, because some of the members came from far away, so I just stayed there the whole day—for choir practice and sacrament meeting in the afternoon. And that's what I did the next Sunday and the next Sunday and the next Sunday.

In some ways it was easy, because that was what I'd always done on Sunday. Ed used to joke that we had never had a date on

Sunday because I was always in church. Well, I think he came with me to stake conference in the Honolulu Tabernacle a time or two, but that was all. I just wasn't available on Sundays.

It was easy, too, because I didn't feel like that strange thing we label a "part-member family." I'd grown up seeing lots of families that had different commitments to the Church or to other churches. I'd see a mother and some of the children going to one church while the father and other children went to another church, or the parents going to church while some of the children went to another church, or one person going to some church while nobody else in the family did. These situations didn't cause family fights. I didn't know any horror stories. They were just the decisions that each family made. And my little branch on Maui accepted me the same way. They were happy to have me there, glad I could sing soprano, and delighted that I was available for service.

Now, it wasn't *totally* easy going to church by myself. When I saw Ed settling down to read the Sunday paper in his bare feet, I thought, "Gee, it would be so relaxing to just stay home with Ed." But when I had a thought like that, I reminded myself of my covenants—not only the covenant I had made at baptism but also the covenant I had made when I made the decision to marry Ed: that I would never let Ed become an excuse for me to be less than the member of the Church that I knew I should be.

So I'd be gone all day on Sundays while Ed would read the newspaper, mow the lawn, then go to his grandmother's house with his extended family to spend the rest of the day playing poker, eating, drinking coffee, and visiting. You should know that we lived perhaps half a block from a Congregational church, but I don't think he went even once. And I didn't ask him about it. I just concentrated on my own religious decision.

I'm glad to say that Ed and I missed each other on Sundays. We were very happy together, and he wanted to spend more time with me, not less. So what were the options? He could ask me to miss church and be with him on Sunday—and he *knew* what the

answer would be if he proposed that! Or he could start coming to church with me.

So, after we'd been married for a couple of months, he casually asked, "What do you do at church all day?"

I replied, "It's kind of hard to explain. Why don't you come see?"

So he came. From there on, it seemed natural. Ed came to the gospel gradually, like a lily of the field unfolding, without any pushing or pulling from me. The next Sunday, without any discussion, he got up, got dressed, and came to church with me again. The members were happy to see him and immediately adopted him into the branch. The missionaries were very welcoming and promptly started visiting. Their explanations made sense to him, and he kept coming to church and learning more about the gospel.

The only thing I did that might have been interpreted as pressure was about the Word of Wisdom—and that was an accident. He always drank coffee, but somehow I never even thought of buying a coffeepot when we got married. I certainly would have made coffee for him if he'd ever said anything, but instead I poured him milk as I was pouring it for myself, and he just drank it without a word. We'd been married for two or three weeks when I suddenly realized, "Oh, my golly, you drink coffee!" I was a little upset with myself, but he said quickly, "It's okay. I'm used to drinking milk already." And he'd stopped smoking and drinking when we were dating, so somehow the Word of Wisdom issue, which can be such an enormous obstacle in making the baptismal covenant, just dissolved like a snowball on the sidewalk.

Ten months after our marriage, Ed was baptized in the Iao Valley, one of the loveliest spots in the lovely Hawaiian Islands. I still remember how lush and green the heavy forest was, how still and beautiful. Ed was smiling from ear to ear, so happy. He looked beautiful and radiant in his white clothes. I was so thrilled and happy and grateful. I had believed that Ed would accept the gospel, but I had never imagined it would be so soon.

After the baptism, Ed and I had a quiet moment together

when I struggled to express the feelings in my heart. I told him how grateful I was that he had joined the Church, how much I loved him, how blessed I felt that now both of us would share the same covenants to the Lord. I remember that I kept saying, over and over, "The Lord is gracious to me." And oh! how I felt the love of our Heavenly Father for this wonderful son of his.

I've shared this very personal story with you to emphasize the importance of cleaving to our covenants. I know those first two or three months of our marriage were important months for Ed, because they were a little bit of a test for me. They showed him that I really meant it when I said that the Church was important to me, and they also showed him that I would keep my promises—my promises to him, my promises to myself, and my promises to the Lord.

I don't know what would have happened if I had been half-hearted about keeping my covenants, if I'd opened my hand and let my grasp on the iron rod slip away. I don't know if Ed would have joined the Church or not. But I do know what an increase in strength and joy we felt, and how our love became even more important to us when we had both made the same baptismal covenants to the Lord and were united within those covenants. And those feelings only got stronger when we could make temple covenants as well.

There will be many times when you will be tried, when your covenants will seem hard to you—even confusing, perhaps. At these difficult moments, cleave to your covenants. Behave with honor and dignity in keeping the promises you have made. Trust the promises of the Lord in return, for there is great rejoicing in store if you do.

I testify with all my heart that the Savior lives and that he loves us, that we can minister to him in ministering to each other, and that whatever rejoicings we experience here are only pale shadows of the divine joy we will experience when we return to his presence. May we live in steadfastness and look forward with love to that great homecoming.

NOTES

Chapter 1
In the Shelter of His Wings

1. Dr. Hyman Judah Schachtel, "How to Be Mature," in *A New Treasury of Words to Live By: Selected and Interpreted by Ninety Eminent Men and Women*, edited by William Nichols (New York: Simon and Schuster, 1974), pp. 48–49.

2. *Times and Seasons*, Vol. 3, p. 668.

3. As quoted in E. Richard Packham, *Born of the Spirit* (Salt Lake City: Bookcraft, 1979), p. 47.

4. Ibid., p. 50.

Chapter 2
Questions for a Disciple

1. Ed Hayes, as quoted in *Random Acts of Kindness* (Berkeley, CA: Conari Press, 1993), p. 72.

2. Susan Easton Black, "My Neighbor," *Cameo: Latter-day Women in Profile*, November 1993, 20–21.

Chapter 3
Steadfast Disciples

1. As quoted in John Dybdahl, "God's War Stories," *Signs of the Times*, September 1992, p. 27.

2. Eric Marshall and Stuart Hample, comps., *Children's Letters to God*, enl. ed. (New York: Pocket Books, 1975), not paginated.

3. Lynette Moss, "Accepting His Will," *Ensign,* March 1994, p. 55.

Chapter 4
Weaving Patterns: Men, Women, and Priesthood Principles

1. Laurel Thatcher Ulrich, *A Midwife's Tale: The Life of Martha Ballard, Based on Her Diary, 1785–1812* (New York: Alfred A. Knopf/Vintage Paperbacks, 1991), pp. 75–76.

2. Spencer W. Kimball, "Privileges and Responsibilities of Sisters," *Ensign,* November 1978, p. 106.

3. Jill Mulvay Derr, Janath Russell Cannon, and Maureen Ursenbach Beecher, *Women of Covenant: A History of the Relief Society* (Salt Lake City: Deseret Book, 1992), preface.

4. Francine Russell Bennion, "Women and the Book of Mormon: Tradition and Revelation," in *Women of Wisdom and Knowledge: Talks Selected from the BYU Women's Conferences,* edited by Marie Cornwall and Susan E. Howe (Salt Lake City: Deseret Book, 1991), pp. 171, 173.

Chapter 6
Knit Together in Love

1. Spencer W. Kimball, "Privileges and Responsibilities of Sisters," *Ensign,* November 1978, p. 106.

2. June Barrus, letter to Chieko Okazaki, January 30, 1993.

Chapter 7
Strengthening Every Home

1. Mike Cannon, "Pres. Hinckley Greets Saints in St. Louis," *Church News,* April 22, 1995, p. 3.

2. As quoted in James Charlton, *A Little Learning Is a Dangerous Thing* (New York: St. Martins Press, 1994), p. 5.

3. Jill Watson, letter to Elaine Cannon, May 29, 1994.

4. Deborah Hedstrom, "Single with Children," *Signs of the Times,* Vol. 121, no. 7, pp. 6–7.

5. Kristin Goodman, "Blended Families: A Brief Review," memo to Chieko Okazaki, June 2, 1994, typescript in my possession.

6. As quoted in *Golden Words of Faith, Hope, and Love,* edited by Louise Bachelder (Mount Vernon, VA: Peter Pauper Press, 1969), p. 8.

7. As quoted in *Great Quotes from Great Teachers* (Glendale Heights, IL: Great Quotations Publishing Company, 1994), p. 13.

8. Martin Luther, *Listen to Love: Reflections on the Seasons of the Year; Photographs,*

Poems and Readings, compiled by Louis M. Savary, with Thomas J. O'Connor, Ruth M. Cullen, Diane M. Plummer (New York: Regina Press, 1971), p. 55.

Chapter 8
Healing from Sexual Abuse:
Eight Messages for Survivors, Families, and Leaders

1. See their addresses in *Ensign,* May 1985, p. 50, and November 1991, p. 69, respectively.

2. Anne L. Horton, "Secret Abominations: Healing and Empowering Survivors of Child Sexual Abuse," *Virginia F. Cutler Center Lecture Supplement,* November 10, 1992, n.p.

3. F. Boulton, L. Morris, and A. MacEachron, *Males at Risk* (Newbury Park, CA: Sage Publications, 1989); and D. Everstine and L. Everstine, *Sexual Trauma in Children and Adolescents* (New York: Brunner/Mazel, 1989), as quoted by Rex Kocherhans, "Males Are Victims Too," in *Confronting Abuse,* edited by Anne L. Horton, B. Kent Harrison, and Barry L. Johnson (Salt Lake City: Deseret Book, 1993), p. 204.

4. Horton, "Secret Abominations."

5. "Sexual Abuse and Healing: Narratives from Latter-day Saints," interviews by Diane Brown, preparation of manuscript by Martha Nibley Beck and Tracey Wilkinson Sparks, edited by Marie Cornwall and Donna Lee Bowen; typescript, August 17, 1992, pp. 16–17.

6. Wendy L. Ulrich, "Not for Adam's Transgression: Paths to Intergenerational Peace," *Sunstone,* November 1991, p. 33.

7. Donna Lee Bowen Barnes, "A Struggle for an Eternal Order," in *As Women of Faith: Talks Selected from the BYU Women's Conferences,* edited by Mary E. Stovall and Carol Cornwall Madsen (Salt Lake City: Deseret Book, 1989), pp. 82–83.

Chapter 9
Good Measure, Pressed Down, and Running Over

1. As quoted in *Golden Words of Faith, Hope, and Love,* edited by Louise Bachelder (Mount Vernon, VA: Peter Pauper Press, 1969), p. 50.

2. Clare Judy, "Water, Shelter, and Love," *Ensign,* July 1995, pp. 68–69.

Chapter 10
Delivered from Bondage

1. "God Touched the Stones," December 8, 1991, typescript in my possession.

2. As quoted in Paul Swenson, "Will the Private Sector Provide Mental Health Parity. . . ," *Event,* February 1998, p. 4.

3. Val Crow, "Lansing Michigan Stake, Jackson/Albion Wards," in *Lansing*

Michigan Stake History, edited by Sue Ann Walker (Chelsea, MI: BookCrafters, 1993), pp. 36–37.

4. *History of the Church of Jesus Christ of Latter-day Saints,* 7 vols. (Salt Lake City: Deseret Book, 1974), 4:4–5.

Chapter 11
Christ and Culture

1. David Heller, *Dear God* (New York: Berkley Publishing Group, 1987), pp. 32, 29.

2. Ted L. Gibbons, "Footsteps of the Father, Shadow of the Son," *Latter-day Digest,* Vol. 2, no. 8, p. 24.

3. Geoffrey Spencer, "Put Out into the Deep!" *Saints Herald,* June 1992, p. 8.

4. Marian Wright Edelman, *Guide My Feet: Prayers and Meditations on Loving and Working for Children* (Boston: Beacon Press, 1995), p. 146.

Chapter 12
Stones

1. Howard W. Hunter, "The Pharisee and the Publican," *Ensign,* May 1984, p. 35.

2. Grant E. Burns, letter to Chieko N. Okazaki, June 7, 1995.

3. José Luis González-Galado and Janet N. Playfoot, *My Life for the Poor: Mother Teresa of Calcutta* (San Francisco: Harper & Row, 1985), pp. 23–24.

4. "They Know Him," *New Era,* April 1992, p. 28.

Chapter 13
Behold Thy Handmaiden: The Answer of Faith

1. Janice Kapp Perry, "A Child's Prayer," *Children's Songbook* (Salt Lake City: The Church of Jesus Christ of Latter-day Saints, 1989), pp. 12–13.

2. Francine R. Bennion, "A Latter-day Saint Theology of Suffering," in *A Heritage of Faith: Talks Selected from the BYU Women's Conferences,* edited by Mary E. Stovall and Carol Cornwall Madsen (Salt Lake City: Deseret Book, 1988), pp. 64–67, 69–70.

Chapter 14
Change, Choice, Challenge, and the Cockroach

1. As quoted in James Charlton, *A Little Learning Is a Dangerous Thing* (New York: St. Martins Press, 1994), p. 101.

2. Ibid., p. 100.

3. Carri P. Jensen, "Judge Monroe McKay, Creating a Commotion," *BYU Today*, May 1992, pp. 27–38.

4. As quoted in *A Thought for Today*, edited by Theron C. Liddle (Salt Lake City: Deseret News Press, 1961), p. 46.

5. Ibid., p. 18.

6. Robert Fulghum, *It Was On Fire When I Lay Down on It* (New York: Ballantine Books, 1988), pp. 171–75.

7. A. C. Carlson, as quoted in *To Your Success: Thoughts to Give Wings to Your Work and Your Dreams*, compiled by Dan Zadra (Woodinville, WA: Compendium, Inc., 1994), p. 66.

Chapter 15
Unsponsored Service: The *Kigatsuku* Spirit

1. Malcolm Muggeridge, *Something Beautiful for God: Mother Teresa of Calcutta* (New York: Walker and Company/Phoenix Press, 1971; large print edition 1984), p. 64.

2. Rachel Crabb, "Insights," *Time with God: New Century Version* (Dallas: Word Bibles, 1991), p. 363.

3. LaRene Gaunt, "One Voice," *Ensign*, April 1993, p. 47.

Chapter 16
Hearts to the Past, Hands to the Future

1. David Lawrence McKay, *My Father, David O. McKay* (Salt Lake City: Deseret Book, 1989), p. 98.

2. Ibid., pp. 149–51.

3. Jill Mulvay Derr, Janath Russell Cannon, and Maureen Ursenbach Beecher, *Women of Covenant: The Story of Relief Society* (Salt Lake City: Deseret Book, 1992), pp. 235–36.

4. Mary Ellen Edmunds, "Blessed, Honored Pioneers," *Ensign*, March 1992, p. 37.

5. Derr, Cannon, and Beecher, *Women of Covenant*, pp. 301–2.

6. Ibid., p. 28.

7. Glenn L. Pace, "A Thousand Times," *Ensign*, November 1990, p. 10.

8. Derin Head Rodriguez, "Reaching Out," *Ensign*, January 1992, p. 68.

9. Susan Cort Johnson, "The Senior Gleaners," *Signs of the Times*, April 1992, pp. 16–18.

10. Adapted from Bertha A. Kleinman and Frank W. Asper, "To Use the Gifts Thou Gavest Me," *Latter-day Saint Hymns* (Salt Lake City: Deseret Book, 1927), no. 243.

Chapter 17
Let Down Your Nets

1. Truman G. Madsen, "Joseph Smith and the Sources of Love," in *Four Essays on Love* (Salt Lake City: Bookcraft, 1995), pp. 12–13.

2. F. Scott Fitzgerald, as quoted in James Charlton, *A Little Learning Is a Dangerous Thing* (New York: St. Martins Press, 1994), p. 36.

3. Andrew Jenson, "Amanda Smith," *LDS Biographical Encyclopedia*, 4 vols. (Salt Lake City: Andrew Jenson History Co., 1901–37; reprinted by Salt Lake City: Western Epics, 1971), 2:795.

4. Ibid., p. 797.

5. Ibid.

6. William James, as quoted in *Random Acts of Kindness* (Berkeley, CA: Conari Press, 1993).

Chapter 18
Lamps and Trumpets

1. Portions of this retelling are based on David Christie-Murray, *The Illustrated Children's Bible* (New York: Grosset & Dunlap, 1982), pp. 102–4.

2. S. Dilworth Young, "Courage to Be Righteous," *Latter-day Digest*, November 1992, p. 60.

3. H. Jackson Brown, Jr., *Live and Learn and Pass It On* (Nashville, Tenn.: Rutledge Hill Press, 1992), p. 145.

4. In *To Your Success: Thoughts to Give Wings to Your Work and Your Dreams*, compiled by Dan Zadra (Woodinville, WA.: Compendium, Inc., 1994), p. 77.

5. Howard W. Hunter, "The God That Doest Wonders," *Ensign*, May 1989, pp. 15–17.

6. Greggory S. McDonald, "In the Midst of Us," *Saints Herald*, July 1993, p. 9.

7. Pamela H. Finlayson, "Let Not Your Heart Be Troubled; Neither Let It Be Afraid," address to the Washington D.C. Stake Conference, October 31, 1992; photocopy of typescript in my possession.

SOURCES

Chapter 1, "In the Shelter of His Wings," was adapted from a devotional address given at the West Valley Institute of Religion, West Valley City, Utah, February 27, 1994.

Chapter 2, "Questions for a Disciple," was adapted from a taped address given to the Young Women of the Thomas Second Ward, Blackfoot, Idaho, April 29, 1995.

Chapter 3, "Steadfast Disciples," was adapted from an address given at a regional women's conference, Centerville, Utah, March 19, 1994.

Chapter 4, "Weaving Patterns: Men, Women, and Priesthood Principles in Today's World," was adapted from an address given at a sunset service in the Foothill Stake, Salt Lake City, Utah, August 8, 1993.

Chapter 5, "Honoring the Priesthood," was adapted from an address given at an adult leadership meeting in Jamaica, February 8, 1997.

Chapter 6, "Knit Together in Love," was adapted from an address given at a tri-ward women's meeting in the Mount Olympus Stake, Salt Lake City, Utah, March 10, 1993.

Chapter 7, "Strengthening Every Home," was adapted from an address given at the Pocatello Idaho East Region Relief Society conference, April 28, 1995.

Chapter 8, "Healing from Sexual Abuse: Eight Messages for Survivors, Families, and Leaders," was adapted from an audiotape presentation of the same title (Salt Lake City: Deseret Book, 1993).

Chapter 9, "Good Measure, Pressed Down, and Running Over," was adapted from an address given at a regional fireside in Honolulu, Hawaii, August 13, 1995.

Chapter 10, "Delivered from Bondage," was adapted from an address given at the Cottonwood Creek Stake education day fireside, Sandy, Utah, March 18, 1998.

Chapter 11, "Christ and Culture," was adapted from the Pioneers in the Pacific Symposium keynote address, BYU-Hawaii, October 8, 1997.

Chapter 12, "Stones," was adapted from an address given at a singles conference in Honolulu, Hawaii, August 13, 1995.

Chapter 13, "Behold Thy Handmaiden: The Answer of Faith," was adapted from an address given at a regional conference in Meridian, Idaho, March 12, 1994.

Chapter 14, "Change, Choice, Challenge, and the Cockroach," was adapted from an address given to the BYU Management Group, San Diego, California, May 13, 1995.

Chapter 15, "Unsponsored Service: The *Kigatsuku* Spirit," was adapted from a devotional address given to the Church motor pool personnel, Salt Lake City, Utah, April 22, 1993.

Chapter 16, "Hearts to the Past, Hands to the Future," was adapted from an address given at the Champaign Illinois Region women's conference, March 18, 1995.

Chapter 17, "Let Down Your Nets," was adapted from a fireside address given in the BYU 5th Stake, Provo, Utah, September 17, 1995.

Chapter 18, "Lamps and Trumpets," was adapted from an address given in the Enrichment Lecture Series for Church employees, Salt Lake City, Utah, June 16, 1995.

Chapter 19, "Rejoice with Singing," was adapted from a fireside address given at BYU-Hawaii, February 6, 1994.

INDEX